THIS
IS NOT
FAME

ALSO BY DOUG STANHOPE

Digging Up Mother: A Love Story

IS NOT
FAME

A "From What I Re-Memoir"

DOUG STANHOPE

Da Capo Press

Hachette Book Group supports the right to free expression and the value of copyright. The purpose of copyright is to encourage writers and artists to produce the creative works that enrich our culture.

The scanning, uploading, and distribution of this book without permission is a theft of the author's intellectual property. If you would like permission to use material from the book (other than for review purposes), please contact permissions@hbgusa.com. Thank you for your support of the author's rights.

Da Capo Press
Hachette Book Group
1290 Avenue of the Americas, New York, NY 10104
www.dacapopress.com
@DaCapoPress; @DaCapoPR

Printed in the United States of America

First Edition: November 2017

Published by Da Capo Press, an imprint of Perseus Books, LLC,
a subsidiary of Hachette Book Group, Inc.

The publisher is not responsible for websites (or their content) that are not owned by the publisher.

Editorial production by Christine Marra, Marrathon Production Services.
www.marrathoneditorial.org

Book design by Jane Raese
Set in 11-point Avance

Library of Congress Cataloging-in-Publication Data has been applied for.

ISBN 978-0-306-82574-3 (hardcover), ISBN 978-0-306-82575-0 (ebook)

LSC-H

10   9   8   7   6   5   4   3   2   1

Dedicated to Mark and Suzie Bazzell

and All the King's Horses and All the King's Men

who helped put Bingo back together again.

CONTENTS

FOREWORD

My first thought when Stanhope asked me to create a foreword to his book was that there must be a mistake. I did indeed ask if he was punking me. That is true—that happened. My reaction must have caught his attention as well, as he included that moment in his story though I still don't know if he is offended or proud of it. After all, he was the same guy who stood on stage and ruthlessly busted my balls without ever having met me! But that was all in our past. I then felt sort of honored. He and I had crafted a friendship across some pretty shitty seas. (If you wish to understand how our friendship blossomed you must read on.) He assured me he was not punking me. Once I realized he was serious I thought, "Well, once he gets the balls, he'll ask his friend Depp and I'll be off the hook." Evidently he never developed the *huevos* to do it, so here I am.

Having studied his opus carefully, I will tell you this is actually a practical parenting guide. I mean, what child does not need the practical wisdom for managing the vicissitudes of entering adulthood with sage advice such as being sure to buy a love seat rather than a couch, so your loser buddies feel so uncomfortable when they flop at your pad that they do not stay, or learning the fact that you can avoid a flight-change fee if you manage to get kicked off the plane for excessive intoxication. And of course every child should understand that threesomes are awkward and weird unless you are completely intoxicated to the point you can barely function sexually and, finally, that you too can bullshit your way onto a talk show if your story is good enough.

Aside from the practical wisdom Doug dispenses, I want you, the reader, to understand something else. Doug has written a story that Hunter S. Thompson would wish he could have lived. This is, I shit you not, a modern story for the ages. Now let me be clear. This is not a story of healthy behavior and surely not a story written by a healthy person. But this is a human story and it is honest and it is somehow refreshing. I love people, warts and all. I also like to help people to change when they *want* help changing. That does not mean I don't love them just as much when they don't want my help and do not wish to change, or are struggling with what it means to be a human being. Doug embraces his human-ness; he celebrates his pathologies and his flaws, terrible choices and their consequences. I don't think he ever really hurts anyone but himself along the way. Mind you, you don't want to be in his crosshairs. Been there—it doesn't feel good. I don't recommend it. But Doug's vulnerability, in the midst of these extraordinary situations you will read about, connects to us on a familiar level. I love Doug for his humanity and, like everyone else, I love him for his comedy. If you are a fan this read will be time well spent. You will feel like you have been on vacation with Doug Stanhope. And although I enjoyed the front-row seat in the adventure that is Doug's life, I found myself more than once worried about my friend's survival.

One day Doug may need or have to change. Maybe one day he will look back on some of these experiences with regret or remorse. But I don't think he will ever regret having lived a life fully lived. And we will not regret the stories and entertainment he has given us. As he says, he has in fact done a lot, if he could just remember it.

So now the warning. Do *not* follow any of the practical wisdom you cull from this book. Do *not* consider this a template for how to live your life. This book should also convince you that if you see Stanhope heading your way, don't make eye contact.

Dr. Drew Pinsky

INTRODUCTION

I usually skip the introduction to a book if it doesn't immediately strike me as important. So I will tell you now, read this introduction. I will assume that you read like I read, plodding and without much patience.

There is no letdown greater for me than reading a bio of a degenerate rocker or an otherwise renowned derelict with sordid stories only to have them sober up two-thirds of the way through the book. You know that the rest is gonna suck but you've invested so much time, you know that you have to see it through. At no point in this book will I find God, go on the straight and narrow or find any higher purpose. You will always find yourself better than me even when I am calling you a nugget of shit. There is no happy ending. There is no ending at all. I'm not dead, at least at this writing.

I also hate reading memoirs when you have to wade through someone's childhood years and their parents in order to get to the good parts. If their childhood was compelling, they would have written the book back then. If the parents were of any interest, they'd have a book of their own. Fortunately I got all of that detritus of being raised out in my first book. I hope you enjoyed it.

Like the first book, I use a lot of fancy words when I can. This has nothing to do with a strong vocabulary. I get excited when I find a big word on my own but mostly I use a thesaurus. It feels like cheating but I pride myself on making decent choices in the absence of actual knowledge.

Here are some of the main people who will come in and out of these stories.

Amy Bingaman, known in the book as "Bingo," is my gal pal of nearly twelve years as of this writing. She has a history of mental illness and being adorable. She is the soul and the muse of the operation. And occasionally the monkey wrench in the gears when her brain goes bad on her.

Greg Chaille, only known as "Chaille" anywhere in the civilized world, is my "tour manager." He is known as my tour manager as that is his one job. Managing the tours. He also produces, edits and co-hosts the podcasts, runs the website, and packages and ships the merchandise from said website as well as selling it on the road. He also drives the van, sets the GPS for the next town's gig and hotel, gets us breakfast and makes sure that the gig has sound, greenroom booze and that we get paid afterwards when we are too drunk to see. He also finds the shortest route from the greenroom to where I can smoke and makes sure I have a stool onstage for my drink. He mules our drugs in his anus even though they are usually over-the-counter drugs for heartburn or seasonal allergies. At home, he is currently fixing the Christmas lights after making me fish sticks. His hobbies include gassing up the cars, picking up my friends from the airport and running sound and lights for comics and bands that perform at parties at the house. He will even fill in on most instruments on any given jam band playing at the house, so long as he can get time away from his one job. Tour manager.

Brian Hennigan, known mostly as "Hennigan" in this book, is a filthy, uncut Scotsman. He is my "business manager" who manages business things like book deals, television appearances and booking tour dates. That means he forces us to make money.

He is evidently sometimes a prick about this with booking agents and in other business dealings, but we try to ignore his barbarous and impolite tactics. Too often, on the road Chaille has been confused for Hennigan because of the common "manager" title. Hennigan has the benefit of being able to hide his fancy-lad Scottish accent when he only has to communicate his boorish vitriol via email. Then when Chaille shows up at the gig, the local booker assumes Chaille was the asshole who the booker had to deal with in order to hire me. Chaille gets all the dirty looks that Hennigan has earned. Chaille doesn't do any of the bookings. He's only got one job and that keeps him busy enough.

Andy Andrist and Matt Becker are two of my oldest and closest friends and two of the funniest people who have ever walked this planet. For that reason they show up in the book quite a bit.

Save for Bingo who runs ten years behind, we are all around the fifty-year mark and we have all been together for many a moon. We probably should have stopped being fuckups a long time ago. That doesn't look like it's going to happen anytime soon.

This book is a journey of a life in the breakdown lane on the highway of fame, a motivational opus for those who strive for the margins. A highlight reel of a life on the stage when most people were looking at a bar fight in a different direction. Often enough, that worked in my favor. Everyone wants to be in the spotlight until it's their own prison break.

Mitch Hedberg had a joke where he said, "As a comedian, I always get into situations where I'm auditioning for movies and sitcoms, you know? As a comedian, they want you to do things besides comedy. They say, 'All right, you're a comedian, can you write? Write us a script. Act in this sitcom.' They want me to do shit that is related to comedy, but it's not comedy, man. It's not fair, you know? It's as though if I was a cook, and I worked my ass off to become a really good cook, and they said, 'All right, you're a cook . . . can you farm?'"

The joke is that it isn't a joke at all. It's the truth with a fantastic analogy. People in the industry look at stand-up as an audition to a shittier platform. If you can do well in a pure, unadulterated and raw format of your own making, then you might be given a chance to be elevated to a place where you can be diluted and neutered for mass appeal. And be made famous.

Like Hedberg, I never wanted to "farm." In my younger years, I thought that was what I should aspire to if only because they told me so. I'm a cook and I've had a lot of fun doing just that. In a sense, this book is akin to Anthony Bourdain's *Kitchen Confidential*. The joys and pitfalls of just being a fucked-up cook. The greasy-spoon breakfast to another comedian's *Zagat*-rated four-course meal.

The stories may seem to weave off topic but that is how my head works. Stay with me. They'll get back to the point eventually. Or maybe not. The tone of my remembrances might also ping-pong from positive to negative. That is because I am a drunk. "I will kill you" can turn into "I love you, man!" over the course of a few salty dogs.

Another thing. These pricks at this book-writing company correct me too often. I like to write stories in the present tense, the same as you'd tell them in a bar if you can tell a story worth a fuck. It makes the listener imagine that he or she is with you as you go. Instead of "So now I'm looking down the barrel of the gun" they want it written "I looked down the barrel," etc. And you never get to feel like you are going to die. For some reason I listen to them. I bet I'm right but I don't have the time nor tenure to argue. If you find some old story written in the present tense, that's one I slipped past the censors.

If you are the fan who's watched every special, bootleg and YouTube clip, listened to every podcast and read every interview, you'll recognize some of these stories. Fortunately most of you are barflies and reprobates who won't remember until you read them again. And if you have your glove that deep in my ass as a fan, you couldn't live without this book anyway.

If you're like most people and have never heard of me, this book should give you some insight as to *why* you've never heard of me.

FUNNY FOR NOTHING

I hope that the president gets assassinated. Not for political reasons. You just have to understand that I drink every single day. And it would be nice if for once I could remember where I was on that one day.

—Norm Wilkerson, Unknown Comedian

Early in my career, a young stand-up comic, Josh Perlman who I knew at the time in Los Angeles, came back from Las Vegas after playing a show at the Rio Hotel. He told me that he'd been lounging late night at the casino bar talking to a prostitute playing video poker next to him. He was interested but he was new to the game, shy and didn't know how to broach the subject. Instead he just continued to make small talk for an eternity, hoping she'd go for the close. Eventually she asked Josh if he'd like to take her to his room for "a dance." He asked how much it would cost and she told him that it would be two hundred dollars. He hemmed and hawed and finally asked her what she meant by "a dance," specifically what he could expect for his money. She paused suspiciously.

"Um . . . are you a cop?"

He laughed and said, "No, no! I'm a comedian!"

She lit up. "Really?! Do you know *Doug Stanhope*???"

● ● ●

6

This is not fame.

"Known in certain circles" would be a more accurate way to put it. This gal in Vegas didn't know me from my body of work and I'd bet that I never found out if she could actually dance. That was decades ago but the times haven't changed. The circle might have widened but the audience has remained within the loop. All for one, one for nothing. Or whatever.

So long as the right people remember you.

• • •

Before I wasn't famous, I was completely unknown. It was so much more fun. When I started doing open-mic comedy, I was only concerned with being famous for that one night after I got off the stage. I wanted someone to tell me that I was great. I wanted the owner to invite me back. I wanted some dude to buy me a drink and some girl to give me a second look. Karaoke famous.

I achieved those goals in record time. Those were the early days of 1990 Las Vegas. I did stand-up as a lark and eventually when a local stripper wanted me to beat her senseless while I fucked her poorly, I considered myself to have been "discovered." As a twenty-three-year-old, in my eyes I'd made it to the big time.

For most of my twenty-five-plus years since in this business, the stage was just the pivot pole, the jumping-off point. The excuse. The baked potato. You would never eat a plain baked potato. You eat it for all of the great things that go along with it. But you still need it as a platform. Eating butter and sour cream all by themselves makes you look like a glutton.

I remember an early open mic in a casino where, after barreling through my set of mostly jerk-off jokes, a Down syndrome man-child ran up on the stage, grabbed the mic and started yelling at me.

"You are *evil*, Doug! The things you say are *EVIL!*"

Now imagine that voice in a tone that would be considered mocking or insensitive if I said it aloud, and you've nailed it. I was barely three steps from exiting the stage and had no idea what to do, nor did the crowd. Eventually someone gently guided him back to his seat, but I never lived it down with the local comedians for the next six months that I stayed in Vegas. Anything that I said off-color was followed by comic buddies mimicking him.

"You ah eeeevel, Doug! Da theengs you say ah EEEvel!"

That's not a bad show. That's fucking funny. That guy made it funny. Without him, that show was just a plain baked potato. Unmemorable.

There was a comic who started his open-mic shows by doing hokey impressions from a wireless microphone in the men's room. I'm sure he believed the audience was confounded as to why nobody was onstage, yet bad comedy still lived in their ears. He'd make his "Ta-da!" moment, revealing himself coming out of the shitter, take the stage and continue to suck. What he didn't know or couldn't see from the toilet was that nobody gave a shit. The only time it was funny was when the other comics got the entire bar to get up and leave the bar as he did his Donald Duck or whoever from the toilet. He went into the bathroom with twenty to twenty-five people in the room and came out to only the bartender silently wiping a glass. Ta-da! I don't think he ever came back to open-mic night.

I remember doing a show for nobody. There was a flash-in-the-pan wanna-be booker we called "Jack the Wig" due to his ridiculous toupee. He'd started a show in North Las Vegas at the Silver Nugget Casino, a casino whose major draw was people coming in to not get murdered in the surrounding ghetto. The show was being held in the "bingo access room," a room beside the bingo hall that could be used to hold more patrons should bingo draw above the capacity in their main room.

The loudspeakers in the casino were announcing "free comedy at eight p.m." every five minutes or so in the hour leading up to showtime. Still, as the hour wore near, there was not a soul in the house. The Wig, in a panic, demanded that the show go on as planned, so on the off chance someone walked past and saw a show in progress, they might venture in. One after another of the local comics went up on the semblance of a stage under a darkened bingo board and delivered their acts to nobody at all. I can't tell you about the tree falling alone in the forest but I can tell you that your jokes still suck if there's nobody there to hear them. We all wished bingo had been more popular and there had been an overflow forcing our cancellation. We weren't getting paid anyway. It would have been better to not play at all for nothing than to play to nobody for nothing. But the story was invaluable. I might not be famous but I could one-up or match any comedian's story of the smallest crowd they've ever played. Nobody for nothing.

People who ask me now for advice about doing stand-up comedy as a profession without having ever stepped on a stage baffle me. Why would you want to skip those ridiculous early days of fucking up and fucking off and skip straight to having to do it for money? I did it as a dare to myself and it took me weeks just to drum up the courage. Asking how to do it for a living is like asking how to be in the X Games before you learned how to ride a bike. Learn to ride the bike first to see if you like it. And be prepared to fall down quite a bit and hurt a lot, knowing that the odds are you will never be X Games good at it.

I got good enough that I found my way out onto the road, playing to a few people more than nobody and for a little bit of money. Off and running.

A SUNDAY
THAT SUCKED

April 18, 1993

Cheyenne, Wyoming, was big city for me and Wiley Roberts on that closing Saturday night on a tour of obscure western towns. It's certainly the only town on that tour that you would have ever heard of, anyway. Lord only knows what horrible gags I thought were funny back then, much less what the people in Cheyenne thought was funny in comparison. Some places, you can be a celebrity just for being willing to actually go there.

I don't recall the show at all but I know that the next day my car wouldn't start and we couldn't find a shop open on a Sunday to fix it. Not only was I stuck but I was also Wiley's ride, so he was stuck as well. Serves him right for making the opener drive on this boondocks tour. The car—actually an old Chevy LUV pickup truck—was so badly rusted that you could watch the pavement go by through the gaping holes in the passenger-side floorboards. Enjoy the view, Wiley.

The car shitting out meant that little or nothing of the week's money that I'd mined out of those Rocky Mountain Podunk towns would probably be left after they gouged me to repair it. Not wanting—or being able to—pay for a hotel, I went back to the bar we'd played and fortunately found the same bartender who'd worked our show. I spun my tale of being shipwrecked and stranded over free beers until she eventually offered up her couch to stay at her place. And with Wiley being included and being the headliner, I deduced that her couch would be Wiley's and I'd be on the floor. Nothing new and not a problem. Beats a cold, broken-down car.

"I hope you don't mind animals!" she said and I didn't flinch when I should have. We drank the day away waiting for her shift to end and then she drove us to her place—which, naturally, was in a trailer park. If I could describe it in detail, which I cannot, it would be no funnier or entertaining than what you would picture when I say "Wyoming trailer park." Yep. It was just like that. Along with a lot of people. Some of them children. And then there were the animals. Six dogs, eight cats and a pig. I'm lowballing the guesstimate on the cats and dogs. I'm deadly accurate on the number of pigs that lived in the trailer.

You mean the animals all lived *inside* the trailer?

Oh, yes. Lived, slept, ate and shit in the trailer. Shit everywhere like they'd thrown it as confetti for New Year's and there it still lay in mid-April, cold and hard to greet the coming spring.

The animals all rushed out to greet their master for dinnertime and the trailer seemed like an ark. I don't know my pigs but had to assume that this was one of those Vietnamese potbellied pigs that were all the rage as pets at the time. But I'd also pictured potbellied pigs to be small, pink and cute like a Disney cartoon. This one just seemed like an ugly, hairy, grunting, stupid pig-sized pig. I've heard that pigs are extremely intelligent compared to other animals and I have no reason to doubt that. I'm simply saying that this particular pig seemed stupid. Not everybody's baby is a prize.

All of the beady animal eyes were now on the mom as she retrieved their food—which all came from one impossibly large thousand-pound sack and was spilled directly onto the linoleum kitchen floor where the stable circled around and gorged. If Wiley and I had been polite at all when we first walked into the place, we had drifted into spewing laughter by now. Every walk to the beer cooler was a dance around the minefield of animal shit and the degree of difficulty grew with every drink, as did the hilarity. Stranger still was that our hosts thought our laughter itself was the amusing part. They saw nothing out of the ordinary in the way they lived. They looked at us like we were some kinda high-falutin' city folk who were witnessing real America for the first time.

Fortunately for me that night, Wiley was a drinker too. Sober people have a harder time finding the amusement in these types of situations. I was also fortunate that Wiley was a better drinker. Meaning he could drink more and longer. It's the only way I can imagine I pulled off stealing the couch. I must have passed out first.

Wiley found himself a spot on the floor just in front of the couch where people's feet usually go, hence a small swath of feces-free acreage. As I was waking up in the morning, I opened an eye to Wiley just as the pig was trying to maneuver his way over Wiley's sleeping head. Wiley woke up in a fit with the pig high-centered and stuck on the side of Wiley's face, his stubby back hoofs unable to vault him the rest of the way towards the remaining pile of animal food in the kitchen.

The next day we sat back at the bar waiting for the car to get fixed, rehashing the details of the night before. And that is the only reason I can tell you the exact date that this happened because, on the news behind the bar, David Koresh and his followers in Waco, Texas, were all being burned to the ground.

That story was towards the beginning of three years of living on the road, aimless and without any expectations. There were other stories but if I had to sum them all up into one, it would be being famous enough to sleep with a pig for free.

●　●　●

I wanted to call Wiley to see if he had any other detail to add to this story but Wiley is one of those old friends who you really only have that one good story you share. Every time you cross paths over the years, you hug it out and eventually you say, "Remember the pig???" and then you exhaust your laughter with a moment-closing phrase like "Oh, man. Those were the days."

The silence kicks in as you both scrape for something more to say. You have nothing. You fake that you're late for an appointment.

●　●

New comedians email me quite often for advice. I don't have any. Early in my career I was giving advice to an even younger comedian after an open mic. Joey Scazzola, a comedian just a little bit more experienced than me, pulled me aside and said, "Hey, don't ever tell these kids what to do because all you're doing is telling them how to be more like you."

That was the best advice I ever got. If a young Russell Brand had asked me for advice I would have told him to quit and buy an ice cream truck. Everybody has a different sense of humor, both audience and comedian. It makes me crazy when I hear someone say, "He's not funny" without acknowledging personal preference. Even comedians do this. Even I do this. I'll catch myself saying something isn't funny even when I'm giving advice to some comedian that I know is only telling them how to be like me.

There is no good advice.

Nothing that ever happened in my career was by design. Every credit on my resume is like every stain on my reputation was something that happened randomly, like stepping in a pile of dog shit. All by accident. Run on instinct and take it as it comes. There was no long-term plan. It has always been living in the moment and Whac-A-Mole. That isn't to say I haven't worked my ass off but I never knew why or to what ends.

There has never been any kind of system that worked consistently. Maybe you try to write about your life. Maybe try to write about current events. Out of the creek in between, you might find something unimaginable that you couldn't have ever "tried" to write. But you wouldn't have ever found it without the trying.

Sometimes you'd have a certain number of drinks before the show and kill only to repeat the same recipe a night later and find yourself slurring. Sometimes bits that consistently destroy inexplicably lie down and die on the night that counts. And later you realize that that night didn't really count at all.

There might be a day where you work out your material so succinctly, adding all sorts of new tags and dead-on segues that you can feel it killing while you write it. But that night the show goes in a different direction. There are hecklers and spilled drink trays and some guy has a seizure during the middle of your act. You prepared but you are so completely in lockstep with what you've memorized and imagined that you can't adapt. And you suck. You should have written seizure jokes.

You learn a little bit more every time but there are no set rules for you as an individual, much less across the board as a comedian. And the more you learn, the more it tears your ass out when you still aren't perfect.

Eat before you drink and make the stage as much fun for yourself as possible. Those are rules you can live by. If you aren't enjoying yourself, what the fuck does it matter. Generally, if you are genuinely having fun, the audience will climb on board. Fuck the ones who don't. If you try to pander with garbage that you yourself don't find funny and you still fall on your ass, you can't even fall back on self-respect. So fuck 'em. There are plenty of other jobs out there for you if you think that the customer is always right.

Giving people advice on how to do comedy is like telling them how to get laid. You try to get laid and when it works, know that you have no guarantee that the same approach will work again. Eventually you might realize that not trying at all works even better or that getting laid isn't worth all the time you put into it.

Here's a piece of advice I hear every comedian dole out right off the top and why I don't necessarily subscribe . . .

GET ALL
THE STAGE TIME
YOU CAN

Bill Hicks—who I'll get to later—had a line where after any particularly caustic bit, he'd finish by saying, "Yes, and I'm also available for children's parties."

Just after I moved to LA, Becker and I played a children's party. Or didn't. But we unwittingly booked it.

We'd run into some tail-wagging new comic who'd been hanging around the local scene. He breathlessly asked us if we could possibly do a private afternoon show in the Hollywood Hills the next day. We knew better. Most comedy veterans will tell you that as a new comic you should get any and all stage time you can when you're starting out. Not necessarily a bad recommendation. But too much stage time in places that will repeatedly suck can demoralize you on the whole.

Matt and I learned early on that you should never try to open for nor do breaks during a live band. And we would still often ignore what we learned. An audience who are there to hear live music don't want to hear you talk, no matter how much your drummer friend tries to convince you that they'll love you. I've been booed off stage by many a comedy audience, but it's nowhere near as defeating as the feeling of playing to a packed bar talking loudly and not even acknowledging that you are onstage. It's worse than playing a show for nobody.

I've done a few private parties for the money or just for the fuck of it even when I knew they would go poorly. One house party for the well-to-do had no mic and no proper room to fit all the guests. I made the call to do it outside at the pool, mostly because it allowed me to smoke. I used the diving board as the stage and the pool as an ashtray and yelled my way through the silence. No refunds.

Another private party was in the living room of a lawyer we'd recently met at a show a few months earlier. The house was filled with his cohorts—cops, attorneys, prosecutors—all easy marks for me at that later stage of my career. Instead of jokes they got a lot of angry opinions and a summary of why they were all the cause of the rot in the core of America. The problem with lawyers is that you can't hurt their feelings. The easy joke is that lawyers do not have feelings but the truth is that they don't need them. They have all the power. The same way you can't shit on white people for being white to any effect. White people own everything and have all of the privilege. They have no reason to be offended.

The lawyer show turned into a drunken heckle-fest and eventually devolved into me leading the whole party through the neighborhood in their gated community, midsummer Christmas-caroling their sleeping neighbors. The lawyer who hired us, Jay Kirschner, remains a good friend and has gotten us out of more than a couple of bad jams in the years since. More of that later.

The next show doesn't really count as a private party but still happened in their own house. Brandt Tobler was a young comedian in Vegas who got tired of the shitty or nonexistent stage time he was getting in town. He was renting a house in a gated community with a large backyard that he shared with a few other local newbie comics. They came up with the idea to just rent folding chairs and hold shows in the backyard. Bring your own alcohol and tell your friends. He'd done pretty well with it. I loved the idea and booked a night, selling tickets on the Internet through BrownPaperTickets.com. The only advertising was through social media, my mailing list and word of mouth. We sold every rented chair and the rest stood. This, I thought, should be the way of the future. Cut out the middleman. Bring the bar to you, book who you like, charge a reasonable cover charge and folks don't have to get jacked up on liquor prices. Invite people you already know on (then) Myspace. Why wasn't everyone doing this? It was the perfect DIY show, sold out and everyone was cool and happy.

Except the neighbors who evidently weren't big fans of my material, the volume of which they could not ignore. I killed and made bank. Brandt was evicted shortly afterwards because of it.

These stories all happened years after Becker and I were asked to perform at that afternoon private party in the Hollywood Hills. We still knew the gig would probably be agony and there wasn't even any money. Maybe we thought it might be good careerwise—what if it was Spielberg's house and we turned it down unknowingly? There must have been a reason we said yes, even if just for free beer.

But nobody had mentioned the children.

Just finding the place in the labyrinth of the Hills in a pre-GPS era was a workload. We found parking about fifty yards down from what seemed to be a 90 percent climb to the house at the top. We could hear the ruckus of the party with a comedian trying to talk over it as we passed the side of the house where ivy covered the chain link before we got to the front door. Allowing ourselves in—talent never knocks—we found our way to the backyard into a full-blown children's party. Not just a children's party but a Hollywood children's party. It was set up to be some type of fundraiser for Arts for Kids. Every kid had a booth set up like a tiny farmers' market. A face-painting or palm-reading booth, a lemonade stand and such. Cute. All the parents were chatting and drinking wine spritzers while the comic who'd invited us was on a stopgap stage, oblivious to the depths of shit he was eating while fighting for their attention. Wine-drunk mommies showed us to the undernourished beer cooler, while their kids manned glory-hole or origami booths for charity. Becker and I started drinking like we'd crossed a desert to get there, depleting their beer stores before settling for their wine.

Our comic friend finally gave up on his set and announced that there was going to be a small break before the comedy resumed. Nobody noticed, nobody cared. Becker and I were already living in the horror of what was to come like a lucid nightmare.

I am a polite person on most occasions, even when I don't want to be. It's a character thing and sometimes a flaw. That day I was polite. I'm also self-aware that I am a one-trick pony as a comedian. I have my material and that is all. I can't act. I don't do characters. I fail at crowd work. I can usually handle a heckler with a quick barb but I'm no improviser. Just me and my act, and my act back then was rife with bits like "Suck Your Own Dick Dreams" and "Bucket of Vaginas." It wasn't gonna play to six-year-olds hitting piñatas with their parents. On the hostess's tour of the house to the bathroom, I stopped her in the kitchen and told her earnestly that we'd had no idea this was a children's event and that Becker and I had no material that was appropriate for the function. We felt bad for drinking all of her beer before we bowed out of the gig but we knew it would be far more impolite to go through with it.

She was completely unfazed. "Oh, don't you worry about it!" Becker and I snuck a sigh of relief as she turned her back. We took that to mean that she understood why we couldn't perform and that we were off the hook. But then she returned to the back-yard, yelling for everyone to gather around, that the comedy was about to resume! Becker and I shit each other's pants through mere eye contact. We thought she understood that our material was too rough for the kids. She was saying that she didn't care.

What happened next was one of those beautiful and all too rare moments between close friends where Becker and I didn't have to say a word. We were staring hard and open mouthed at each other having a telepathic emergency meeting, when the comic who'd brought us to this gig wandered towards us. Without any audible discussion, we pulled the kid by his shirt through the front door, yelled, "GO!" and started running. We ran like heap-footed fat convicts past the side of the house where the voices dulled from frivolity to confusion as they heard the trampling going down the slope, skidding in the loose gravel, our wheezing and giggling as we sprinted for our lives. Fight or flight in the absence of communication skills, only making the half scream, half laugh of girls on a roller coaster as we fled. I threw the key into the ignition before I even shut the door. As I jammed the Oldsmobile into drive and spit unnecessary amounts of rocks and dust into the air, I could see our hostess at the top of the hill standing with her arms wide, palms out, incredulous as to what had caused such a panic. She probably thought we'd stolen jew-elry from her bedroom. She will never know that serious a fear. She will never know the need to run or the ability to trust your instincts in those situations, even if they would be deemed un-professional or impolite.

So my advice to those who ask is to do all the stage time you *want* to do. Personally, with shit gigs for no money being involved I'd balance the story value against the pain threshold. A Klan rally or a swingers' orgy have to be worth the risk just for the story. The company Christmas party for Dell computers will simply deaden you more and nobody will want to hear about it.

Private parties are for crashing, not performing.

PARTY CRASHING

S ometime after I'd just moved to Los Angeles, my neighbor told me she'd found out from an industry friend that Bill Maher—then the host of Comedy Central's *Politically Incorrect*—was having his annual Fourth of July party and had gotten an address should we want to crash it. I wasn't even that well known in comedy circles at that point. But I lived next to people who knew people who worked for people who represented some famous people and in LA—it's all about who you know.

We'd crashed a few parties at that point. One was at some producer's house where I stood next to Oliver Stone while he smoked a joint that I would have shared with him even though I don't smoke pot. But he didn't offer. I later went into a bedroom looking for a bathroom and walked in on Ellen Barkin and Howard Stern, who I hadn't yet met at that point. Unfortunately there was nothing going on. They were just grabbing their jackets to leave. If they had been fucking I might have blackmailed them. Or some other harebrained scheme. In reality, I just stood around and apologized to nobody listening. Aside from some names to drop when I got home, it was pretty much like any other party back then. Stand around and nobody talks to you and if they do, you have nothing to say in return.

Around the same time one of our friends had found a flyer for a bondage-themed house party that was just a few blocks away from my apartment. We were already drunk at home when he brought it to our attention. I broke into a sprint trying to figure out what kind of slapdash, poor-kid-on-Halloween S&M outfits we could put together. I was breaking my arm patting myself on the back when I came up with my idea. Simple duct tape. I didn't pause to think it through. By the time I'd covered myself from midthigh to near my belly button, someone else spotted the flaw in the theory.

"What happens when you have to piss?"

I paused waiting for the solution to appear like a lightbulb over my head. After those few fruitless seconds, I found none and proceeded to the bathtub and to the agonizing process of ripping duct tape off of body hair.

●　●　●

Crashing Bill Maher's party required no special dress code and although I didn't know him, I knew he was a comedian. I figured there'd probably be other comedians in attendance and if I knew another comedian there and I got busted crashing, maybe they'd vouch for me. Also, my manager had already been talking to Maher's people about getting me on his show. So I had that. I was really overthinking it. I couldn't have known it at the time. When you live and work in the industry, especially in television, you meet so many people that it would be impossible to remember them all, even the ones you should. Bill Maher probably couldn't remember half the people he'd actually invited much less know who they were bringing as a guest or the ones like me who just came on a hot tip.

We walked into the party like we were walking onto a yacht. It was obvious that nobody was checking IDs against a guest list. No muss no fuss, no need for a fake mustache. In fact it was just the opposite. Nobody looked or cared. I made myself well acquainted with the bar and looked for familiar faces. The only person I remember seeing who even talked to me was Jeff Cesario, a comedian I didn't know personally but was and is well respected, and I'll always remember him for being friendly to me that night. Bill Maher hadn't even shown his face before I was well torqued up on his liquor. Everyone else was seeming to pace themselves, sipping their wine and aw-shucksing at the offer of a second glass. I didn't care for it. I bided my time waiting for comedians to take over the pace of the party. They never showed. So in a burst of genius, I shed all of my clothes, ran through the party and jumped into the pool.

These things have to happen sometimes. A lot of stagnant parties need one guy to set the bar by being the first to look like an idiot. Especially at an LA party where the talent doesn't want to fuck up in front of the agents and the agents don't want to fuck up in front of the execs. And everybody is afraid of the people they don't know because they could be anybody. Then some asshole who is too drunk too early comes screaming through the evening air butt-naked and belly-flops in an otherwise empty and placid pool.

You see, what happens is that everyone can now relax and step it up a notch. Trade in the wine for that bourbon. Take off your jacket and spread out a bit. Tell a bawdy joke or salty anecdote. At least you won't be the naked idiot splashing around and trying to drink beer underwater. You've rewritten the code of conduct to where they can get far more loose while still remaining in the middle.

I'd expected immediate results. I was imagining throngs of people following suit like I was the Pied Piper but I was still ignored. Yet as new people started to arrive, a few people started to filter into the pool, keeping a wide distance from me with my dink and berries floating free. But coming in nonetheless. One girl swam towards me. She evidently didn't know anyone there either. I imagine Bill invited any random hot chick he ran across or could yell out a car window at. She was—get this—a Swedish flight attendant. And no, I didn't steal that from Fonzie from an episode of *Happy Days*. He would have had Swedish flight attendant twins.

Soon after, Bill Maher made his grand entrance from upstairs, coming down in a ridiculous Apollo Creed–as–Uncle Sam costume, cocktail swinging in his hand, bringing the level up to ten. He went through the throngs of guests like a regular Hugh Hefner and after not too long he saw people in the pool and jumped in with a thousand lemmings right on his heels.

The pool was quickly mobbed and except for occasional forays to the bar for more drink, I stayed floating in a corner with the Swede. As the party started to wind down and people left the pool, she and I followed. Only we had no towels and by late night it was fucking cold. Yes, it can get really cold even in LA in July, especially when you're wet and naked. So I beelined her into a bathroom with a shower and turned it on as hot as was possible. There was no fucking going on, just teeth-chattering survival. After several minutes, Bill Maher came barging in, saw us and screamed, "Hey! No shower scenes in my house!" before slamming the door. He'd probably done inventory of the available hot chicks who were left and was then unpleased that I might have pilfered one.

I sheepishly walked out, grabbed my clothes and tried to sneak out, only passing him briefly where he shook his head in contempt and made some kind of "Not cool" utterance.

The next day, my manager at the time caught wind of my high jinks and castigated me for cock-blocking her efforts to get me on his show and suggested I send a letter of apology. I'm not big on apologies but I did send a letter with a key to my place inside saying, "Dear Bill. Thanks for the party. Enclosed is a key to my apartment located at 12— Avenue #9 Los Angeles, CA 90046. Feel free to stop by anytime, run around naked, drink all my beer and fuck up my stuff."

I still haven't heard back so many decades later but I did keep the "jump in pool drunk 'n' naked" thing hip-pocketed for other similarly awkward events. I think my comedian friend K. P. Anderson and his new bride were a little pissed off at me for a brief while when I did it to break up the monotony of their backyard wedding, but a lot of their friends and family seemed amused.

The last naked pool-dive I remember was in *The Man Show* days at legendary producer Robert Evans's grotesque mansion where he was hosting a premiere party for Comedy Central's new-season shows. I guess he had some cartoon coming out on the network. I was with Andy Andrist and after Andy was loudly berated by the fully deranged Gary Busey for cutting the buffet line, we determined it best to just get shit-housed and find cocaine. Robert Evans was legendary for his admitted cocaine use back in the seventies and eighties. The problem was getting to him. He was seeing people by appointment only in the main room of one of his houses but only after some network geek came to find you and tell you it's your turn to see him.

Our turn came and we were led in by our Comedy Central liaison. Robert stood in the foyer flanked by assistants and flunkies, a wax figure in the receiving line at a stranger's wedding. Andy and I were introduced.

"Well hello, gentlemen. Welcome. It's a pleasure to meet you."

"Yeah, thanks for having us, Bob, but let's cut through the bullshit—where can we get some blow?"

"Ooh heh-heh-heh. Heh, I don't mess around with that stuff anymore. But I'm really looking forward to a successful new season on Comedy Central for all of us!"

"Yeah, yeah, Bob. But seriously. Where's the blow?"

He kept a vacant old-man smile and muttered something about how since his previous cocaine issues he couldn't even get a speeding ticket. And with that, the mortified Comedy Central lady shuffled us off into some more-private party in the back. I found drinks and Andy found Craig Kilborn with a harem of ladies in a hot tub.

"Hey, Kilborn, got any blow?" says Andy.

Without getting an answer he followed up with: "C'mon Kilborn. You gotta have blow. These ladies ain't with you cuz you're funny."

One of the gals took great exception to this and protested in a way that made us all the more certain that they must have had blow. We didn't keep pushing.

We went back to the front of the main house where we ran into Slash from Guns N' Roses. Gold mine, you'd think. But Slash said he was on the straight and narrow. He'd even quit smoking, which sucked because I was out of cigarettes. Andy asked Slash where one might find cocaine at that party and Slash told him: "I dunno. Try the bathroom."

"Sure," says Andy. "Maybe that works for *you*."

As we were about to have our limo summoned, I noticed a pool up near where the valets come around. It wasn't technically a pool. It was a fountain. A giant fountain the size of a pool. I dared Andy to jump in naked. He was only a writer on the show; how much trouble could he get in? He said he'd meet me halfway by jumping in with his underwear, which was meeting me none of the way for the dare of jumping in naked. So I had to strip to actual naked and jump in too—so as to not come off as lightweights. As our limo was coming—to the delight of most everybody there—I got dressed in the driveway while Andy went to the bathroom of a guest house to put on his clothes. I assumed it was his Slash-inspired last check of the bathroom for coke until I saw him awkwardly shuffle back out with an obvious square in his pants and hurry into the limo. He'd stolen Robert Evans's graduation picture off the bathroom wall.

• • •

I used to get invites to Sarah Silverman's notorious annual shindig, which always surprised me because I didn't think she even liked me. But the invites came every year long after I'd moved to Arizona—and always when I was on the road so I couldn't go even if I wanted to fly out to LA for it. A couple years back I finally got the invite on a year when I wasn't working and I bought a plane ticket immediately. First I went to a party at Drew Carey's house where someone—or seemingly everyone—offered me Ecstasy. I was reticent at first because I didn't want to be too lit up and make an asshole of myself with the Silverman crowd. But I succumbed to peer pressure within three drinks and took it anyway. Sarah's party was delightful and to the best of my recollection, I didn't say anything off-putting, was well mannered so far as I know and had a wide-eyed, smiling good time. I didn't steal anything or even think to jump in a pool naked.

And I've never been invited back to her party since. Maybe I wasn't living up to my reputation. Or maybe she'd forgotten that she didn't really like me.

FUCKING THE WAITSTAFF

I don't know the temperature of the current comedy club landscape but I do know that for a while in my earlier years, most comedy clubs would try to implement a "no fraternization" rule between comedians and waitresses. That means "don't fuck the waitresses." The motivation for this rule was never clear. It may have been so that comics didn't relentlessly hit on uninterested waitresses while they were trying to get their side-work done after a show. It may have been that the club owner was trying to fuck all of his waitresses himself and didn't want to compete with talent. It may have been that they wanted to use a big word like "fraternization" in a sentence. I've done the same with big words in this book.

Clubs would always have a yellowed copy of these type of rules listed on the greenroom wall. I always took that as a list of dares. The list of comics who fucked waitresses regardless would be longer by far. Many of them are still together, some now with families. The rule might as well have included "don't fall in love."

I fell in love with a comedy club waitress in the mid-nineties. It didn't work out. She's now married to some other guy and they own a coffee shop together in Switzerland. Not that I still stalk her on the Internet like I did in person back then.

People are always quick to justify the aftermath of a bad relationship by simply using standard and somewhat empty words to describe intangible emotions. "I thought I was in love but it turned out I was just obsessed," they'll say, as though they'd just gotten the results of lab work done to pinpoint it. It's a common cover story for the relationship that ended when she had to change her phone number to get away from you.

I'll call this girl Krystal. She was one of those girls, one of those circumstances that I couldn't be held responsible for. I was a victim of her beauty and her mystery, as mysterious as any girl could be at twenty-one years old. Mysterious and mischievous, the kind of girl who'd talk you into having sex in public only to walk away just in time for you to get caught all alone with your pants at your ankles, and then giggle while you were hauled off to jail.

I met her during a two-week stint at a comedy club in Minneapolis in the summer of 1994, after having lived on the road for a little over a year and a half. She was one of two out-of-my-league women who decided in the same week to show interest in me, leading me to buy my own press and suddenly dismiss a lifetime of being ignored by hot chicks as a fluke, a mere oversight on their part. I left town feeling like a pimp on navy payday and imagined both of these ladies crying into a pillow at my absence. I never considered the possibility that they may have only shown interest in me because I was leaving town. It didn't occur to me then, nor did it occur to me several weeks later when, on seeing an empty couple months on my calendar, I decided to return to my waiting angels.

My cockiness quickly ruined things with the other girl within a very short time of my arrival but it didn't matter, as I was sure Krystal was the one I really wanted. For one reason, she was the one I hadn't had sex with yet, and two . . . Well, there was no reason two. Reason one was plenty. And I was so sure she wanted me that I honestly hadn't detected her obvious sarcasm when she'd said on the phone before my arrival: "Sure. You can stay with me. My mother will love it." Now I was scrambling for a place to stay.

I wound up doing couch time at my friend Paula's house and spent my days corrupting her thirteen-year-old son Jonathan. My car had shit the bed a hundred miles outside of town so I showed up broke, homeless and without a ride or a place to be. I was no longer the life of the party. Krystal would take me out and get crazy on occasion at best. One minute she was giving me a noncommittal and unsolicited hand job while we sat in her car and the next minute she'd go out of town for days with friends that she didn't want to talk about. She'd fuck me and a week later deny to me that she ever had, straight-faced save for a devious sparkle in her eye. It drove me mad.

One time whilst I tried to make the love with her on Paula's couch, she became bored and said, "Just rape me."

"Whu???"

"*Rape* me!"

Spindly as she was, I couldn't even pin her arms. She'd just throw me off of her and onto the floor. I'm the worst fuck alive.

She blew me off a few times on plans we'd made and started to become more distant. I became stalkery but in inventive and entertaining ways. She had a day job as a secretary for some classified ad circular. I got a job there telemarketing for a day, just to see the look on her face when I punched in for work. I put on a big fawning display of bullshit in the interview and the boss couldn't have been more impressed. Krystal hadn't seen me come in but was at her desk when I walked out with her boss—perfectly timed—telling me: "Well, we look forward to seeing you first thing Monday morning." I put on an over-the-top, cheese-dick smile, looked right at her and said, "Oh, believe me, I'm looking forward to working here, too!" She tilted her head back, rocked it sideways and yawn-laughed in defeat. It was funny until I had to do telemarketing for a few hours that Monday. As soon as Krystal went to lunch and the joke had run its course, I went permanently AWOL.

It was clever but eventually that type of nonsense wore thin. Krystal told me she had another boyfriend and that I should, in so many words, fuck off. I was devastated.

I had gigs coming up out of town and got myself together to get back to life on the road. The night I was set to leave, I took out the trash at Paula's apartment complex and noticed an enormous box next to the Dumpster filled four feet deep with brand new stuffed animals. I couldn't imagine why anyone would throw them away. So I got the bright idea and headed off to the club where Krystal was working. I found her car, a tiny old Honda Civic, unlocked, and as my parting romantic gesture, I filled it to the walls with stuffed animals, covering every inch but the driver's seat. I called her drunk late the next night after a gig in Sault Ste. Marie, Michigan. She seemed mildly amused at the stuffed animal gag, only because I had left town more than likely. But the conversation wound up in one of those sad, slurring "I loved you and you didn't care" diatribes where you could hear her eyes roll. She called me a psycho and told me not to call again. I'm sure I did a few more times till she took the phone off the hook. I woke up with that familiar stink of shame and left it to actual road miles to distance me from the embarrassment.

About a year later I made contact with Krystal and we went out for lunch.

"Remember how ridiculous I used to be back when I was young last year? Ha-ha, those were crazy times."

Eventually conversation turned to that night with the stuffed animals. After several minutes of "Oh my Gods" and light histrionics, it finally came out that she had driven around for weeks with the stuffed animals in her car only to have her and her boyfriend wind up catching a vicious case of scabies from them. Scabies are much like pubic lice that crawl down into your hair follicles where they party and lay eggs. She said they were everywhere—heads, eyebrows, everywhere. She said the boyfriend still had scars in his genital region from scratching so much. She'd thought I'd done it on purpose. I wished I had. I just couldn't understand why anyone would chuck out perfectly good stuffed animals like that.

She used to come out to shows now and again after that when our paths crossed and we always had fun. She had the greatest laugh and she somehow always made me a thousand times funnier.

I haven't heard from her for several years and finding out she married another guy in the Alps on Facebook, I'm not sure that we're ever gonna take our friendship to the "next level."

Love and obsession are the same emotion, only love requires the obsession of both parties to lay claim to the title. Being obsessed with someone who is obsessed with you, fleeting as it may be, is quite possibly the best feeling in the world. Being in love with someone all by yourself and unreciprocated just ends up making you feel like a chump.

Still, I may fly to Switzerland and apply for a job at her coffee shop. It's only funny if you actually do it.

● ● ●

The first time I worked at the Improv in Tempe, Arizona, was December of 1995 so the Santa hat I'd taken to wearing year round didn't look as ridiculous as it had in July. The staff were cool and let me in a football pool of some kind. A cute waitress was grandstanding and gloating about having won the pool the week before so, under the pretense of "chicks don't know dick about football," I made her a side bet of something deviant in nature, which she laughingly but not seriously agreed to.

This wasn't too long after I'd had similar success with Bobbie. If you are new to my work and don't know that story, I'll gloss over it quickly. Bobbie was a girl I'd met after a gig in Minneapolis and ended up going to a Twins-Red Sox baseball game with, each of our home teams. After some shit-talking when my team was being crucified, I made her a bet that would require that she put out if she lost. And she lost and she put out. That is the quick and unfunny version. The full story, however, to this day remains my most downloaded track on iTunes. Go have a listen.

I kept that "talk shit and then bet her" move up my sleeve from then on, as though it was the move itself that worked rather than an idiot's luck.

This time I just lobbed the wager out there like it was a joke, as it was in the presence of other staff, one of whom I was to find out later was her boyfriend. She didn't tell me about the boyfriend at the time of the bet because they were keeping their relationship a secret. Evidently that club had a "no fraternization" rule that applied to interoffice love as well as with the talent. The waiter wasn't really taken aback by the bet, as it was all done in a jokey-flirty manner and, you know, I'm a comedian. Of course I'm kidding.

The drink policy for comics at the Tempe Improv was that you were assigned a member of the waitstaff each night and you would order through that person rather than going to the bar yourself. That night this same guy had been assigned as my waiter and when I tried to tip him a buck for a beer, he'd politely refused my gratuity. Yeah, it was only a buck but I wasn't rich and with as much as I drink, a buck a beer will add up. But he wouldn't take my money so I knew he wasn't pissed off about the hitting on his girl thing. Just a joke, see? But I still thought I might be able to fuck her.

After the last show of the week, a Sunday, the three of us met up with some other staff to go to a disco night at some dance club and started in on the Goldschläger pretty heavy. At one point in the evening the boyfriend was out dancing while the girl and I were talking about road trysts. She asked me, hypothetically, that if she were to sleep with me, if I'd respect her in the morning. She actually used that 1950s cliché. And I'm sure that it may have been strictly hypothetical but at the time, in my saturated head, it meant she was going to blow off her boyfriend and fuck me. We stumbled out at last call and they drove me back to the comedy condo, the boyfriend driving her car with me in the back trying to focus, somehow thinking I could still pull this off.

They dropped me in the parking lot and I said goodbye and thanks to the boy and then leaned through the passenger window and gave the girl a big sloppy kiss good night, smiled and weaved my way inside. I stood in the condo laughing for a few minutes listening for the car to drive away, part of me actually thinking she might leave him with her car and come inside. I could still hear the car running after a while so I walked back out to see what was going on. The boyfriend was standing outside of the car, yelling through the open window to his lady: ". . . no, he owes you an apology!"

I went over and said that if anything, I owed him an apology but I'm sure I said it in a way that insinuated that I didn't owe her an apology at all since she wanted to fuck me.

This seemed to rile him up even more, who'da guessed, and after a long exchange of words he grabbed me by the throat and slammed me into a car. The girl dragged him off of me (probably leading me to believe she wanted to protect me, her secret love) and tried to cool him down. I went back over, full of adrenaline and beer-bravado and after another few heated words, head-butted him in the mouth. This was another poor choice in a long night of them but the ensuing scuffle was brief and again, she pulled him away, sat him on the curb and tried to calm him down while, perhaps, devising a plan to give him the slip and come fuck me.

Now, as he sat enraged on the sidewalk, I had a hilarious idea to diffuse the situation. I walked over and said, "So hey. I guess you want that dollar now." This set him off completely.

He sprang from the curb breathing fire and chased me as I ran airplane style around parked cars, adding in a few Three Stooges Curlyesque "Woo-woo-woos" before quickly running out of gas and falling down in the parking lot, where he promptly began delivering a well-deserved ass-beating.

I've always had a problem with nervous laughter, one that's gotten me hit by any number of girlfriends in the heat of an argument. The more you yell at me, the harder I laugh. I can't help it. I wished I could at this point because, as the waiter sat on top of me punching me in the back of my head, I continued to laugh. Which only seemed to goad him into hitting me harder, which made me laugh more, etc. And he was really beating the fuck out of me.

Finally somebody came along and tried to get him off of me, to which he replied, "He tried to beat up that girl!" It was akin to me tapping out in MMA and having my opponent tell the ref that I was still good to fight.

The passerby chimed in with: "Oh, you like to beat up chicks, huh?"

I managed to squeak out: "No I didn't, go ask her!" The passerby asked the girl and she of course denied that I'd tried to beat her up. The pummeling stopped just as the police showed up. They separated us and sent us on our way, him with the girl (who after seeing how much punishment I could take, most certainly wanted to fuck me) and me with a broken nose, chipped tooth, various contusions and a commitment never to drink Gold-schläger again. Brand-shaming.

The next day I talked with the manager of the club after he'd spoken with the other two and I found out that the only punch I'd landed in the fight aside from the head-butt was a nice closed-eyed roundhouse that struck right at the point when the girl was leaning in to break us up. It had landed on her head, not his.

I've never been anything near a fighter and probably wouldn't have done any better sober, aside from not getting myself into that position in the first place. The manager asked if I wanted to take any action against the waiter and I told him no, that it was certainly a beating I was asking for. In fact, when I look back over the years, I'm surprised that I didn't get my ass kicked a lot more often. One heavy-handed trouncing in all these years of being an asshole is pretty good odds and I think I'll quit while I'm ahead.

The beauty of the story was that when I returned to LA with two black eyes, everybody asked me if I'd gotten a nose job. In a way, I had. When I'd tell them the truth, that I'd been a drunken dick and somebody stoved my head in, they felt sorry for me. Sorry that I was too embarrassed to admit that I'd gotten a nose job. It was like being a girl in a town full of wife beaters, trying to convince everybody that I really just fell.

COMEDY STILL
ISN'T PRETTY

f you follow your dream of fame all the way to Hollywood like Becker and I did, you may find out that you are too ugly for television. This is far more likely to happen if you are overwhelmingly considered unattractive by most people. Statistically.

It is widely reported that the media is responsible for what men find attractive in a woman. I've always contended that my dick tells me what I find attractive in a woman and that I've never woken up to find my dick reading a *Cosmopolitan*. We are also repeatedly told that women are more attracted to a man's personality than his physical attributes. So where a lady might find herself too fat, I should find myself too uninteresting.

More than that, we have always been told that there is someone for everyone. I've met too many people who have never found anyone much less the right one and they are far too old to have hope. Maybe we should stop listening to what people tell us we are supposed to believe.

Becker and I—with new confidence since my "nose job"—went to an audition for a rebirth of the game show *The Dating Game*. If you are too young to remember, it's a game show about dating. Figure it out.

This was a big show in the seventies and now in the nineties they were trying to bring back an updated version. Updated usually means "less funny." We tried to make it more funny.

The cattle-call audition had roughly twenty to thirty people in a large room that started with all of us filling out a questionnaire about ourselves. It was very tense. Becker and I being the only comedians felt undue pressure. You know, because ladies like personality. We were lacking the Hollywood looks. And there was only one girl who you would need to bank on personality over looks. She was a Sasquatch she-monster, six foot at least if she could ever straighten her spine.

Then they called people up one at a time to answer questions from the producers like when you had to speak in front of your middle-school class. Becker baited the waters of the questionnaire with a joke I'd heard him riff before.

In the "Previous Accomplishments" part of the questionnaire, he'd written that he was the winner of the "Hydrocephalic Comedy Competition."

That was the bait.

The producers bit on it like starved carp.

"It says here that you won the . . . *Hydrocephalic Comedy Competition???*"

With perfect beat and false humility, Becker says, "Yeah. But I'm trying not to get a big head about it."

I was the only one who laughed. Again. Hard laughing. Banging the table laughing like I might choke up puke. It was the same odds as Becker pulling up a trophy marlin on one cast of a night crawler on a bobber. I apologize for the comedy-meets-gambling-meets-fishing references. But that's how it was.

The questionnaire part was only the first round of many. Only Becker, the Bigfoot lady and me were politely excused after the initial questionnaire round. Sometimes you find out that you are ugly, uninteresting, unfunny and unwanted all in the first cut of one game show audition. Or so they tell you without actually saying it.

YOU ARE NEVER TOO UGLY FOR GAY PHONE SEX

The reason I got a job doing gay phone sex was not that I needed a supplemental income, not a job I had to take when I was struggling to make ends meet. Not even for the free, hot, gay phone sex. I took this job to make a point and also because it sounded like it would be hilarious.

The problem started with the fact that I lived in LA and my apartment soon turned into a youth hostel of friends migrating there to take their own blind haymaker at fame. And none of them would find a job to support themselves while they made a campsite of my couch. My friend Big Fat Ron Putnam stayed for three or four months and he wasn't even trying to get into show business, much less find work. He had no reason to be there. Towards the end of my rope I was giving him shit one day for not seeking employment. He responded in all seriousness and without taking his eyes off the television that he'd called about a job as a bounty hunter and was still waiting to hear back. He must have been answering ads out of *Soldier of Fortune* magazine.

It got to a point where I'd be looking for jobs for my friends. Usually while they napped on the couch. The one job I always saw in the classifieds was for gay phone sex. It's the job I would have taken if I needed a job. It paid enough, was nearby and required no skills other than the ability to bullshit and the sense of humor to actually do it. My friends had the "no skills" in spades and they could have used their experience in squatting on my couch for free as a reference for "ability to bullshit."

None of my friends ever bit. I thought they were assholes and I thought they were crazy for missing out on what good material it would make. At some point during a bout of exasperation I said, "Fuck it. I'll do it." Just for the story as much as making the point. I went down and applied for the job and, of course, got it. There wasn't a heavy vetting process, no calling previous employers nor did they ask where I saw myself in ten years. They were going to start me on graveyard shift, which worked out perfectly as I knew I'd be liquored up by then. I also had a bag of mushrooms I'd kept in the freezer for the last few months waiting for a special occasion, and this was it. I went to the Coach and Horses, had a few drinks and choked down the mushrooms before Big Fat Ralphie May drove me down to the job. I was certainly too drunk to drive myself.

The first night was a complete anticlimax (scuuze da pun) where they had me stuck on some monitored trainee line where I only got about six calls in six hours, mostly hang ups, and the mushrooms never quite kicked in.

Not the good story I was looking for, although I did gain a sincere respect for people who work for a living when I got yelled at for taking thirteen minutes on a ten-minute smoke break. Evidently there are people out there who want their cocks mocksucked now, not later! This kind of shit for six bucks an hour. Six bucks an hour was just the base pay. You made your money by keeping them on the line. Even the name of the company was something to the effect of "Premium Hold-Time." Subtle.

The other thing that was surprising to me was that I was not allowed to talk about graphic sex on a 900 line. I don't know if

900 numbers even exist anymore but back then in the late nineties, if you wanted hard-core phone sex you had to have a credit card and call in on an 800 number, the theory being that it will keep minors from getting through. The suckers who called 900 lines can say anything they want, but the operator is supposed to steer them away from sex talk while keeping them on the line as long as possible. Ask them questions like "What do you look like?" and "What are you wearing?" As though you're about to start talking nasty but you never do. A complete fucking scam. No jacking off without proper credit. What a country!

I loved how the laws even separated the vices that were allowed. I could talk graphic sexuality onstage in a nightclub for a living but if you want to hear it over the phone, bring your Visa. Of course, you couldn't jack off when I talked dirty in a nightclub (not that you'd want to) nor could you smoke a cigarette afterwards with your cocktail. You could go to a titty bar where you could have a cocktail and see partial nudity. You still couldn't jack off or smoke, and if you wanted to see full nudity you could but you'd no longer be allowed to have a cocktail and chances are she wouldn't talk dirty to you unless you got too handsy. The only place the girl could legally touch you was in a massage parlor but she couldn't be naked, wouldn't let you drink or smoke, probably wouldn't talk dirty and could touch you everywhere but there. You could see an actor naked and hear them talk dirty in an R-rated movie but then you couldn't drink, smoke, jack off or even heckle for that matter.

So you go back home to drink, smoke, get naked and jack off to porn. Your cable porn wouldn't show penetration and porn without penetration is like hockey without the fights, so you go out in those pre-Internet glory days to rent some real porn but you couldn't rent real porn because you don't have a credit card!

Besides, if you jack off too much you'll go blind, and if you're going blind that's the only way they'd allow you to smoke a joint.

Well, there you have it.

I went back to my gay phone sex job the next day only on the assurance that they'd let me work on one of the hard-core lines. I spent six hours making the most perverse prank calls ever, all at a cost of $4.99 a minute to the customer. This was a precursor to my days "baiting" online, my time fucking with online pedophiles, but it was the same type of monkeyshines. It's amazing what a guy will listen to or pretend not to hear when he's right about to come. If I started off too goofy, they'd just hang up but if I played along at first and waited for them to really get into it, I could say anything.

"Oh ya, I'd love to fuck your ass! Oh baby, yeah. I'd love to have you fuck me up the ass but I just found out today that I have colon cancer and it's spread to my lymph nodes and it doesn't look very good . . . But this probably isn't the time to talk about it. Go ahead, fuck my ass! Pound me right past that malignant lump all the way to the bottom, baby!"

It was the same as if a girlie told you she had worm-riddled diarrhea as you were close to coming. You try to ignore it as best you can. I tried to make them ignore the worst possible scenarios.

"I just had my first black guy last week. I swear, he had an eleven-inch cock and when he pulled outta me, my ass slammed shut like a car door! It shoved my stool up into my lungs! You ever cough up feces? Anyway, what do you look like? Me, I'm a sixty-one-year-old Korean War veteran. I used to drive cross-country tractor-trailer until diabetes took away my legs. I have three and a half inches of uncut, twisted, herpes-scarred penis and one ball. Geez, I guess I shoulda made something up right there, huh?"

When I felt like I was losing them, I'd go back to serious gay jack-talk. Only long enough to get them back to not hanging up. Then I'd go right back to warped.

"I used to use gerbils but that got too pricey after a while and I think the pet store was catching on so now I like to get a big string of rats on a rope, shove them up my kucky-hole one at a time and then yank them out just when I start to come. By the way, do you know anything that will get shit stains out of a Persian cat? My mother is going to kill me!"

I was hoping to get fired but no one in charge seemed to be paying attention. I just kept getting more vile and abusive until my shift was over and I was in pain from the laughter. I don't think I ever went back for my paycheck but if you've read my *Best of Baiting* book, now you know the catalyst story.

And if there's a lesson to be learned for new comics, it's "don't own a couch in LA." Get a love seat. That way, your friends who sleep on it will cramp up with scoliosis after a few days and move on before they become a burden.

IF SOMEONE IS A CUNT TO YOU, HOLD IT IN YOUR HEART FOR LIFE

My early life in the wilderness of the road seemed nothing but a happy time with all the comedians having a certain bond. Even if we hated each other, the audience was always our common enemy. We were weak and outnumbered. And we mostly sucked, so we were usually fighting uphill.

When I moved to LA, I had that same innocent, naive assumption that all comics were a tribe.

Let me cut straight to the shit-talking. I got my first Comedy Central television spot on a show called *Premium Blend*. It went well by my standards of not having many standards at all and I was jubilant. The theater where it was being filmed had a bar attached, much to my appreciation. California had just passed their first smoking ban that only allowed you to smoke in bars but not restaurants. I strutted into the bar with my hot redheaded actress girlfriend, finally feeling like I deserved her. I wanted a beer and a cigarette and polite round of applause for my genius performance, but mostly the cigarette. My heart sank when I saw that the bar was full. That was my pole position. The nonsmoking restaurant side was nearly empty but the bartender said that the corner horseshoe booth between the two sides—the DMZ if you will—was still smoker friendly. I looked in that special booth

45

and I saw David Cross holding court with other people who I assumed were comedians and friends from the shows that had just taped.

I knew this table from the road. All the comics on the road would hunker down in a safe place in the back corner and distance themselves from the plebes in the audience. Comics were all friends from my limited road experience. My gal was getting impatient as I waited for any seat at the bar or that table to open up. Finally a few people left David Cross's table and I breathed a sigh of relief. I could smoke and drink and be the guy who just killed on his first Comedy Central show.

"Thank God."

That's what I remember saying as I pulled into the booth with my gal and lit up a cigarette.

David Cross looked at me incredulously, like I'd just pissed in his calamari.

"Um . . . I'm *with people???*"

He couldn't have said it cuntier. I felt like I'd just walked into a wedding and knocked over the cake. I thought I was sitting down at the regular road comics' table after the show. To say that I felt humiliated is not strong enough. The fact that it still bothers me some twenty years later is telling.

Having nothing else to say, I almost begged for forgiveness at a transgression I didn't even understand. I stammered that I was sorry and that I was told this was the only table I could smoke at.

He looked at me like I was throwing bad excuses for trying to get past the velvet rope into his VIP section as he pointed to all the empty tables in the restaurant. I was too embarrassed to explain the recent smoking ordinances, much less how I thought comedians were all a tight-knit group of friends. It wasn't until later that I realized that "road comics" were generally derided in those circles as boring hacks. That wasn't wrong for the most part. I didn't know that "alternative comedy" meant a bunch of elitist, exclusionary piss-jackets until around that time either. Or at least a few of them.

You shouldn't label. Even when it generally works. Be polite and find exceptions to the rule.

I've hated David Cross ever since—even though I like a lot of his comedy and the fact that I've probably been that much of a self-involved asshole to many more young comedians in my later years. I was just trying to take up a corner booth with friends and have a quiet conversation. But I never would be a cunt to anyone who just wanted to smoke. Even when I won't give homeless people money, I will never deny them a cigarette.*

Randomly, as of this last draft of this book, David Cross followed me on Twitter. So maybe he's not that bad after all.

Fucking ego.

---

*I've caught myself at least thirty times denying homeless people cigarettes since I wrote this. I'm a hypocrite.

NEVER SHY AWAY
FROM A CHANCE AT
A GOOD STORY

A lot of people don't remember how huge *The Jerry Springer Show* was when it first came to prominence in the late 1990s. Some of you weren't even born yet. At its height, the show was beating Oprah Winfrey in some markets. I'd schedule my day around it, not that my days back then were clogged with appointments. Half the fun of the show was trying to figure out the real brawls from the staged ones, the Hulk Hogans from the Mike Tysons. I could come up with less dated references but that would be disingenuous because those are the last wrestler/boxer names I remember. But knowing that some of the shows were clearly bogus, I'd often considered staging an episode myself. I'd also considered quitting drinking, spending more time with my girlfriend, writing a screenplay, etc. that I never got around to doing.

Then I ran into Tom Ryan. Tom and I were booked together at the Laff Stop in Houston, Texas, and were talking one day about *Springer*. Tom told me that he had a stripper friend (every good comic has at least one) who was going to do an episode and needed people to go with her to play different roles. Her motivation for going on the show, he explained, was to push her new literary achievement, *How to Be a Successful Stripper*, or some such horseshit that she'd evidently penned between spins on the brass pole. He said that his stripper friend, Suzanne, had spoken with the *Springer* people who'd shown interest but said she needed to come up with a storyline around which she could push her book.

Figuring a storyline for *Springer* was about as difficult as writing a porn plot, I called Suzanne immediately and started devising possible scenarios. Her only concerns were being the only blond girl in our segment and, of course, pushing the book. Don't forget, she had a message.

Before I could even pitch a simple pizza-boy plot, the producers called up Suzanne and told her they'd come up with a storyline of their own. I would be brought to the show so that my "girlfriend" could reveal to me her secret life as a titty dancer. I would act as though I had been kicked in the nut. Then a second girl, Suzanne, would come out as my girlfriend's new lesbian lover. A kick to the other nut. Adding more insult to injury, they'd then perform a striptease for the audience, during which I was to go apeshit. End of segment. Suzanne would now seek out a girl to play my girlfriend while I worked on getting into character, pretending to hate titty dancers while my friends took turns kicking me in the nuts.

I first spoke with a segment producer about a week before the taping. He briefly went over the storyline, asked a few pertinent questions and told me that I could not, at any time, for any reason, tell anyone that this story was anything other than the truth, including my own friends. My friends laughed when I told them this.

They'd arrange my airfare from LA to Chicago where the show was taped. The taping date was, appropriately enough, April Fool's Day, 1998, although we'd get there two days ahead of time to rehearse.

A limo waited for me when I landed at Chicago O'Hare. No matter how many times I get in a limo, I always look around first hoping that someone I hated from high school is panhandling nearby. No such luck. As I waited in line at the hotel check-in, I noticed a young trailer-trash couple ahead of me looking completely out of place and had to assume they were also there for the show. I listened to their conversation with the front-desk girl as they told her about that day's taping. These two were for real. They didn't need any coaching, I'm sure. I'd bet they fucked in the limo, not sure if they'd ever see the inside of one again. I bet they fucked in the shower for the same reason.

I met with Suzanne and her friend Danielle, who would be playing my girlfriend, in their room where they were waiting on the segment producer. Both seemed pretty war torn, Danielle from a two-day Ecstasy binge and Suzanne from too many years of titty dancing. It was obvious why she left the lap dance for the laptop. Danielle, however, was young, twenty, and many years and rehabs away from writing her memoirs. She was somewhat attractive in a low-grade kind of way, like she could have been voted prettiest girl at Job Corps. But pretty has a lot to do with attitude and with that in mind, Danielle was as ugly as pigs fucking.

It was also clear from the beginning that we weren't on the same page. My plan was to be so outrageous that we were shoo-ins for the *Too Hot for TV* video, the uncensored video they sold in infomercials. That was my goal even if I had to punch Jerry right in the face. Suzanne wanted absolutely no violence. She was very "Gandhi-like," if Gandhi were an obsolete stripper with a tit job that looked like it was done in an auto body shop. Danielle actually said she wanted our segment to have "a little class." I waited for laughter but none came. I was definitely a man alone.

The producers, who couldn't produce a loose stool after a hard "Cinco de Mayo," exuded all the class and competence you'd expect from a show of this caliber. They arrived late and began spitting out greetings, directions, flirtations and questions like they were fresh from an Adderall tasting party. We were handed outlines of the show we'd be doing. It wasn't a script, really, as it contained no actual dialogue. Just the basic beats of the segment. Danielle will tell Doug that she lied about her secret job as a topless dancer, Doug will become upset and so forth.

We were warned not to let the outline leave our rooms, as they'd be taking them back before we taped. We were also warned not to talk to anyone if we were approached in the hotel, as the investigative television show *20/20* had been snooping around. With that said and done, we started rehearsal, which mostly consisted of having the ladies strip. Over and over again. It was clear, if only to me, that this wasn't all in an effort to make a quality television show, but merely a perk of the job. I mentioned this to the girls afterwards when we were alone but they defended it, saying it was the production's job to make sure it looked perfect. If it looked perfect the first four times, why the fifth and sixth times? More blank stares. My fault for trying to point out blatant sexual harassment to vapid titty dancers. I didn't bother to point out that at no time was there any mention of promoting Suzanne's book.

I was still a man alone and now the numbers against me were mounting. I went back to my room and in the morning I had my agent put in a call to *20/20*. Shortly afterwards my phone rang. A woman named Penelope Fleming was on the line from New York. She was vague and would not commit to the fact that they were indeed doing a story on *Jerry Springer*. She listened to my story with a distant interest and said she'd call back.

Soon my phone was ringing off the hook. On the next call Penelope remained vague but "happened to have" someone in Chicago now and would have them call. Next a guy named Glenn Ruppel called and I reiterated my story. He asked for a copy of the outline. I told him I'd leave it partially sticking out under my door so he could come pick it up and copy it while I was at another rehearsal. I told him to do it quickly, in case they asked for it back. Fortunately the *Springer* people were hours late again so I waited in the hotel bar. Glenn and his assistant wasted no time getting in and out. I was still in the lounge when they came down from returning the outline to my room. I pegged them immediately, as they looked around, walking like they had rods shoved up their asses. They were either the 20/20 people or rookie narcotics officers destined to have memorial highways named after them. I made eye contact, gave them the high nod, did everything but scream "I'm from *Springer*" through a bullhorn before they sidled up to me at the bar. They positioned themselves to look like they were only talking to each other and told me to call them as soon as I was out of rehearsal. I felt like I was Deep Throat in *All the President's Men* and I liked it.

As soon as we were done, I called Glenn and arranged to meet him somewhere up the street at another hotel lounge. From there we hopped in a cab and I was secreted off to an office building where a camera crew was waiting to do an interview. Had I known I was going to be on camera I might have showered or maybe combed my hair. But probably not. Nonetheless, we taped the interview and before I knew it I was back in a cab and on my way back to the hotel, without a kiss goodbye or a Handi Wipe to clean off with. I felt like I should have been graciously heralded as a hero for blowing the lid off this case.

The next day in the studio we were separated into groups, segregated from any other person in our own segments. I was sharing a dressing room with three other guys from different segments, all of which they readily admitted were contrived. We were outfitted by the wardrobe people and given contracts to sign. I asked for a copy of mine but was denied.

Shortly after, some producer came crashing in like a drill sergeant, shrieking at the top of his lungs: "ALL RIGHT! I WILL NOT HAVE ANY PUSSIES ON MY FUCKING SHOW! I DON'T WANT ANY BULLSHIT! I WANT FUCKING ENERGY OUT THERE!!!!!" It was hard not to laugh but I'm sure with some of the dunce caps they get on this show, it's sometimes necessary to focus them.

He went through each person's dialogue and then brought them out one at a time as each new segment began taping, mine being the last. Once onstage, everything went as planned. The horrible secret revealed, me spouting my disdain for the field of titty dancerdom, the lesbian lover, the nudity and my going apeshit.

"How would you like it if I came on national TV and said I was gay and took off my clothes?" I said, jumping up and dropping my pants. "Hey, Jerry, look at me! I'm half a fag! Ya, c'mon, dance with me, Jerry, I'm a homo!" I was quite the riffer. I walked off the stage and they went to commercial. We all went back out for the final segment, answering questions from the audience. No one had any questions for me so I just sat there until it was over.

At that point a half dozen of us (neither of my girls) were taken directly to the airport where we were all on the same flight back to LA. I talked with a few of the other guests on the plane and we went out for sushi and drinks back in LA. Most of them said they had done the show for the "exposure," as though Tarantino would be sitting on his couch with his hand down his shorts watching *Springer* looking for the next Uma Thurman. We exchanged numbers and called it a night.

The next morning I woke to the sound of shit spraying through the fan. It was the *Springer* people on the phone.

"What the fuck is going on, Doug?" I was caught completely off guard.

"What'dya talking about?"

"Why did you tell *20/20* that your story wasn't true?" they asked.

"I don't know what you're talking about." I can't lie for shit straight outta bed.

"So you're saying *20/20* is full of shit?"

I paused for a second, then said, "I can neither confirm nor deny and have no further comment" and hung up the phone.

The next call was from Penelope at *20/20* wanting to know the names of the people in the limo pictures and how to get in touch with them. She needed someone to corroborate my story. I gave her the little information I had. Meanwhile *Springer* people were busy calling everybody from the show, reminding them of the consequences and threatening lawsuits should they talk. I was unconcerned. Those were risks you could take when you didn't have any money. Suzanne retained an attorney and stopped answering her phone. *20/20* went so far as to send someone to her house. She wouldn't say a word. The *Springer* people got a sworn affidavit from Danielle saying that our story was completely accurate, that I'd never known Suzanne until she came out on the stage. I faxed phone bills to *20/20* showing calls to Suzanne from a month before to prove otherwise, but it wasn't enough.

20/20 couldn't air my interview without someone else coming forward. It was scheduled to run on a Monday, which was then three days away. Without corroboration, they would have to run with their original piece on Springer that they'd been working on, about him degrading unsuspecting people on his show. Either way, they were going to cash in on his popularity.

Over the next three days, right up until hours before the *20/20* show aired, we tried to get another source. I went down to a theater where one of the girls from the plane performed in an improv group. She said she couldn't talk to me because the *Springer* people might be watching. Like it was the CIA. And she was serious. Finally, *20/20* went with their original story.

About a week later we caught a break when the show *Extra* came up with a group of people who said their *Springer* shows were all rigged. The story made it to every local news channel that day and I made sure to call every one of them, scratching for my fifteen minutes of the pie. I got on a few local news channels, including the NBC affiliate, which passed me on to *Dateline NBC*. *20/20* got the people from *Extra* and ran a drastically different story than the one a week previously.

In the first exposé, Jerry Springer was spotlighted as being bad for exploiting his guests. Now, Jerry Springer was bad for not really exploiting his guests. Poor prick couldn't win either way. *Dateline* sent a crew to my apartment. The producer told me to pause before I answered the questions so they could cut Maria Shriver in later, pretending to be in my apartment asking the questions. I said, "So you want me to pretend that you are Maria Shriver and tell you how Jerry Springer is all bullshit?" They said, "Heh-heh."

In the end, *20/20* and *Dateline* cut my interviews down to a few benign words, focusing mostly on the people whose episodes had already aired. I got a few sound bites and, what I was looking for initially, a great story to tell my friends. A story I got sick of telling almost immediately.

Sometime a while later, when I was on the road in Texas, I saw the *Springer* episode I'd been on. They had cut my segment out due to the publicity but they couldn't cut me out of the last segment where everyone takes questions from the audience.

There I was, for seemingly no particular reason, sitting Gump-like, looking stupid.

I'd get calls from friends with every repeat of the show. "Hey, man. I think I just saw you on *Springer*. I musta been in the kitchen during your part but I swear I saw you right at the end."

Famous.

PRANKING THE MEDIA

Excuse me while I go all over the map for a decade or so while I tell you about some other fuck-withs I am proud of. I'll get back to the nineties eventually. I assume. But now we're somewhere around 2005.

Joe Rogan and I happened to be playing San Francisco the same weekend and just down the street from each other. He was at Cobb's playing four shows to a six hundred seater while I was just up the block at the Purple Onion playing two shows to sixty. I was excited that we were both sold out.

After my Friday show, Bingo and I hoofed it down to catch Joe's late show. We spent most of the show outside smoking and passing around a bottle in a paper sack that our old friend Hags had shown up with. We could still hear Joe through the door, along with the monstrous waves of laughter shaking the place. It was nearly last call by the time the show ended. We waited for Joe to get done with the pictures and pressing hams before hitting the bar like people clean grocery store shelves before a hurricane.

The place was still lousy with comics after the regular folks were shown the exit, so the bar stayed open late for us. Somebody offered up cocaine. I was trying to be fairly responsible because I had agreed to get up at some ghastly early hour to do a spot on local TV news to promote my show. Worse, it wasn't even gonna be in studio. I had to go to some fairgrounds or convention center for a live feed from a car show.

Now, maybe you're not a comedian but put yourself in my shoes and go down the reasons you don't need to show up for this interview. First, as I said not humbly, my shows were already sold out. Second, it's already 2:30 a.m. and I'm drunk and doing coke. Third, it's going to air early on a Saturday morning. Nobody is going to be watching, at least nobody who would like me. Fourth, the station has no idea who I am. They only agreed to have me because they were sold on the fact that I was the host of the new version of *The Man Show*, which everybody hated. Lastly, I should blow it off because it would stink. There's nothing I could do that would represent my act that wouldn't have me quickly cut off the air. The alternative was me just plugging the club so they get free advertisement and I look like a dullard.

These reasons went through my head in the amount of time it took to douche my nostrils with Miller Lite. I went back and focused a bit more on number four. *They have no idea who I am.* I turned to a local comic, Jason Downs, who was hanging out.

"What are you doing tomorrow morning?"

I bet he was expecting me to invite him to brunch.

"I dunno, why?"

"Do you wanna be *me* on TV?"

I explained my thinking and then continued into overthinking in the way an amphetamine tends to make you do. I'd give him my trench coat and knit winter hat that I was fond of wearing back then. No, wait! I'd need that to get back to the hotel. Otherwise I'd be cold. Wait, I got it. He'd come all the way to my hotel in the morning and get my coat and hat. *Then* he'd drive all the way to the civic center or the horse track or wherever the fuck.

I don't know if it was my enthusiasm for the gag or the gag itself that sold him on the idea but he was in. He was Downs!

When the morning came too quickly, it was him knocking at my hotel room door. I probably just shoved my coat and hat at him through the door and mumbled a good luck. It still hadn't dawned on me that if they don't know who I am anyway, wearing my trench coat and longshoreman's knit hat is a completely unnecessary step that he drove across the city to fulfill. But some great plans have a lot of fat that could have been trimmed.

The irony—as the British don't understand—is that instead of sleeping in, I had actually set a wake-up call for when I/he was going to be on live television. I even videotaped it from bed with my feet sticking out from under the covers framing his face. The graphic under his face on the television feed read: "Doug Stanhope: Host of *The Man Show*." He played it straight and dull like I would have had to if I didn't want to get the hook. My attire did not hide the fact that he was about eight inches taller and twelve years younger than me. The anchor didn't have any idea that he was being duped but during the break someone caught wise. I/he was supposed to do a second break but during the commercial, Jason Downs saw a producer rushing the furlong from the control booth towards him talking hurriedly into a headset. Jason knew the jig was up and pounded turf to get the fuck out.

He could still get away with it today, twelve years later. Only he'd be wearing a different unnecessary outfit. They still wouldn't know who either of us are.

•   •   •

Jason Downs does a far better impression of me than I do of Johnny Rotten. Let me start by saying how much I loathe doing radio interviews, especially by phone. There are always too many people talking and a delay that makes everyone talk over each other. There is no face to read that tells you when you're going too far or when they're trying to wrap up. I'd rather play the sixty seater by word of mouth than have to promote a bigger show. But sometimes you are contractually obligated to promote.

This time I was obligated to promote something that included a telephone radio interview, pre-taped for a later air date. It would also be transcribed as a print interview for *Huffington Post*.

My phone was ringing at six-thirty in the morning. I ignored it. It rang again and by the time I picked it up and screamed, "WHAT THE FUCK DO YOU WANT???" I realized I'd missed the call and was yelling into a dead line. Then I got angry when I heard the beep that there was a voice message. I wanted blood.

"Hey, John . . . This is [name not remembered] and we have a phoner scheduled. It'll all be pretty simple stuff, just a few questions about PiL and your upcoming tour. Gimme a call back . . ." etc.

I knew that I had a phoner scheduled for 11:30 a.m. and even in my delirium I was sure that it was not 11:30. I'm no fan of music but somehow I put "John" and "PiL" together and realized it was the same radio guy I was supposed to talk to at 11:30 a.m. fucking up his contact info and calling to interview Johnny Rotten.

My contact lenses were still blurry as I pulled up Johnny Rotten on Wikipedia and returned the call. For the record, I've worn contact lenses since my twenties and sometimes go a year without ever changing them out or even taking them out. They will tell you two weeks or a month at maximum. I think they are full of shit and so far, so good. Sometimes the only downside is when you are trying to read the Internet at an inhuman hour of the morning, trying to read some facts about a person you are pretending to be. I faked a British accent as well as I could (and can't at all) and started the interview.

It stinks when you have a golden comedy opportunity like this but you don't have the faculties. I had that one strand of sense memory that connected PiL to Johnny Rotten. That was the extent of my knowledge. I'm squeezing my eyes to fight the gunk on my contacts trying to read the computer but it didn't matter.

The questions were all softballs and I answered with bunts. I apologized for being extremely hung over—neither of us knowing that Johnny Rotten had long been sober—and when I got stuck on a question, I'd fill my mouth with water and spew it into the toilet to create the sound of violent blood-vomits. I kept making references to my wife divorcing me, neither of us knowing that his wife had, in fact, died. All in all, it was a good interview.

Eleven-thirty a.m. came around and I was wondering if the phone would ever ring for my actual interview. When it did, I was wondering if the *HuffPo* guy was gonna be unloading a truckload of shit on me for pretending to be Johnny Rotten. It was the same guy but he went straight into interview mode, asking a lot of the same questions he'd asked me earlier when he thought I was Johnny Rotten.

I played that interview straight as well, knowing eventually he'd figure it out and neither interview would ever air. But I was wrong.

Several days after, the fake Johnny Rotten interview aired. They edited out all of my fake vomiting and any vulgar language, killing all the funny I might have added. The interview went out and it eventually came to light that it was bogus—only when we posted it on my website with the full story behind it. The Rotten camp wanted it taken down. The interviewer begged us to take it down. He was afraid of being fired. He wasn't aware that nobody gave a fuck about me OR Johnny Rotten, much less him for that matter. And besides, he'd cut all the funny out of it. At six-thirty in the morning, I could only focus on believable and I failed miserably even at that, so maybe he should have been fired.

• • •

I'd done the same thing in Tampa, Florida, only live, in-studio. Thanks to social media I rarely have to do terrestrial radio anymore and I no longer work full weeks at comedy clubs that require it. It used to be that clubs would have you go out and do any radio station they could get you on, regardless of the audience. Of course, on regular radio you have to keep it clean so I'd have to show up at whatever zombie hour of the morning when assholes sit in traffic to not do my act. On rock-and-roll stations you could dance around language and still stay within the parameters of "decency" that are legally required. But then I'd get stuck doing country-western or sports talk a.m. radio where I have no business being nor would their listeners have any interest in seeing the show I was promoting if they knew what it consisted of.

Here's where I'd have a decision to make. I can play it straight, have a few timid yucks at the expense of the town or the news of the day, keep it light, get your plugs in and get the fuck out. The problem with this is the deception of it. Here I'd be selling a product that doesn't exist. Your listeners would all think I'm some family-friendly cruise ship act and then they show up to a litany of fist-fuck jokes, blasphemy and abortion stories. I'm basically inviting complaints and walkouts. This makes me the asshole.

Or I can just talk about the same kind of things I do talk about onstage and, even without the obscenities, I will be shuffled out of the studio and possibly burn the club's bridge with the radio station. I'd ruin it for all the upcoming comedians whose personas are better suited for that market. This also makes me the asshole.

A lot of times the clubs and radio stations would try to alleviate the problem by calling me "X-rated." This is also dishonest.

This can lead people to think that what I do is just a lot of swear words and fuck jokes. In truth, my language and my fuck jokes were the last thing people would complain about. That was the soft stuff. The people who hated me were the ones who took exception to my opinions. Plenty of folks would have no problem seeing an X-rated show but then go apeshit when I start shitting on religion or yesterday's plane crash. My apologies. I'm sorry you brought your wife out to an X-rated show and then I'm wrong for making fun of your Lord and Savior. My bad. But still, "X-rated" gives the illusion that there will be sexual penetration at some point in my show and maybe that's why you're scribbling angrily in a comment card. I guess I'd be really upset if I bought an X-rated movie and it was just some dude talking for an hour.

In Ohio one winter I did a station where I had a window view of the bleak, industrial landscape and its utter lack of prospects. As I implored the listeners to skip work and keep driving south to Florida and a better life, I made the mistake of describing their existence as "Dickensian." The jocks were so panicked that this X-rated act was going to swear and get them fined by the FCC that they jumped to the five-second delay as soon as the "Dick" part came out. Censored for a literary reference and I've never even actually read Dickens.

Back to Tampa. This was probably late 2005 when my life was in full "who gives a fuck" mode. Brendon Walsh and I were doing two morning radio shows, both stations in the same building, Chaille and Bingo in tow. As you may know, we're fond of thrift store shopping and back then would find the most ridiculous outfits we could pick out to wear to the shows. We'd found Muslim prayer robes on this trip and thought it would be funny to bring Bingo to the station like this, head shaved bald, bare footed and wearing a hijab. We told her to just look at her bare feet and mumble to herself and we'd act like there was nothing amiss. The banality of the hosts was offending. The female of the duo capped any and all stories with a drawn-out and unsultry "Aaah, good times," like she hadn't listened to a word. All the time Bingo was doing a short shuffle in a corner, eyes crossing and chewing her thumbs. When Bingo and I stepped out during a break, the host asked Brendon gently what the story was with the bald gal.

Brendon put on a full-panic face and told her that he didn't know. He told her that I'd picked Bingo up in a truck stop, that he thought she might only be sixteen years old and that he was so creeped out that he was thinking about quitting the whole tour. Then we walked back just in time to go back on the air. The tension was crawling but not a word about it was spoken. Bingo got more spastic, intermittently squeaking sounds and picking invisible bugs off of her scalp.

"Aaah, good times."

We finished the first station and stepped out front to smoke, killing time until the second. A woman pulled up in her car and jumped out, obviously harried. When she saw us standing there disheveled and leaning against the wall you'd have assumed she was terrified of us. Instead she ran up and asked me: "Are you Steve???"

I told her that I was not Steve. And immediately Bingo corrected me.

"Yes, he is Steve."

Evidently this complete turnaround didn't raise any red flags. She apologized for being late. I forgave her as I, Steve, am a decent person. She guided us to the station where Steve was to do an interview. She filled me in on the basics, that we'll be doing so many minutes and this and that. Chaille had been fond of filming everything—back then with an actual video camera before phones were all-capable—so he had pulled out his camera and started filming right away. When the nice PR lady asked why we were filming, we told her that we were doing a "little documentary." Again, she asked no more questions.

We got to the station—fortunately not the one that I'd already done or the one I was scheduled to do next—and she introduced me to the jock. He told me what she'd already told me and that we'd be going on the air in about five minutes. He reassured me that he'd received my press release from my office. I asked to see it so I could make sure my secretary had sent the updated version. He gave it to me. Now I could read who I was and why I was there.

I was Steve Yerrid and I was there to promote the Tampa Bay Lightning hockey game that night where they were having some kids with cancer event during an intermission. Like Johnny Rotten, I played the interview vaguely straight. At some point the lady DJ complimented Bingo on her bald head, ignoring the robe and bare feet. I told her that Bingo had shaved her head out of solidarity for the kids with cancer. The lady thought that was admirable. She continued on that not a lot of ladies could pull off that look.

"Well, our kids with cancer can."

I said it with a damp contempt and let the awkward moment fester.

We wrapped up with the plugs on the one-sheet and nobody was the wiser. But now "Steve's" liaison was trying to take us to yet another station while we were trying to get to our actual station that I was afraid we might have already missed. We somehow ditched her and found the place that I, Doug, was just in time to do.

I rushed through an explanation to the new jocks of the gag we'd just pulled and was almost in the clear when the PR lady found us in studio. By now she'd realized our ploy and was very upset. I laughingly begged my way out. I reminded her that her guest hadn't even showed up and, without me promoting it for him, those kids with cancer might as well be dead. I did have a point. She eventually relaxed a bit except for the thought that she might be rightfully fired for being stupid and late.

The next day we got reprimanded softly by the club for fucking with the radio spots. Turns out that Steve Yerrid was a fat-cat attorney who sponsored kids-with-cancer kinda shit. He'd fucked up which day he was supposed to be there and had done his interview later. No idea if they ever mentioned my interview as him from the day before or why he was there to promote last night's hockey game. But we googled him. His claim to fame was that he'd won the biggest lawsuit against Big Tobacco in US history. And his PR woman believed that I was him, in a group of derelicts, in my pajamas—smoking cigarettes.

So far as my target audience goes, no radio is worse than country-western. Now imagine having to promote my show on the top-rated c-w morning show in Shreveport, Louisiana. On the day after the second election of George W. Bush.

I was with my friend comedian Brett Erickson. The station was seriously concerned due to our reputations and we were repeatedly warned by the club that this was tight-ass conservative radio, that the station was very important to their livelihood and to please not go too far. We chose to, instead of toning it down, just go in the opposite direction. We'd go hardcore in favor of the hosts and the listeners. Hard right wing and wiping it in the non-listeners' faces.

"George Bush won so just suck it up, liberals! Kiss my butt, Michael Moore! Accept the fact that YOU LOST!" We wiped our asses on the Hollywood leftists and all but blew the troops who were dying for your freedom.

We kept pounding away on that course for the entire show. They loved us and we knew their audience loved us. And they showed up in droves. You'd think we were Jesus and Larry the Cable Guy on the same bill. We, of course, stuck to our regular acts once these minions had paid the cover charge. They would have walked out on Erickson's act alone if he'd told them the entire radio show was a ruse. It should have been obvious by the content of his material. Maybe they were confused and thought he wasn't the guy who had been on the air and that I—their Republican Hero—would be coming up next to save the show.

I would go into my regular set until I could see the tardive-dyskinesia twitching ripple across their faces and then I'd wait for them to fully convulse.

"By the way, if you heard us on the radio, that whole 'Yay, George Bush' thing was all bullshit. Fuck that guy. I just figured that if you're gonna hate me, you should pay for the ticket first. I don't want you to get to hate me for free on the radio. It was just a bait and switch scam. Like when the cops tell you that you won a free television and then they bust you for a warrant when you show up to claim it."

Then the walkouts started.

"Have a nice night. No refunds."

It was hilarious to us the first night. But we had five more shows to do that week. Crowds of people hating your guts night after night, show after show will wear you down, no matter how much you tout yourself for not giving a fuck. By the end of the weekend we were miserable.

Erickson and I were at a bar late night on the Saturday after the two last shows of agony and we were grinding our axes with alcohol. Fuck all these people. Brett was hanging with some stragglers from the staff and I'd somehow gotten into a conversation with some military guys expounding my views on the war and 9/11. Needless to say, we had differences of opinions. Two shows of shit that night weren't enough. I had to start a third. Plus, they were only air force, which in my porous mind meant I could take them.

If I had a case to be stated, my mouth couldn't seem to put it together. If I'd been more sober, I probably would've been beaten immediately. You know, for my freedom. Instead these guys were encouraging my stumbling diatribe. Even that drunk I could tell they were just goading me to talk more shit so that when they did eventually hammer me, all of America and the cops and bar staff could feel it was justified. I was going along for the ride and kept pushing the issue.

At some point Erickson caught wind of what was happening and about to happen. He walked up to the table, politely excused the interruption, stepped in, tilted my head back and plunged his tongue deep into my mouth for an extended period of time.

"Sorry, guys. I think that means it's time to go." I smiled.

Shock and awe. Nothing stops sadistic military guys cold in their tracks like raging public acts of homosexuality. They sat there dumbstruck and we walked out without another word spoken.

● ● ●

The old Allen Park Inn in Houston had everything a comedian could ask for except porn. They had a bar, restaurant, room service, a pool. Perfect save no in-room porn. This was in the prehistoric, unthinkable days before the Internet. So for a young comedian to beat his meat after a long hour's work, he'd have to use his imagination that he'd already used up onstage. I had early morning radio the next day and needed the sleep that beer and a porn yank could deliver.

They did have HBO and *Trading Places* was on. I remember thinking that I could possibly time a jack to the sensational three-second tit shot of Jamie Lee Curtis. If I were thirteen years old, maybe. In the movie she plays a streetwalking prostitute who happens to be hot as fuck. So I blame the media for my decision to grab the weekly and dial up a hooker on that lonely night.

Escorts in the classifieds didn't have pictures, so you'd go based on descriptions. And you believed what you wanted to believe. If it said "Blond, 5' 2", 125 lbs." your boner would imagine those stats in the best possible light. You don't think, "Well, it doesn't say if she has arms and legs or skin or anything."

The woman who showed up at my door was blond, 5' 2" and probably 125 pounds. She had arms and legs and skin. Otherwise I would describe her as "hard to market."

She looked like an insurance agent. She was my mother's age. She wore a business suit and carried a briefcase. Without it you'd picture her on a porch in West Virginia with a Pall Mall staining her creased upper lip yellow. She excused her garb saying that she dressed in business attire so that the front desk wouldn't suspect she was a prostitute. If she were dressed exactly like a Halloween stereotype hooker you still wouldn't suspect she was a hooker. You'd think it was casual Friday at the insurance agency. I was flummoxed. There was no possible way I could have sex with this woman, nor could I be rude and tell her so. I was stumped for an exit strategy. She started to get undressed and her midsection seemed the casualty of a dozen fat babies. Laid back on my bed with my pants off, I could only sit and pray that she was really a cop.

She crawled up on all fours and started to blow me, her breasts hanging like leeches on a dog's belly. I tried to look at the television. She crawled up with intentions of mounting me. I stopped her, thought quick and said, "You know what I'm really into? I want you to sit on the other bed and watch me jerk off."

I'd gone from not wanting to jerk off to Jamie Lee Curtis to jerking off while pretending this woman wasn't in my room. Through some act of transcendental flight from reality I was able to deploy an adequate amount of seed that would fulfill my side of the bargain and sum up our transaction. Thanks for coming by and be careful on your way out. But she didn't leave. She told me that I had plenty of time left for the hour rate and she started to chat. If you haven't had experience with prostitutes, this doesn't happen. Hookers try to make you cum as quickly as possible and then get the fuck out, hence their popularity. This gal wanted to tell me about her problems. And I listened, happy just to have our clothes back on. Eventually I told her I had an early meeting and had to get to sleep.

The next morning on the radio I launched into the story on the air. At first they thought it was a bit that I was doing, but eventually they realized I wasn't kidding. I told them that I had the number for the escort service that sent her and wanted to call them live on the air to confront them about quality-control issues, like the nightly local news guy who busts shady businesses. They were up for it but before we could, the program director shit-canned the idea and said they could get sued. Getting sued by a prostitute for slander—surely unprecedented in the halls of justice—would be a much better story still and no jury on earth would believe this woman could have gotten paid to have sex.

HOOKERS

A s I've said onstage, I think a lot of women look at hookers like scabs crossing a picket line. "You can't just go out and sell it! We're holding out for so much more!"

I still believe that. I see nothing wrong whatsoever in a woman's choice to take that career path. The moral conundrum lies in *why* she chose that road. When I used to get a lot of escorts, I wasn't fully aware of how many were doing it through coercion or to feed addictions—how many *had* to do it. I imagined them all to be savvy self-made businesspeople who had figured an easy way out of the daily grind of the nine to five, sleeping on barrels of cash in the mattress, saving up for that trip to Tahiti and that degree in mechanical engineering.

I even had the hubris to think they'd be really happy to fuck me. I imagined that most of their calls were hairy, corpulent men who sweat a lot and treated them like litter. Won't she be thrilled when I open my hotel room door to find this pleasant, young, long-haired kid offering her a seat and a cocktail! I had one escort in Seattle who I was so sure had fully enjoyed our time together that I sent her off with an autographed copy of my first CD, *Sicko*, which had just come out. Like a parting gift, so she knew she had fucked someone famous. I told her excitedly that there was a good hooker story on it she'd really like. I imagined her and all of her hooker friends at the hooker dispatch station sitting around listening to it and laughing and coming to my show the next night. Hookers are never happy to fuck you. You just have to hope they can act like they are.

● ● ●

The only exception to this rule that ever happened to me was when I was in my early twenties living in North Vegas in an extraordinarily skeezy trailer park. It was the only time in my life that I'd occasionally play around with meth, which back then was called crystal and you only snorted it. Or that's all I knew to do with it. My neighbors were a couple and were hardcore tweekers, staying awake for five and six days in a row on that poison and telling me about their shared hallucinations. They would see the same elves on fence posts. They were also where I scored meth. Right next door.

On an afternoon after work—I was still a telemarketer back then—I had plans to drive to Pahrump, Nevada, to visit my first-ever legal brothel. I was very excited and told my neighbors about it over some bumps of crystal. You'd think I was talking about going to see my favorite band, I was so anxious. They asked what it was gonna cost and I told them I figured I could get outta there for under a hundred and fifty bucks. He looked at her for a beat or two and said, "Well, shit. You don't have to drive all the way to Pahrump. She'll do it for fifty bucks."

The fact that I'd already been drinking and doing meth made this sound like a grand idea. Plus I could continue drinking and doing meth without having to worry about driving. Win-win. I took her back to my trailer and pooned her in short order. It didn't feel wrong until after I came. You know the feeling. I didn't want to go back and have to look at her husband after that. So I stayed alone in my trailer doing meth and drinking beer. Later that night there was a timid knock on my door. It was the neighbor lady coming back for seconds. This one would be on the house, she told me. I banged her again but somehow felt a little ripped off. If she had done it for free to begin with, I kinda wanted my fifty bucks back.

• • •

Some prostitutes were kind. My second-ever escort offered a "twenty-minute quickie" deal for sixty bucks, which was most of what I had to my name. I was twenty-two or so and not very astute in the ways of the call girl. She came in, peppy, friendly and talkative, wanting to know all about me. She took a beer, used the bathroom for a bit and then came out and slowly got undressed—real slowly—making a show of it.

By the time she got down to her crotchless fishnet onesie as I was literally inches away from plundering her, she pipes up with: "Oh I'm sorry, baby, your twenty minutes are up." Bu-bu-bu whaaaaa??? What a scam! After I begged and pleaded and told her that was all my money, she took pity on me and allowed me the seven to eight seconds I needed to finish and be simply ashamed instead of both ashamed and bamboozled.

• • •

Another lady of the night years later in Florida who only did in-call at her house cost me nearly a seventy-five-dollar cab ride to get to in the wee hours. I hadn't known quite where I was at the time in comparison to her town. She was sweet and let me stay the night. Unheard of. I walked the beach for a long while in the morning before getting a cab back to the condo. I almost wrote "back home" there. I've found myself saying that about random hotels or comedy condos over the million years on the road. Back home.

• • •

Sometimes we'd call escorts just for fun with no intention of having sex with them.

Not long ago, my podcast co-host Chad Shank was on tour with me and Chaille in Montana when we tried to get an escort, only this time it was strictly as a podcast guest. She could be completely anonymous, talk about real-life stories from her career and get paid the same money, plus tip, for the hour. We couldn't get a single girl willing to do it. They'd suck your dick for money but an honest conversation—like kissing on the mouth—was out of the question with a Montana hooker.

Andy Andrist and I were somewhere on the road in Tennessee when we crossed paths with Henry Phillips, who was also in town on a shared night off. According to Henry, Andy and I evidently ditched him at some biker bar close to the hotel by miscommunication or by design just to fuck with him. Regardless, we all met up back at the hotel and the talk turned towards calling an escort. I probably started these conversations. I was the only one with disposable hooker funds at the time.

The joke conversation turned into a knock at the door. We'd answered an ad for a "dancer" who was available for 24/7 outcall services. You know, in case you have an event where nobody will dance at two-thirty in the morning. The joke was that we just wanted her to dance. We set up a hidden video camera, poorly camouflaged on a nightstand. She showed up and we told her that we were big fans of dance, an art form largely overlooked in this part of the country. We asked what type dance she excelled at, what was her passion. Salsa? Swing? The Forbidden Lambada? She waited for us to break face but we did not. We wanted dancing. Just what she advertised. She would have been less trepidatious if we said we wanted to triple-team her bung-pipe.

Stymied and stuttering, she finally fell back on the excuse that she had no music. No music? What dancer has no music?

No problem. We put on the radio from the shitty alarm clock radio on whatever station came in the clearest. I would have asked her to dance to *Coast to Coast AM* George Noory conspiracy talk radio. Whatever we played, she did the best she could do under the circumstances. At some point either Andy or Henry let loose with the fact that I was currently the host of *The Man Show* and lied that I was auditioning gals for the show's end segment, "Girls on Trampolines." She went from dancing poorly to jumping up and down on the bed.

"Nice. We'll be in touch."

She left with a story that probably nobody would believe if there was anyone she could tell it to. Good stories for comedians aren't the same as a good story for a prostitute. I don't have to hide the fact that I'm a comedian.

● ● ●

The "let's call a prostitute as a joke" drunken conversation can wind up with the joke being on you.

I was working with Daniel Tosh in West Palm Beach back in the late nineties when the idle, late-night perusing of adult classifieds turned immediately into action when Tosh said, "I dare you." Tosh hadn't believed that I'd actually called and ran to barricade himself in his bedroom when she arrived. Being aware of how drunk I was—one of the primary keys to longevity in being a thriving drunk—I'd already hooker proofed the place, hiding any valuables under my bed.

I was paying by credit card so, from the front room, she was the go-between on the phone with the service. She asked for the Visa number and then repeated it into the phone. She asked for the expiration date and then repeated it into the phone. She asked for the Social Security number and it wasn't until she repeated it into the phone that I realized they don't need to know your Social to pay for a call girl. I made a mental note to cancel that credit card in the morning.

Now she told me that she needed to use the bathroom. The problem was that the bathroom shared doors from both the hallway and the master bedroom where I'd hidden all my stealables.

So, like the Houston insurance salesperson hooker, I invented a fetish as a security measure and told her that I wanted to watch. She happily agreed and hovered high over the bowl while she urinated, making heavy eye contact with me standing at the door.

"Do you want me to piss *on* you?"

Nice of you to ask but I'm good right here.

All my shit was still there under the bed in the morning. It wasn't until years after that I figured out I'd been robbed. I got a letter from a collection agency for an outstanding phone bill from PacSouth where they'd used my identity to set up a bogus account.

I'm sure that if they looked back now, they'd be sorry they hadn't stolen Daniel Tosh's identity instead. He's worth quite a bit more nowadays.

●　●　●

The one time I made it to a legal brothel in Nevada was while filming for *The Man Show* for a couple of days. Brothel owner and grand self-promoter Dennis Hof was a fine host, as were all the gals who worked there. I was in a the kitchen one day between shoots and met a gray-haired older guy and we struck up a conversation. I'd always loved disappearing from LA when I had time off and just driving the vast, empty and endless back roads of Nevada and passing the small towns that dot them. Tonopah, Goldfield, Ely and Elko. He said he loved to do the same. He even ran out to grab me a book he had detailing the roads of Nevada. He was a regular guest—actually more of a friend—of the Bunny Ranch.

Later on Dennis Hof asked me if I'd met Bob Zmuda. Bob is the legendary coconspirator of Andy Kaufman and the founder of Comic Relief. I told Dennis that I hadn't ever met him. He rushed me back to the kitchen to introduce me to the man I'd just spent forty minutes shooting the shit with. Imagine that. Fucking Bob Zmuda. I didn't recognize him not dressed as Tony Clifton.

Dennis told Joe Rogan and me that he'd comp us any girl we wanted. He went on to tell us all these celebrity names of clients who frequented the place. Joe declined the offer. If nothing else, he didn't want to be included in the list next time Dennis was rattling off names of famous clients. (Dennis later explained he only dropped names of people who themselves had publicly acknowledged being clients.) I didn't mind my name being mentioned except that I had a lady at the time. The one prostitute I'd been hanging with the most while I was at the Bunny Ranch was the legendary "Air Force Amy" and she was a fucking riot. Somewhere between Roseanne Barr and Mae West and a veteran hooker. I could drink with her seven nights a week.

The last night as the crew was breaking down gear, we all hung at the bar, slamming drinks. Knowing that Dennis would pay for her time, I felt like I owed her for keeping me laughing for the whole shoot. I figured it wouldn't be cheating if I just jacked off while she dildoed herself. It's in the rules. I blew a festive load all over my T-shirt and we went right back to laughing. As for the shirt, that would be wardrobe's problem. I walked back into the bar where a few people knew where I had been. One who didn't know was Man-Dick. He was some assistant producer who we loathed and our working relationship was contentious on a good day. His last name was Mandrake or Mandrick but he became "Man-Dick" to us. I think he thought we called him that in fun. He was just passing the bar coming towards me, splattered in my own nad-matter.

I raised my arms.

"Man-Dick! Great shoot! Congratulations!" as I went in for a long bear hug. A couple of folks put it together when I started rubbing my chest back and forth against his, and their laughter made him jump back.

"Jesus . . . is that . . .? OH Fuuuuck!" and he sprinted out, pulling his shirt away from his body like he was on fire. We all cried laughing. Nobody liked Man-Dick.

* * *

The only other legal brothel I've frequented is in Costa Rica at the Hotel Del Rey. Light a cigar and picture Havana in the 1950s. I know. I wasn't there either but you've seen it in the movies. The Hotel Del Rey has everything you want in Costa Rica except the beach. It's got a fantastic bar, restaurant, full casino—antiquated in that the roulette is played with an old hand-spun bingo ball hopper instead of on a wheel, but quaint—as well as sixty to seventy prostitutes roaming the floors along with decent enough hotel rooms upstairs to take them.

I don't remember who tipped me off to the place but I went there on my first trip to Costa Rica in 2002. I went on one of my most unbelievable roulette runs of all time, hookers draped on both sides. I couldn't miss.

"How old are you?"

"Twenty-three."

Giant stack of chips on twenty-three red and it hits.

"Do you think it will hit again?"

She shrugs, the question probably beyond her grasp of the language.

"I don't think so, either. Let's move it to thirty-six. That's Jesus's number."

Thirty-six red hits.

Avalanches of chips were coming my way. I waited for a pit boss to have me thrown out, as I was taking them for so much. I'm not really good with math and exchange rates. I was beating the knees out of the odds but basically all those chips were nickels.

But those stacks of nickels bought me four prostitutes that night, the first two at the same time and then two others between more rounds of roulette. Before that, my record was three in one night but those were escorts in the middle of a cocaine binge where I was too fucked up to come—or realize that fact, evidently. This Costa Rica barn burner was a straight-up Viagra binge and gambling has the same effect on me as coke except for the shrink-dick repercussion.

I had copies of my first two CDs with me and I had all four women pose holding them naked for my website. I apologize if those pictures being on the Internet have affected their later careers.

* * *

I've gone back to the Hotel Del Rey a few times since but only as a drinker, a gambler and a tour guide. It's an astounding place. I brought my old gal Renee there shortly after *The Man Show* had started airing. We went directly to the bar after the long flight and chaos cab ride. We sank in and as our eyes adjusted to the darkness, a face across the wide horseshoe bar began to look familiar. When I was fairly certain, I yelled out.

"Bob?"

Nothing.

"BOB!"

Zero notice

"BOB ZMUDA!!!"

He looked up and said, "Oh hey! How you doing! Hey, you ever read that book I gave you?"

Fucking Bob Zmuda. Twice in two whorehouses.

●   ●   ●

Brothels existed fairly openly in Anchorage, Alaska, from the time I first played there in 1995 up until the early 2000s when they started shutting them down. They'd never been legal but a milky eye was turned away from them and they were all located within walking distance of the club I worked—Chilkoot Charlie's—aka Koot's.

When you are a young artist performing with your main objective being planting your dick in an unfamiliar place, having four or five whorehouses within a cold stroll takes the pressure off of actually working the crowd and having to try hard. I didn't have to lie to a girl in order to bed her down. Instead I could be gallant and pay a girl to fuck me without having to be dishonest. Like a gentleman.

Koot's is the biggest bar in Alaska, holding something like twelve bars under one roof, all the floors littered in sawdust and every room holding expectations of fistfight or strange pussy. Becker and I were about to do mushrooms. I didn't want to be tripping and thinking with my dick in this cavern full of chaos. Your drunken dick makes just as poor decisions as your tripping brain. By my estimation, my best bet was to take the mushrooms and then duck out to the Ravenite—a whorehouse a block away at the time—dump my genetic instinct into a willing surrogate and then meet up with Becker at my hotel afterwards.

I got to the whorehouse just in time. They were closing soon at one a.m. Why the brothel would close three hours before the biggest bar in Alaska closed was unfathomable to me. Today as an old rummy who has seen a lot of last-call drunk dudes, it makes perfect sense.

I walked in just as the wobbly knees of the mushrooms started to wreck my confidence. The rubber legs were soon joined by the perma-grin smile. I was afraid to be there but at the same time was ready to connect with a girl. There were only two girls still working, as they were about to close the doors, and both were as attractive as they were ready to leave. I took the blonde.

She brought me into a room, disrobed and matter-of-factly asked if I wanted to go missionary or doggie style, the same way a waitress would ask how you wanted your eggs cooked. This might seem like a no-brainer to some of you kids. But there is math and physics involved that you only do backwards, after the fact.

Any young man who is not a veteran would say doggie style. It is a "style" as opposed to missionary, which is a "position." Style counts. What you don't consider is the person you are playing against. She is a tired prostitute who is just waiting to fill her last order so she can go home to the rest of the wreckage that drove her into this life to begin with. I hadn't considered this either.

I hadn't considered that she'd probably spent the whole day being plooked by fat, unwashed businessmen tourists from the lower forty-eight fresh off a week of salmon fishing or moose hunting, with her having little time or need to clean herself between rounds. I didn't weigh in the fact that the mushrooms I'd ingested would have my senses piqued. I could've smelled a gnat fart from the corner of Northern Lights and Spenard. I didn't even put together the basic variable that stink, like smoke, rises.

Doggie style was the equivalent to putting fire bellows into her and blowing out a long hard day's worth of fuck-stench into my trip-aware olfactory. My boner collapsed like the controlled demolition of Building 7. It was still important to be polite. I blamed my erectile dysfunction on the alcohol, which would normally be the problem. I did not tell her that her gash stank of a mouth riddled with periodontal disease. I will tell you that with a last-call hooker who asks you to choose between missionary and doggie, treat it like a house fire. Stop, drop and roll.

There is a DVD that I put out in 2002 called *Word of Mouth* with bonus footage of me and Becker—by then tripping hard—in my hotel moments just after I'd arrived back from that debacle. It's twenty-five minutes of bawling with laughter so hard that the conversation is mostly indecipherable but now that you know the backstory, you might be able to catch some references.

"I have hooker money and my life is still a shambles!"

KOOT'S

The first time I played Koot's was December of 1995 and I got off the plane wearing a Santa hat and sporting two black eyes. You all remember that waiter in Tempe.

I'd been trying to play Alaska since I was an open micer. My old flame Jacquie Trinka from Vegas was a musician who played Koot's. When she heard they were going to start doing comedy, she asked the booking agent to get me in and he did. I didn't know him then but I do now. That guy was Greg Chaille.

I've been banned, fired or ignored by so many clubs across the country for any reason from vulgarity, drunkenness, or antagonizing the audience to simply pulling my dick out onstage. It was all of these behaviors that endeared me to the people at Koot's. And to this day, the Koot's folk are still the best friends I have, regardless of how often we—or even if we don't ever—talk.

This place was wall-to-wall chaos. Trinka led me into a world of depravity that she only allowed herself to be on the outskirts of. Trinka was and is a good girl. Especially by the standards of Chilkoot Charlie's. Doran the owner regaled me with tales of the old days of Koot's during the 1970s when it was all oil money and blow, fistfights and gun play. The only difference I could see was that Ecstasy had joined the party. All the rest were still in the works.

Day drunks slopped over the bar in silence from the minute they opened until people who wanted to have fun started trickling in later on in the early evening. Smiling customers had a way of gentrifying the bar around happy hour. One of my first days there I was in early to watch Trinka play her solo lounge act during this changing of the guard. Some gurgling old rummy was pent up and angry about being cut off at the bar. He told the security guy that he was going to come back and kill everybody and such and so forth. He was shown the door without notice, as though threats of mass murder were a local way of saying good-bye. An Anchorage "aloha."

Soon a group of Hooters waitresses just off work took up the main bar ("South Long" for the Koot's folk) by the front door where Trinka played beside the door facing in. I remember Trinka playing "Lady in Red" when I saw the old drunk burst back through the door, eyes barely able to focus, with 9-mms in each hand. I was standing right in front of him ten feet away with only the door security between us. Security tried to calm him as the Hooters girls leapt over the bar for cover. The bartender leapt over the Hooters girls to back up security. I stood there smiling like an imbecile. Trinka yelled for me to get away but the drink had taken away any natural fear I should have felt. I didn't want to miss the story. Security calmly motioned his arms up and down, palms down in a "just relax" fashion, until he'd inched close enough to grab both wrists, at which point the bartender bum-rushed into the guy's ribs and tackled him. What happened to the guy between that and when the cops came I don't remember, and nobody saw a thing.

Clan X was the house band doing disco covers during that run, so named for their rampant use of Ecstasy. Yes, I did Ecstasy back when it was called X and meth when it was called crystal. We tripped quite a bit and the "X party" became an annual Christmas tradition for years to come. (Although the first Christmas party I remember instead doing acid and mushrooms at the same time. Which seems wrong somehow. It's like having a chicken omelet. Or a pie filled with cake.)

I was drinking at the bar on North Long after one of my first shows where we were usually followed by the band. A stripper who I had to assume worked only morning shifts or national disasters asked me for my Santa hat. I told her she'd have to blow me for it. I wasn't being rude. I was responding in kind to the way she said it. I didn't know she would do it right there and then. Nobody noticed, nobody cared. Every night was some new buffoonery.

Enter the midgets. I met more midgets in two weeks of Koot's than I had in the rest of my life. To be exact, Koot's beat life 3–2. Kenny and Dave were two of the dwarf regulars. I call them midgets because they called themselves midgets. They didn't give a fuck. They bragged about being thrown out of a "little person" convention for whatever chicanery far more felonious than simply using the term "midget." We became fast friends and eventually had them in black Santa hats selling my T-shirts table to table towards the end of the shows. Then we had them in the cages with the dancers while the band played at the company Christmas party. By the time I left they were neuvo-legend and were getting fucked in storerooms. Not long after, Koot's built Kenny and Dave their own little bar to tend called Emerald City where they served little beers and little shots and had a yellow brick road painted from the front door all the way to the little bar. Doran even made them half-sized business cards. This was disbanded when it became rapidly apparent that the midgets were not responsible barkeeps. People would buy them shots and due to their diminutive size, they'd get shit-pummeled in two drinks and then they'd be trying to get girls' panties off. That would have been the best episode of Bar Rescue ever.

DJ Bob pulled double duty. He was the morning show radio host at KWHL that sponsored the club but was also the DJ at Koot's on the dance club side (South-siiiide!!!) during the week. I met some nice lady after a show and after having little to say, we went directly to fucking. It was a weekday and the Loft Bar above Southside was closed. I gave a nod and a smile to DJ Bob as I slipped us under the velvet rope to go upstairs. He kept the dance floor rolling downstairs as we made romantic love on a barstool above. At some point I noticed the midgets peeking with their big noggins three-quarters of the way up the staircase, giggling and giving thumbs-ups. Then the song would end on the dance floor below and I'd hear DJ Bob.

"Hey, is everyone having fun tonight??? Well some of us are having more fun than others!!! Go, Dougie, Go!!!"

The midgets had been relaying the play by play from the stairs to DJ Bob the whole while we were dunce-fucking in a closed bar above but out of sight.

I knew DJ Bob would bring this up on radio the next morning and was happy to have something fun to talk about. What I didn't know was that the girl had been the fiancée of one of the KWHL interns. Fortunately I was only doing a call-in. By the time DJ Bob had me on the phone he'd already told the story on the air, mocking his intern about it with the hackneyed cruelty that a morning radio jock treats a supplicant.

I played the diplomat and made the most apologetic fun of destroying a relationship as was possible. Everyone was fucked up all the time back there and then. You have to excuse some bad choices. Sometimes people drink and fuck and regret it. Sometimes a girl will fuck a guy just because he was onstage and sometimes a guy will fuck a girl just because she's willing. I can't explain or apologize for these facts. I heard afterwards that they got back together, got married and moved to Seattle. I wish them the best and thank you for the story.

• • •

But this is just the beginning of my first trip to Alaska.

I'd been booked for two weeks, the first to headline and the second just as the opening act to hang out longer through Christmas. I'd done so well that by the second week I had people coming back to see me, and others just on word spreading. I'm not bragging. My act was as dumb as the crowds were back then so I was destroying—to the great misfortune of the guy who was booked to headline on the second week. He was some poor fuck who'd been booked as a favor, some sad clean and sober guy, trying to get back into comedy after a hiatus. And I'm assuming that it was comedy that had taken the hiatus from him. He did political jokes of politics years gone by with references nobody remembered or cared about. I don't even think he mentioned his cock one single time onstage. They hated him. He lasted two nights before the owner called an audible and switched the order. It was uncomfortable to say the least, as we were not only performing together but also sharing the band house for the week. Me all drunk and having the time of my life, him all dejected, demoted and desperately clinging on to his sobriety in this circus of depravity under the same sagging roof.

Nobody who played Koot's came back without talking about—usually loudly complaining about—the band houses. These were three houses across from the club where the bands and comedians would stay. I explain this because I know I need to for some people. A band house is different from a comedy condo in the same way a comedy club greenroom is different from a band's greenroom at a rock-and-roll club. Bands tend to destroy things, leave cigarettes burning on television sets or carpets, piss in trash cans and draw crude dick pics with Sharpies on the walls. The band houses at Koot's were the worst of the worst. The furniture all looked like the stuff you see behind a Salvation Army where even the thrift store rejected it. The windows were so filthy you couldn't see through them more than to tell if it was daylight. I loved it. It was drunk-convenient being so close and it was an endless source of material to ball-bust the club owner during the show. One night, to prove that I wasn't exaggerating the filth, I brought a bar of soap onstage that had been in the shower. The soap itself was covered in black mold. That's a whole deeper level of grime when you can grow fungus on an antibacterial product.

I swore that Bill Burr hated me for years for recommending the gig just because of the hideous accommodations. Glenn Wool got bedbugs from a newly installed couch probably salvaged from some Dumpster. When Sean Rouse played there I called ahead and told the bar to kibosh the imminent rounds of shots that would be sent to the stage. Sean has the tolerance of a fainting goat and tends to bite people for fun on his way down. The bar thought that my warning was sarcasm and doubled down. Sean had to be carried off the stage and took a header on the ice outside, tearing half his face off trying to get home. I'm sure the band house still wears his bloodstains as well as those of James Inman's whiskey vomits. Ralphie May was the only comedian I knew of who weaseled a hotel room out of the notoriously cheap owner, Doran. But that was only because of Ralphie's weight, well north of the four-hundred-pound mark. They didn't think the decaying floorboards of the band house could handle the payload and that a hotel would be cheaper than the inevitable legal and medical costs, much less price of a rug to cover the hole.

On what would sound like a plus side, the club provided you with a band car. This was not because they cared about you. This was so they didn't have to shuttle you to and from morning radio several times a week or pay for a taxi. Doran literally bought most of these cars for less than a round-trip cab fare. "The King of the Fifty-Dollar Car" was a common moniker for Doran and when you'd call him that, he'd be quick to boast of the time he talked a destitute speed freak down from fifty to thirty-five.

Early on in that first run, the radio station KWHL held a forty-eight-hour marathon for Toys for Tots from an RV in a mall parking lot. It was common for people to bring free shit to the station—donuts and whatnot—but now we were soliciting toys and beer. The toys were for those tots. By noontime we were shitfaced and pushing the envelope on the air. On my first night there, Trinka had pointed out a state senator in the bar that she'd gone on a date with who she said kept hounding her relentlessly by phone afterwards. At the time he was on the dance floor cutting a rug with what I assumed was a transvestite. I caught her alone later that night and made comment about her and the senator. She wasn't shy.

"Oh Jesus! That guy has a huge dick and he knows how to use it but now he won't stop calling me!"

I guess he had a pattern.

Pie-eyed in the RV, I told the story on the air and a dim lightbulb went off in DJ Bob's head. He knew the senator's secretary and got her to trick him into taking a call on the air.

"Hey, senator, are you a magician? Because we heard you had a big wand."

"Who is this?" As we tried to stifle giggles like teenagers.

"Was your campaign slogan 'Speak softly and carry a big stick'?"

"Who am I speaking to???"

"You must have a pretty big office cuz we heard you have a huge staff!"

We got as many grade-school, radio-friendly dick jokes in as we could before he hung up and then laughed ourselves silly into an even drunker afternoon. All for the tots without toys.

Later that afternoon, Doran informed me that the senator was on a manhunt for me. He'd stormed into the club demanding to know where the comedian was, threatening alternately to either sue or kick the shit out of me. Doran reminded him that we'd merely referred to his giant cock and that would be a tough lawsuit. The senator was more upset about me referring to his stalker behavior. So upset that he was now stalking me.

After the show that night we were tanked and back on the RV marathon, shilling more Toys for Tots, a charity run by the Marine Corps. It so happened that there was a case looming in the news at the time of three marines accused of raping a kid in Japan. Somewhere my comedy brain connected these dots on the air and I said, "Hey, come on down to the Sears parking lot and drop off a toy for a tot! And if you don't have a toy, maybe you can drop off a twelve-year-old Okinawan girl for the marines!"

I hadn't even remembered this part of the adventure until I called Doran to fact-check some details of the senator story.

"Don't you remember? I got a call at three in the morning saying that I have to get Stanhope out of there because the marines were there and gonna smash your teeth out."

And the memory was rekindled in this call to Doran.

Oh yeah! The Okinawan girl joke! The fact that I told it after having given my exact location in the RV didn't register until it was too late. Who knew that anyone was listening at that hour. Fortunately the Koot's security had a corps of their own with a similar "no soldier left behind" policy who ferried me out in a hurry. I woke up in the band house with all of my big yellow teeth intact. For the remaining nights, I'd have to look over my shoulder. Like the formulaic movie where the guy finds a suitcase full of cash and next thing he knows, he has both the cops and the mafia coming after him, only for me it was an angry senator and the marines. And it was all over jokes instead of a briefcase full of money.

All of the fact-checking with all of the original Koot's gang could not come up with the details of how the senator and I eventually made up. But I know that he came to one of the last shows on that debut Anchorage debacle and we were friendly. The band car that I'd been given by Doran had failed to start in the front parking lot of Koot's so we spray-painted it with "Re-Elect Big Dick the Senator" on the side.

Koot's made me feel like a king and also like I would be dead by the time I was thirty. There was a night that I got up hang-ball naked to do "Rapper's Delight" with the band Clan X. I knew enough of the verses that I still had plenty left when security came to pull me off the stage. I told them that I was only naked so people didn't notice that I couldn't sing. Fortunately as they were escorting me to the door, we passed Doran. He asked his bouncers what the problem had been.

"He was onstage completely naked!"

"Really? Is that true, Doug?"

"Yes, sir."

"Well, we can let him stay if he promises he won't do it again. Do you promise, Doug?"

"Yes, sir."

The security brutes were outraged but couldn't do a thing but shake their heads. I was given absolute power and I was absolutely corrupted.

•   •   •

If this were just you and me in a bar conversation, I would go on and on with Chilkoot Charlie's stories. I'd tell you about "Pipe-Bomb Barney" or Flounder and Longo with the 9/11 dildos. I'd tell you about the night with the nut butter and the liquid latex. I'd blather on about the mornings of waking up in that attic surrounded by a minefield of spent nitrous cartridges so deep that it looked like Flanders Field. There's one story from years later about a vacuum cleaner salesman that sounds like bullshit because just the phrase "vacuum cleaner salesman" sounds like bullshit unless the story was from 1975. If this were a conversation, I'd eventually get drunk enough that I'd spill the beans about the night with the meth and the poppers and the pull-tab girl.

Fortunately you wouldn't know her and fortunately this isn't a conversation. It's a book that needs to move forwards so I will move on to other stories about pulling out my dick onstage and in other inopportune places.

NOTHING TO SEE HERE

The first time I was naked onstage—at least at a gig I was getting paid for and risked losing—was at the Cap City Comedy Club in Austin, Texas, on a Valentine's Day and it wasn't very romantic. I'd headlined two shows that night. A third show was scheduled for late night called "The Midnight Blue Show," where a bunch of the local comics could go up and clean out their notebooks of all the filth they could never do in their regular shows. I was scheduled to close out that show as well. The problem was that the majority of the audience were holdovers from my previous show who were told they were welcome to stay for free. The few who stayed sat through six or seven more acts doing their finest vulgarity before I was due up again. As though I had material even more obscene or dark that I'd been holding back earlier. I did not.

With nothing left in my act to top what was my normal level of "blue," I just went up naked and started doing bad, hackneyed airline jokes until the manager rushed the stage and draped my overcoat around me. When the booking agent heard about it he canceled an upcoming week in San Antonio "on principle" and banned me from his clubs. I still defend my actions as appropriate under the circumstances.

A few months later at the Montreal comedy festival, the same booker was running a show at the fest called "The Danger Zone." One of the nights he had comedian Craig Campbell going on naked to read a poem about circumcision. The festival wanted to make it a theme with other naked art. They got the legendary "Spoonman," made famous by the song of the same name by the band Soundgarden. Spoonman would play spoons naked. Then the booker saw that I was in town and asked me if I could do any other kind of reading naked. I don't know how many people had to decline before he was forced to come to me, the guy he'd just fired for doing the exact same thing. One day's pink slip is the next day's job offer.

Campbell did his naked poem to a packed house. Then I came out naked beside him and read a passage from Bukowski's *Tales of Ordinary Madness,* where he talks about being more afraid of constipation than cancer and how sometimes he would try to suck his own dick to unclog his system. Bukowski goes on to a beautifully poetic, graphically judicious narrative about attempting such an act. At the conclusion of the reading, Craig Campbell and I laid on our backs with our knees at our ears, trying to suck our own dicks while Spoonman played his silverware in the buff. Mitch Hedberg, who I'd been naked in public with plenty of times but who had declined the offer to participate this night, had watched in the wings.

"Man, that shit was *ridiculous.*"

From what I know, nobody talked about that show ever again during the festival. What caused such a ruckus in Austin was a nonevent in Montreal. Not even water-cooler talk. Everyone talked about Hedberg and he got a half-million-dollar deal out of that festival, fully dressed.

• • •

If nothing else, that show put me back on the good side of the Austin booker and he gave me another week at Cap City. Again there was a late late show that went on after the bar closed. The same manager who had thrown my overcoat at me the first time I'd gotten naked on his stage now told me that it would perfectly legal for me to do it again, since this time there was no alcohol being served. I sent someone to the 7-Eleven to get a Bic razor. I went onstage and told some elongated road story sitting on a stool while the ticket-booth girl carefully shaved my balls. And this is where I got fired from the same booker again, this time taking the club manager down with me.

"But the manager told me to do it!"

· · ·

From this point, I'd pull my dick out on- and offstage out of spite. It didn't cause anyone any concern or heartache and is hardly intimidating. Then one night in Utah it went badly.

It all started back in Omaha with my old friend Dr. John.

Dr. John was a fine citizen of this earth and also a smut entrepreneur of unequaled integrity. He ran smut shops, Dr. John's Lingerie and Adult Novelties in Omaha and then Midvale, Utah. Or at least he tried to.

I first heard of him when I was playing Jokers Comedy Club in Omaha where Dr. John was being brutalized and beaten down by a puritan city hall and its team of vice cop flunkies. Evidently making large rubber phalluses available to the upstanding folk of Nebraska threatened the wrong people in high places. They liked the fabric of their morality to be thick like their Carhartt dungarees. John had been arrested on a variety of obscenity charges and at the time was in the news while appealing a fifteen-month sentence in Nebraska . . . for selling dildos. I took up his cause on every radio station I did, as well as on the stage.

Dr. John could have opened sex shops anywhere but he liked to go to places where he could cause outrage. I'm sure that's what endeared him to me and me to him.

We became friends in Omaha. He would give me free smut gear to hand out after shows to promote his shop. He even let me drive his rig. He had an old square-back ambulance with working sirens, lights and screaming PA system. He'd painted it with "Dr. John's Love Unit #1" on the side along with "If We Build It, You Will Come!"

I remember banking a corner too sharply and having a "Door Ajar" warning light come on the dash. It was then I realized that one of the back doors had swung open and sent all the free dildos and butt plugs rolling across the street. The sight of me with my ambulance parked sideways across the street, running around and picking up double-dongers and the like must have been startling.

It was March and some guy I'd met at the club told me he was running the sound at the St. Patrick's Day parade on that Saturday. He said he could get me and the ambulance into the parade. I doubted him, knowing how much Dr. John had been a pariah in the town and in the local news, but I showed up early at his place just on the off chance.

Sure enough, the guy weaseled us into the parade, right between the Vietnam vets and the Midland South High School band. Parents and their children with faces painted green stared gape-jawed as I went by, speakers blaring as I hit the PA.

"Come to Dr. John's Smut Emporium—Seventy-second and Pacific—because those kids didn't come from Immaculate Conception!"

"The Midland South High School has been drinking since six a.m., ladies and gentlemen. I watched the tuba player puke green beer through his instrument not one hour ago!"

"Look! It's the grand marshal of the Omaha St. Patrick's Day parade, a regular customer of Dr. John's Smut Emporium—Seventy-second and Pacific!"

"Oh shoot, there's a cop—hide your beer."

All curveballs meant to stay above the heads of the kids, while amusing or disturbing the adults.

Dr. John opened another store in Midvale, Utah, another puritanical outpost with a glaring absence of vibrating latex or any other product that might make one remember that "sex" thing that has been so popular in other regions of the world.

I happened to play at a club called the Comedy Circuit in Midvale as well, where they put comics up directly across the street from Dr. John's new shop. Utah didn't take kindly to John there either and immediately started harassing him through any means possible, from fines to vice stings to general police harassment. I'd noticed that they had a cop stationed in the parking lot across the street every single night when I'd be coming home, no doubt to dissuade anyone who may have drunk away some of their Mormon-enforced inhibitions from risking a DUI in order to have something soft and lubricated to accompany their genitals.

On hearing about Dr. John's Midvale arrival and subsequent molestation by the powers that be, I again took up his cause in my shows and on radio as I had done in Omaha. Dr. John had hooked up a cross-promotion with Spin, the owner of the Comedy Circuit, who would pass out all sorts of complimentary adult products from Dr. John's during the shows. Dr. John was everything you'd expect from a smut peddler. Round, bald, bloated, clammy and a bit high strung but really, really eager to please. Extremely generous as well. Every time I visited his "boutique" he loaded me up with any and every free item I could imagine. If my girlfriend might like it, if I could bring it onstage and make a joke out of it or if it might simply fit in my ass, he gave it to me and wouldn't take a nickel.

I call it a boutique because it wasn't a skeezy jack-off joint. There were no viewing booths or live nudes. It was a boutique. A boutique that sold remote-controlled vibrating leather underpants, but a boutique nonetheless.

The night John came to the show in Utah was a very special show, the tenth anniversary of the Comedy Circuit that promised to be, if nothing else, very, very long. Spin had brought in four headliners to fill out the bill for the big event. I'll call the other three Carl, Lonnie and Lou. You wouldn't know them anyway but I'll just change their names now and have one less note from the lawyers. The show lasted over three hours. I couldn't watch Hedberg, Jesus, Hitler and Brett Clawson do three hours if they were all back from the dead. All I want to do when I'm part of shows like that is apologize and go short. And let me add that Lonnie and Lou were no Jesus and Hitler.

Dr. John took us all back to his store afterwards for celebratory cocktails. The store had offices on the second floor that looked out over the front counter and part of the showroom. We all sat in one of the empty offices—Spin, Lou, Lonnie and Dr. John, along with a couple other Comedy Circuit staff and a few cases of beer—and we proceeded to curb-stomp our livers. All the while we are sitting behind a security window pane watching fine Mormon couples at the counter below discover lubrication and other brave new ideas. At one point, someone leaned over and banged on the one-way glass while an overweight girl and her boyfriend—who could have been the cop from any caught-on-tape shooting of an unarmed black guy—were stocking up on Anal Eaze or 3X crotchless orthopedic fishnets. Or something else that internal affairs and the church would certainly frown upon.

The guy was wearing a handgun openly on the small of his back, more than likely just for the trip to the porn shoppe.

"Okay, baby, we'll go get you a nightie," he'd probably said as he loaded a fresh clip, "but if any faggots in there look at me . . ."

They looked around self-consciously after the glass-banging, as anyone would do in this place, wondering who was secretly watching them. I stood there, behind mirrored security glass as they both stared up, dropped my pants and pressed my cock against the glass. They continued to look around like cows and we all had a little chuckle.

None of us ever gave it a second thought as we continued getting piss-ugly trashed. Not another thought until a sweaty and wide-eyed Dr. John came running in, half laughing, half screaming.

"What the hell are you doing showing your cock to the customers?!?!"

Evidently what I'd assumed to be mirrored security glass was not that at all. It was good old-fashioned, see-through, clear-as-day, squeaky clean and well-lit glass that I'd smashed my lunch against. I'd been a naked Dustin Hoffman in *The Graduate* to the horror of this pair of bazzoons at the counter. I told John that I'd thought it was one-way glass and he told me not to worry about it, that he'd given the guy his order on the house to placate him. We carried on and soon I got as drunk as one man can get on 3.2 beer without bursting from the quantities.

The party started to break up as we went downstairs. Lonnie and Lou went into a back storeroom with Dr. John to pick up some complimentary smut videos while Carl and I took the opportunity of being alone to do some shoplifting. Dr. John would have given us anything we wanted for free but sometimes it's more fun to steal. Besides, there are some things you don't want a guy to know you're using. So while they were still in the back, we went out the front door with our booty.

Carl's "booty" consisted solely of a pair of silky panties that he was now wearing over his shaved head. I had my plunder under my black overcoat and we headed for the car. We sat down in the backseats to wait for Lonnie and Ludo when three police cruisers pulled into the lot, parked and headed into the store. Afraid that the state legislature had made some late-hour ruling against rubber vaginas that was now going to be enforced by all available officers, I waited for the cops to go inside and then ran across the street with my wares, back to the condo we were all sharing. Carl went back inside the store.

About twenty long minutes later, Carl returned, still wearing the panties on his head as he had done throughout his entire conversation with the Midvale police. They had come, not to raid the place, but to investigate a report of a man in a long black overcoat who had exposed his penis!

That gun-toting piece of shit had taken his free goods and called the cops anyway! What the fuck is that? That's like getting a free meal for finding a hair in it and then proceeding to clean his plate regardless.

And he called the cops because he saw a dick in a smut shop?

If there is one thing you can be guaranteed to see in a smut house, it's DICK! Pocket pussy, maybe. Anal beads, perhaps. Big Rubber Fist, on a good day. But DICK? Every shelf, every direction. Dick. At what point had he seen too many?

"Well, what do we have here? Dick, dick, dick, dick dick, dick, double-dick, black dick, pink dick, strap-on dick, dick, dick . . . Hey, what's that? Look up there! It's a diiiiiiiiiiiiick!!! Hello, 911? Hurry, quick, there's a diiiiiiiiiick!!!"

Fortunately I'd been out the door when the cops got there. That was the good news. Even more cops had shown up after I left, six or seven total, leaving me with the impression that the size of my cock must have been really blown out of proportion in the report. The bad news was that Lonnie had made the poor fashion choice of wearing a long, black overcoat just like mine and had been promptly and viciously detained by Midvale's finest. And to hinder him even further, he was piss-drunk and only got surly with them, refusing at first to even show them any ID or cooperate in any fashion. He did not know what had happened; he must have stepped out during my pants dropping. All he knew was that he didn't do shit and didn't care for these pigs saying that he did. It had, by all accounts, gotten very ugly, with Lonnie barely avoiding arrest.

He didn't know that it was me all along. He would have turned me in if he had. Only afterwards did he find out and now Carl was warning me that I may want to hide under a bed or something, cuz Lonnie was violent, drunk and looking for a fight. I could hear him from the parking lot when he got there, screaming and hollering to his wife that he was going to kick the shit out of me, and his wife threatening to kick his ass if he did. Finally I went out and told him to just come up and kick my ass quietly in the apartment so the neighbors could sleep.

He came in the apartment and continued to slur and fume. He'd drink a beer and start to calm down but then he'd do more coke and get mad all over.

"Well, what the fuck?" he'd stutter and half yell. "You pull out your . . . your fucking dick? What is that? I don't get it?" As though there were some deeper meaning.

"You got me arrested, you fuck!!!"

I pointed out that he hadn't gotten arrested.

"Ya, well, they wrote down my fucking name, man!"

I continued to apologize just to shut him up but it only irritated him further. I decided not to argue and let him sleep it off.

The guy was burned out, washed up and in bad shape anyway. I knew as drunk as we both were, it was best to go to bed. Who could be mad about something so ridiculous the next day?

Lonnie could. Still just as angry the next day. Having his name on a notepad in some cop's pocket somewhere had turned this man into a hysterical housewife. I apologized again and he said that he appreciated the apology but he was still angry and would continue to be angry.

"I still don't get it. You . . . pull your dick out???" He was saying it as though I'd thrown a baby in a sewer drain on a lark. I was at a loss for words.

I'd already been warned by the city of Midvale after my first appearance at the Comedy Circuit eight months earlier. At the end of the show, Spin, who would sing and dance in his act as the house MC, would bring out the comics to take a bow. Then he would do a little dance move and point at you to do a little dance move in return. Not being much of a dancer, I decided instead to just pull my dick out. Spin found that inspirational and had me do it at the end of every show for the rest of the week. When I returned months later, he had a letter from Susan B. Shreeve, the city's business license wonk who had gotten a complaint about my exposure and threatened to pull his beer license should it happen again. I'd spend all of that week reading the letter onstage, trashing her mercilessly. I still keep a framed copy on my wall like a diploma or a commendation.

Ironically, her husband was a sergeant with the Midvale police and was the one trying to take Lonnie downtown that night at Dr. John's. Coincidence? Conspiracy? Or Cock-Haters?

Eventually I started writing material that upset people by challenging their beliefs or ideals rather than just yanking my cock out of my pants. Some nights I did both.

THE SECRET TO
HIS SUCCESS

The year after my failed self-fellatio and Mitch Hedberg's half-million-dollar deal in Montreal, we found ourselves together again at the Chicago comedy festival. This time we had swagger. Hedberg was now rich and I'd tried to blow myself onstage. I don't know if we felt that we had nothing more to gain but we carried ourselves that way. We'd done bigger festivals and knew how they worked. Industry gets trucked in, let their guard down and get sloppy drunk with their peers and the comedians pretending to like them. Most industry have no sense of what is funny, much less important or translatable. They just listen to other people talk about which comics are hot properties, what comics are the "buzz." Every comedy festival had a comedian who was the buzz, one that everyone was talking about. Hedberg and I came up with the idea to try to create a fake buzz about a comic randomly. We poked through the "New Faces" section of the festival program and deliberated. Out of a dozen or so comedians and based on nothing concrete, we chose D. T. Tosh.

For the whole long weekend, anytime we found ourselves at a bar, in the hotel elevator or anywhere in earshot of any kind of a network suit or an agent, we'd complain loudly that this D. T. Tosh was blowing up the whole festival, how we deserved it more and how the whole festival is bullshit. Nothing spells "rising star" to industry more than bitter rival comedians grousing.

By the end of the festival, sure enough D. T. Tosh—or Daniel Tosh as you now know him—was the Queen of the Ball. I have no idea how much our shenanigans played a part but I knew we were secretly high-fiving and taking a lot of credit at the time. On the last night—the wrap party essentially—while Tosh was walking on the sunshine of all the greasy attention, we told him how we'd orchestrated this whole ploy, putting more effort into getting him recognized than any work we'd even put into our own shows. Daniel was pissed off initially, as though we'd stolen something from him, but eventually he came around to see the funny.

DT and I would go on to share that hooker story in Florida. Hedberg would go on to be dead. DT would go on to change his name back to Daniel, the way his adoptive parents wanted him. Renamed.

And look at DT now. He's a brilliant gay millionaire and I'm a drunk loser. He sometimes brings me back on his show the same way Steve Martin put his derelict father in small roles in a couple of his later movies, hoping still to somehow gain his love. I always loved D. T. Tosh. I just never knew how to show him. But I would still bust his balls that he wouldn't have been where he is now without me and Hedberg. We made you and we can break you.

MILLION-DOLLAR IDEAS

D aniel Tosh had a million-dollar idea with *Tosh.0* and he ran with it. That's because he's gay and detests women. Power-gay. He rapes priests and murders any woman who was witness. Lawyers will have no problem with this as Tosh will happily admit it. It made him a millionaire.

Women ruin million-dollar ideas just on vanity. I know. I was a victim.

Becker and I once had a million-dollar idea and our lady friend Luker ruined it. Or she saved our careers. You be the judge. We were all out at dinner with the Alaska folk and the subject of *Bumfights* came up, a video series that was then all the uproar and anger in that new age of Internet fame. It featured some *Girls Gone Wild*–style abusers, coercing homeless people into all sorts of fucked up things, from violence to self-harm, in return for cash or booze with the producer shitheads filming it and mocking them openly. After deciding to track the hosts down and kill them—we are idea men but rarely closers—the conversation turned to how much money they had made from selling those videos. As the wine poured, we started pitching a friendlier version of the same kind of video. Pranks without the exploitation, without the evil. The ideas got better with every glass as ideas tend to do. And then the million-dollar idea came up. Turns out that Koot's owner Doran had a dog that was scheduled to have his leg amputated. I assume because his leg was fucked up. I'm sure that it wasn't cosmetic surgery. One drink leads to another and the plan was in play.

We would pretend to be a documentary crew and ask to film the amputation for a television documentary. Then we would cut to a shot of Becker in a chef's hat on the set of a cooking show, breading the amputated leg in a pan. Becker would give cooking directions, tell you how to spice it appropriately and how long to bake it. Then we'd cut to Becker removing the dish fresh from the oven, garnished and presented like a *Zagat* guide meal.

Then Becker would feed it to the three-legged dog.

Masterpiece.

You know for a fact that a dog would eat its own leg. We were so sure that this could be the centerpiece to a newsworthy, controversial Internet video that we were—in that drunken moment—committed. We thought it through and debated the morality of it. The dog was losing his leg regardless. A dog eats anything and wouldn't care if it was eating it's own balls after being neutered or chewing on your used tampon that he pulled from the trash. A dog eating its own leg would appear cruel and unimaginably distasteful while actually victimless and fucking funny. A win-win. We could figure out the rest of the content later.

The problem was that Doran couldn't keep his fucking mouth shut and he told Luker. She went appropriately batshit and said that there was absolutely no way she would allow that to happen. Doran—having cost us a million dollars with his big mouth—picked up the dinner tab and we went home.

I went back to LA but Becker didn't give up. He sidestepped Luker and actually tried to accompany Doran to the amputation with a video camera. The vet told Becker that there was no way he would be allowed to film the surgery. Our million-dollar idea died again at the veterinarian's doorstep.

I will still battle the morality of the fact that our idea would in no way have hurt the animal. Those cunts that made *Bumfights* probably thought they could justify their torment as well. Our argument would have won easily over theirs should it have gone to an Ivy League college debate. But the general public may not have seen either side as anything less than memorably deplorable. I looked up the *Bumfights* fucks online while I was writing this and went back to plotting their murders for fun. It passes the time.

Luker might have been wrong logically but she was right in the long run. We could have been famous for the *Dog Eats Own Leg* video. *Bumfights* famous. Way worse than karaoke famous or never even being noticed at all.

AND THEN YOU
ARE THE DICK

After twenty-five years on the road, week after week, town after town, I have met and made more great friends in short spurts than is imaginable. Or feasibly sustainable. Comedians, fans, club owners, bar staff who make your night or weekend fantastic. At some point you realize there is no way you will ever be able to keep in touch with all of the people who've made the best parts of your life so memorable, no matter how blurry or absent the memory. Even if you made it your life's work, you couldn't keep up.

And then you feel like a dick.

Horse was one of my first "fans," someone who had heard my stuff on the Internet before ever seeing me live and drove a lot of hours to a show because of it. I've never felt comfortable around fans and for the first several years, that was never a problem I would even know. Those were years that the audience came to a comedy club to see comedy. Not a particular comedian. No specific genre, no certain style. Just comedy. You'd have bachelorettes or company Christmas parties or a simple date night, all assuming that you were gonna be like that one comedian they fell asleep to on late-night network television. To most of the pedestrian audience, comedy was all as interchangeable as soy sauce, where brand doesn't matter. Until it was something odd and distasteful like my brand. Then it was my fault for ruining the noodles.

With no other art form would you do that.

Nobody would say they wanted to go to a concert because it had music without asking what type of music. Comedy is different in that people will say, "That isn't comedy!" simply because they don't find it funny. You wouldn't say that music wasn't music just because you didn't like the category and you would still call a sculpture a sculpture even if you hated that specific piece. Bagpipes are still considered music even if you showed up hoping for hip-hop. People will say that it's not comedy because they didn't laugh. But no one will say bagpipes aren't music because they didn't dance. And nobody goes to the opera hoping they'll stop the show to pick on the birthday boy.

Sure, over the years I'd filter some people out of any given audience who were really into my act and those who you went out with after a show to get liquored up and cause a ruckus. A lot of those would keep an eye out for when I was coming back and those were generally few enough that I'd usually remember them.

Eventually someone made me a website with a mailing list so people would know when I was coming back to their town. Then someone else made a forum for my site so that not only could I interact with my audience, but now they had a place to call each other vicious, awful things and post pictures of inordinately oversized objects stuffed into ill-suited orifices. The Internet was made for my people. And soon enough, these people started coming to clubs to see me. Not just arbitrary comedy.

In the days before the fall of Napster as their court case was winding down, someone showed me how to steal music and download it onto CDs. I don't really listen to music or enjoy it unless I'm completely fucked or generally melancholy, but given a deadline and the last chance to get free shit, I jumped on the last-call of Napster. I spent full days trying to remember songs I liked and putting them on CDs. After that, I started stealing comedians and spoken word. I even enjoyed Henry Rollins for a minute. On top of that, I was starting seeing a lot of people downloading my own stuff. I'd made a few CDs of my own by then to sell after shows and was happy that people were finding them and actually showing interest in pilfering them. I'd message them to thank them for stealing.

Napster's home page had a list of categories and just before their courtroom demise, they finally added "Comedy" as a category. I was the first and only comedian highlighted in the featured Napster comedy section—a coup pulled off by a fan who worked there—before they were smashed into obsolescence by the legal system. Napster was at the time the most popular site on earth. They were eradicated within days of adding my name to the home page. I've sworn ever since that if that runny little fuck drummer from Metallica ever ventured into my show, I would have him loudly removed for spearheading the lawsuit against Napster. Metallica only became known through people copying and sharing cassette tapes of them. They were all for it. No mainstream radio would play them. Now that it became easier to share recordings and they were famous, they flexed and defecated on my own personal parade, the same parade that built them in the first place.

I came close to that dream years later when the burn victim guitarist from Metallica was in the audience at a show in Mill Valley, California. I didn't have him thrown out but I did voice my displeasure in how they fucked up a good thing that had just started working for me and spewed a string of abuses to pass along to the smarmy drummer fuck. I took from the smirk on his face that he hates the drummer too. Or maybe that was just scar tissue.

The Internet still survived in the wake of the Napster ruling as did stealing shit, and my shit was getting out there. Here and again someone would email me and tell me they liked my ill-gotten tracks and were coming to a show. My show. Not just comedy and not just some dudes I'd dropped acid with two years ago in Seattle. Actual fans.

Horse may have not been the first one but he's the first one I remember. Horse had found my stuff online and drove several hours with his wife to a show on a Wednesday night, a night where only about eighteen people who actually lived in that city bothered showing up.

That made it even creepier, figuring this guy must have been under some unfortunate assumption that I was popular.

After the show, I went next door to some sweaty bar for beers and invited Horse and his missus along with me. He was my first fan—at least on that level and, fuck, they'd got a hotel for the night and everything. I felt like apologizing for some reason.

So I got juiced up, and we played some pool. He and his wife not only drove a long way to see me but brought gifts. Like I was a big shot. He brought me a sweater based on a rubber-fist joke from my first CD, a joke that I didn't remember, a joke which he had to repeat to me. I drank with them after the show even though I had nothing to say. I was so perplexed that I had actual fans from this new world of the Internet that I felt an obligation I didn't know how to handle. I wanted to pay him gas money for his trip. Instead I suggested we have breakfast the next day. I say a lot of things when I'm drinking that I won't mean in the morning.

My social skills are dependent solely on my alcohol consumption. Breakfast with me consists of silence with my head buried in a newspaper and zero eye contact. But breakfast we did, followed by some photos and a quick ga'bye.

Through no fault of his own, I'd given Horse every indication that this was the start of a close friendship rather than an extended "thank you for coming."

Horse emailed more and more and each one got longer. Lots of personal stuff that I wouldn't even want to know about my actual friends. He'd come to every show anytime I was in the area, always bearing gifts, and sometimes staying at every show for the full long weekend. I was on the verge of hiring writers to come up with things to say to him while he was busy saying anything and everything about nothing to cover the painful silences. Usually, if I have anything to say at all, it's only what I have to say onstage.

Don't get me wrong, Horse wasn't a bad guy. I'd overcompensated and led him to believe this was more than a comedian-audience relationship. And I couldn't find an easy way out of it. I started it and didn't know how to tell him that the show was over. It felt deceitful to read awkwardly intimate emails that one should only be telling to a deeply trusted confidant.

Eventually I decided to handle it the way I do most sensitive situations. I got drunk and said it rudely. Horse and I were not destined to be brothers in arms, do a cross-country road trip or sit in our golden years looking back at the good old days. I'm sure I hurt his feelings at the time, especially in the way I conveyed it. I was without question the dick. But we got past it and we've still shared an email here and there over the years. Usually it's when he's dying of cancer or is considering suicide again because of it. But now we can laugh about it without him thinking I'll be a pallbearer.

Horse taught me an important lesson as my first fan who traveled a long way to see my show. Like they tell rookie athletes who overcelebrate a minor accomplishment:

Act like you've been there before.

Just don't be a dick about it. The way David Cross was to me once and I have been to people far too many times since.

This is not to let the audience off the hook altogether.

* * *

There is a little-known phrase I've recently learned for a person, called a "shot-clog." It is used to describe an irritant who is only tolerated because he is buying the drinks. I know him well. In the early years of living glass to mouth, we as young, broke comedians—we needed that guy. Later he became my reason to flee the bar. Now I may have become him. Who knows.

What I do know is that there is no such thing as a free drink. I've never bought a drink for a lady who I didn't know just because she looked thirsty. There is always some level of expectation, if only a thank you.

Most times, someone buying me a shot after a show is just a common way to say thanks. But then there's always the one guy who needs way more than an hour of laughs. He probably hated the fact that he had to sit through the show to get to the part where he needed the "more." He needs someone to talk to, he needs a friend. He's heard your stuff and knows that you and he are so much alike that you should listen to his ideas or his jokes or his outlooks. And if you do that, he will still need more.

He will need you to leave a voice message on his friend's phone. The friend wanted to be there but is on house arrest. He will tell you that the friend's name is Chance so you should "fuck with him about that," as though the name is somehow inherently funny. You go along this far because you can't find a way out. He smells that and buys another round of shots. Remember, this is a guy who didn't even buy your DVD at the merch table. That would have been an even trade that was quick, cut and dried. He wanted to buy you a drink so you would owe him your time.

Now he wants to take you to his favorite bar and it's really close and it's fucking wall-to-wall pussy and you'll love it and he's fine to drive. You look around and all the people you really did want to talk to have left, and the comedy club is closing so you capitulate and agree to go with him. His car is a 1984 Pontiac Fiero and you shouldn't mind all the stuff on the floor. The bar, it turns out, isn't very close at all and he wants you to listen to a cassette tape of his trance music he's been working on. You try to be polite and listen but he keeps turning it down to explain what inspired it or to apologize for the quality of the recording or to ask if that's a cop behind us. Then he calls his friend and says, "You won't believe who is in my fucking car right now!" You cringe as he tries to explain who you are, right in front of you, to someone who doesn't know or care. He offers to pick the friend up while you make passive-aggressive gestures to the fact the car is a two-seater. He tells you not to worry about it, that his friend won't mind jamming in. You pick up the friend and have to sit sideways as they start talking in disjointed stories that were really funny to them but you really had to be there and you'd have to really like the band Yes.

You get to the bar and it's a near-empty rib joint where he used to work and he was hoping that his other friend would be bartending so he could get free drinks, but the other friend got called back up to active duty and was about to be shipped off to war. This casts a pall over your hosts, who start parroting CNN as though they are political majors while the bartender says they are closing early. You ask to buy a round because somehow you feel like you still owe him. You ask for a beer but all they have are local craft brews. You ask for the one that tastes most like Miller Lite and the bartender looks at you like you're a peasant. The guy who brought you sees that look and says, "Do you even know who this motherfucker is? Oh, man!" but then gets distracted before you even get credit for being a comedian. Any comedian.

You overtip and drink a beer that tastes like socks while he orders only a Coke under the auspices that he has to drive. With the bartender having his head in the cooler, your guy pulls out a flask to spice up his soft drink. He winks at you to assure you've seen him pull the Big Con. Your only hope is that you will now be going home since this fantastic bar is shutting down. But then your guy starts telling you about an even better bar that you have to see and tells you not to be a pussy. You order a shot just before the bartender locks the cabinet and he glares at you like he'll have to milk the liquor out of his own prostate. The other friend who sat half on your lap in the car has left with a waitress and yelled that we'd "meet up" at the other place.

Follow this through as long as you like. This guy will never have enough of you. You could be doing prison time for him so you wouldn't be a rat. You could be midwifing his illegitimate child so he didn't get busted for cheating on his old lady. You owe him for that drink.

No matter where or under what circumstances you finally walk away from this guy, he will tell you that you are "all Hollywood and shit."

And then you are the dick.

* * *

I have found three sure-fire ways to get out of these situations after a show when you just want to decompress and have a lonely drink at the bar. Three ways to get away from That Guy.

One, tell him you will be right back, that you have go to get paid. He will not come between you and cash, especially since he thinks you must be rich anyway since you were onstage and all. He will think that money is probably gonna come back and pay for all of his hospitality. You know, since you guys are friends now.

Two, look over both shoulders and tell him in a hushed tone to stay put, that you're about to hook up some drugs. Don't be specific about what type of drugs. Leave it open in case there's a drug he wants to be in on. Even if he doesn't do drugs, he will immediately feel like he is "in the loop," a confidant and a trusted lookout or a getaway driver.

Number three is pussy. If you tell a dude that you have to sneak out because you're about to get fucked by a stray chick from the show, he will back off and most likely fist-bump you. If he tries to stop you, he's your brother-in-law. And even then he's a dick.

As bonus advice, this also works in reverse with hitting on a chick after the show. Tell her you are trying to avoid some drunk dude and that the only way he will leave you alone is if he thinks you're about to get laid. That allows you both to "pretend" to be flirting. And drinking leads to dancing.

Also, don't give away your trade secrets in a book. Now they will see it coming when I tell them that I'm about to get laid by the drug dealer who is going to pay me for my show. All Hollywood and shit.

Wiley Roberts bugging out after sleeping with a pig.

My alleged Jerry Springer conspirators.

On set of *Tosh.0* with Bingo, Daniel Tosh, and Joe Rogan.

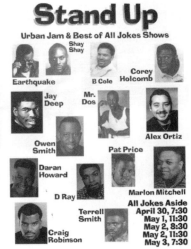

The year we made D.T. Tosh a star!

It's funnier to lift your kilt and show your dick at a karaoke singer if he's blind.

Chicago Comedy Festival 1998. If you look close, you'll spot Louis CK, Mitch Hedberg, Tom Rhodes, and others getting famous and me about to pull my dick out instead.

Costa Rica, Working Girls/Spokespersons.

Naked at Koot's with Matt Becker, Midget Dave, and Kenny Midget.

In the UK with Bingo.

With protesters in Madison.

Chaille and me ready for the road.

At the AVN Awards with Chloe and Nina Hartley.

TO ALL COMICS:
Please no fucking,
licking, or hand job
with
our help
or
our customers
or
any male or female
hookers

Acme Comedy Club Green Room notice to comics—specifically me. The broken English of owner Louis Lee bleeds through.

Florida jock strap.

Allison Pearson article asking "What Planet Are They From?"

Even Bingo has fans with bad tattoos of her.

With Dr. Drew.

GETTING AWAY
FROM IT ALL

'd set a 4:45 a.m. wake-up call with the front desk to get the hell out of Costa Rica, unaware that my bowels would be twisting me awake on their own merely ten minutes before the phone rang. My guts shed one of those evacuations where you're afraid to look down afterwards because it feels like it must have been all hot innards. That much blood spilling out of you wouldn't leave you a lot of time to cancel the taxi and say your goodbyes.

Turns out it was just perfectly timed, gut-wrenching water-shits. I was just getting off the toilet when the front desk called to send me on my way. It's odd when you want to high-five your own violent diarrhea for it's fantastic timing.

Bingo had skipped her sleeper pills so she wasn't so hard to prop up in the elevator to the taxi. Her regular meds make it difficult enough for her in the morning. Sleepers and an early flight on top of them would make her so comatose that some valet is gonna need to be overtipped.

We'd had problems at Liberia airport the previous year from a loud-mouth passenger and this time we got it from the pigs. Costa Rica has come into the new millennium when it comes to overzealous, undertrained and simply dirty, mean and bumbling police work.

The gals at check-in were cheery, probably glad they didn't have to be working in a brothel to make a living but that's just a guess. I guess the same as when I see girls working the Arby's counter and they aren't unhappy.

One asked Bingo if she was okay—Bingo's eyes were at half-mast—and Bingo said she was just tired. It was 6:30 a.m. and we'd just taken an hour-long screaming cab ride, like a flat roller coaster with potholes and livestock on the tracks. Any person would look like they aren't all there.

While I was trying to con my way into first-class upgrades, the chummy girl wandered off to talk to some other airport employees. She motioned towards us, I assumed trying to get me an upgrade. Nothing seemed amiss.

After we got our boarding cards and fond farewells from the happy cunts at the check-in, Bingo and I went out front to smoke our final "we only smoked because we were out of the country" cigarettes. We'd quit for nearly a year going into the vacation but smokes were something like seventy-five cents a pack in Costa Rica. It felt like we'd be losing money not to start again.

There were rows of seats four to a section facing each other in four different groups. We sat on a couple of chairs and lit up. A couple sat directly across from us. They had tags around their necks yet were in street clothes. They appeared to be low-level employees who'd probably have enough access to steal from your bags but would still have to take off their belts to get through security.

The guy was scary, an attribute as rare in Costa Rican men as "gorgeous" is in their women. They have smoking-hot hookers in Costa Rica but those are 99 percent Colombian or Brazilian imports. This guy was Turkish scary. If this were *Midnight Express*, this guy would be Hamidou, the sadistic prison guard. And the girl with him looked Costa Rican.

I was smoking and begging for time to pass so I could fall asleep on the 8 a.m. flight when I saw that prison guard guy was giving me death-eye. If it was merely stink-eye I would have chalked it up to simple "I hate Americans" and I would have had empathy. But this was seething death-eye. Someone who wanted to fuck you up, and right now for no discernable reason.

Angry paranoia is as much a part of my mornings as coffee is in yours but once Bingo noticed, I knew it wasn't just a delusion. Bingo isn't observant. She wouldn't have noticed if we boarded a sailboat home instead of a plane but she noticed this guy. This was something personal. We got up and moved to the next row of seats where now our backs would be to them. They got up and moved with us immediately like shadows, sitting straight across from us again, and staring. We were like boxers between rounds in our corners.

Now that we knew it wasn't an accident we moved once more, very deliberately, and once again to the last row of four seats. Seconds later there they were across from us, fixated and glaring like angry hypnotists.

"What the fuck do you want?" I said more like a beleaguered time-share sales mark than someone who wants a confrontation.

No reply.

The sense of dread that was coming over me shot my booze shakes into full rattle. And I could feel another wave in my colon rumble. Bingo followed my lead and we got up to ask two uniformed police officers nearby if there is a smoking area inside, past security. They said there was. It was the only direction to go that was away from the creeper couple and towards our goal of home. We put out our cigarettes, took our bags and headed that way in a hurry.

The goon duo followed us and when we went through the metal detectors, they went around security without a word spoken or a question asked, like it was their own home. Now we knew we were fucked. They had to be undercover cops. We got through security with no issues. The two had disappeared into the airport as we collected our bags from the conveyor belt. All the while I had to shit but now I was afraid the door would be kicked in as they thought I was flushing whatever they thought I was hiding.

They were waiting for us in the smoking area inside the boarding area. Crafty cunts. Now we had to go to them. And although we now knew they were caging us, we weren't going to leave our secret smoking vacation without burning a few more cheap cigarettes.

We walked into what would be ten square feet and two benches of smoking area with just the four of us. I wanted to cut to the chase.

"Can I help you?" I had a tremor in my voice.

Then Bingo chimed in—which she tends to do when she should absolutely not. Bingo can never grasp the good cop–bad cop play. Anytime I go bad cop she goes all the way into Chicago cop.

"Why the *fuck* are you following us around? What the fuck do you want?"

"We are the police."

"Well, what did we do? Did we do something wrong? Are we not supposed to smoke here?"

"No, you did nothing wrong."

And then back to the blank devil stares. The dead eyes of the robot-dyke were now as frightening as the raging young tico.

After a cigarette, two more men in sport coats and badges showed up with that smiley cunt from the check-in counter, the one who'd pointed us out. She said, "These are government men and need to talk to you."

Of course, these government men spoke no English so she began talking for them.

"What do you do? Why is she not well? Where did you stay? What hotel? Do you feel ill?"

"I am a stand-up comic. She is mentally ill and her drugs make her drowsy. We stayed in some place in Flamingo. What kind of mental illness, you ask??? Schizoaffective, bipolar disorder? Why? Are you familiar with it? Are you a doctor? We have the prescription drugs in her checked bags if you'd like to see them."

Then it got very scary. "They need to separate you to interrogate you."

I sincerely believe that the word "interrogate" was just a poor translation choice when she really wanted to say "ask you some questions."

Which would secretly mean "interrogate."

It would have made sense if I'd been dodging the questions, but having no idea why I'm being detained, haven't been accused of anything and having just come in hung over from a wedding when I'd sworn I'd never go to another—it was terrifying. These were the people in the movies who bring you into a dark room and beat you with phone books. Your guilt would not be in question. It would just be batting practice for these crazies.

I was brought back to the baggage area where they'd pulled our bags off the plane and were now waiting for us. They began to go through everything including the most awkward things— one was a ridiculous televangelist hairpiece that I'd brought for the wedding as a joke but now made me look like an entry-level spy with obvious disguises. Then they started going through my notebooks. They were scrutinizing each page without having anything but a cursory knowledge of elementary English—and then I am watching an officer find an old set list that he went back to twice.

It was all cryptic bullet points that would read like song titles. If you know my act, you can imagine this list.

"Stinkless Pussy"

"Spinning Dildo"

"Dominatrix Health Care"

"Abortion Is Green"

I hoped his reading of the language was as poor as his speaking it. He asked what it all was and I tried to explain that I was a stand-up comedian, which is difficult to pantomime, especially in a country where stand-up comedy doesn't exist. I don't even think they have laughter native to their culture. They only hear it from tourists.

Looking back I'm glad they were confused by this. If it had been clear to these third-world people—eking out a merciless existence by terrorizing tourists for pennies a day while their daughters work the bench in a brothel, sleeping in huts made of coconut shells and using every part of the goat—that I made my living just by talking into a microphone, making jokes based on all of those subjects, in fact, they may not have been able to contain their hatred. As it was, Hamidou was still leaning into me with his nostrils flaring, all but cracking his knuckles for theatrics. The plane was getting ready to leave and I couldn't see Bingo. And I really had to shit. So badly that I might have even taken a plea bargain.

Right then, Slap-Happy the Check-in Narc brought Bingo back around and told us we were free to go. No apologies, no conciliatory upgrade, no explanation as to why we'd been stopped and menaced by these barbarians in the first place. Other than Bingo looked sleepy. Now she looked confused and terrified. I wanted so badly to launch myself on Hamidou and bite out his eye that I looked him square in his block head and apologized for any confusion. They followed us all the way onto the runway—they don't have jetways in open-air airports in destitute, rogue terrorist nations, only rolling, rusted staircases like on *Fantasy Island*— and they continued to mad-dog us all the way onto the plane like they might change their minds at any moment.

We were indeed the last people on the plane but it wasn't like anyone was waiting on us. Everyone was still milling about. Thank fucking Christ. Our seats were in the back half of the plane, two rows behind bathrooms in the middle. I launched my backpack onto my seat and prayed to any god listening that the toilet wasn't occupied. If it had been, it would have been a long, wet, pungent ride back home.

Time slows down when you're attempting to yank your pants down just enough so that the arc of your loose, streaming stool doesn't catch the back lip of your belt loop. Time slows enough that you can even calculate that, in an airplane bathroom, you'll be close enough to lock the door after you've hit the shitter, saving a precious second that could have been your doom and your telltale dripping stain.

Even on the runway, an airplane has enough white noise that I wasn't concerned about anyone hearing what I was doing to that lavatory. But I immediately knew that the odor might have the entire flight grounded. You always know when you think you've destroyed the toilet air for others but it's rare when it actually sickens *you*. On a plane, you already have less air than in a casket and that air was immediately filled with an eye-watering stench that was almost acid infused. Like nervous sweat, there are nervous shits. It wasn't a long process but for the short time I was on the bowl, I poured like a broken faucet. It stung my skin. Hog slop. Chernobyl. Rotting citrus. Like someone had cut open a blister on the corpse of a skunk on the side of a New Mexico highway. In the summer.

And now I'd have to leave and resume my seat for take-off.

I slunk out and took my seat two rows back. I withered and waited. After a short pause, I watched all three seats in front of me—the people right behind the befouled toilet—fumble for their overhead air vents as though it were synchronized.

The flight attendant was coming down the plane shutting the overhead compartments and slowed in front of the bathroom I'd just ruined. Her face turned in and wrinkled like a raisin. She made eye contact with the people in front of me and sniffed the air.

She leaned her shoulder into the closed bathroom door—as though somehow it could be closed even more—and said, "Whoever done that coulda done it INSIDE the AIRPORT!"

I almost jumped out of my chair to shriek:

"I WANTED TO DO THAT *INSIDE* THE MOTHERFUCKING AIRPORT BUT I WAS BEING HELD FUCKING PRISONER BY THOSE FUCKING ANIMALS!!!"

I shut up and got home.

Instead, to this day, I just spread bad rumors about Costa Rica such as their penchant for raping white women on their honeymoons as a fertility ritual, using the vomit of child slaves as a lubricant. Their cocaine is anthrax and the faucets run with raw sewage. The surf teems with MRSA and body parts at high tide. Their major export is anal lice, which they breed like trout farms in hotel pools. The sunsets are in black and white and you can only watch them through a pinhole in a cardboard box or you will leave as blind as their cab drivers. All of which I can't help but believe are true.

Costa Rica actually does have an "exit tax" of twenty-nine dollars per person. You have to pay to leave. You know how they can get away with that? Because they know it's worth it.

FAKE IT UNTIL YOU MAKE IT

On a separate occasion coming back from Costa Rica through US customs, I was in my usual morning mood. Angry and irritated by the long line, with some travel drinking since the Liberia airport floated on top.

The customs agent fell into his *First 48* interrogation routine, waiting for me to slip up. Sober, I would usually feel like I am about to fail a test even though I've done nothing wrong. I would be afraid of getting caught for things I did years ago, possibly behind the back of a girlfriend or maybe cheating on a test in middle school. That morning I was drunk and having none of it.

"Where are you coming from?"

I wanted to say that it isn't any of his business but I didn't. I wanted to go home. I told him where I was coming from.

"What was the purpose of your travel?"

I internalized the same and answered, biting the inside of my lip.

"Where did you stay?"

Eat your hate. Swallow it and become full.

Finally he asked me what I do for a living.

"I'm a stand-up comedian."

I said it with a disdain that showed my cards, that expressed my true feelings. This question had nothing to do with my citizenship nor was it any of his business.

He lit up like we were having a conversation at a hotel bar.
"Really??? A comedian? Like all over the country?"

With all of the sarcastic reserve of Jerry Seinfeld and the cockiness of Dice Clay, I rolled my eyes and broke into him: "C'mon! I'm DOUG STANHOPE, man!"

As though anyone on God's dying earth would not know who Doug Stanhope is and that he's being a shitworm by pretending not to know me.

And it worked.

"Oh. Uh . . . I'm sorry. I don't have TV."

He shrank in embarrassment and waved me through. I choked down my laugh until I got around the corner.

The problem with visiting other countries is that, like bars, it's usually mostly the doormen who are the dicks.

• • • •

ICELAND, THE EXCEPTION TO THE RULE

Our friend Shawnee came over to the house one day and randomly said that he thought Iceland might be a fun place to go to for Christmas. He knew that I often fly anywhere around the world at the end of the year to achieve airline status. I agreed if only to get out of a morning conversation. Yet it happened that I'd just read a news story about a comedian who had run a joke campaign to be the mayor of Reykjavik—the only city in Iceland—and had accidentally won.

After the economic crash of 2008, Jon Gnarr decided to start his own political party—the Best Party—and run for office along with a handful of other rogues and artists. At the time he was a well-known comedian there and star of an Icelandic television series called *Night Shift*. Long story short, the joke backfired and he was now the mayor and his party held six of the fifteen seats on the city council.

The story was compelling enough that I tracked him down with a search of "mayor of Reykjavik" and although the website was all in a foreign tongue, I could figure out that a link was to the mayor.

I sent a missive.

To The Honorable Jon Gnarr,

My name is Doug Stanhope and I am the greatest comedian of all time, according to a recent email from a fan. It is my intention to come to Reykjavik on a diplomatic mission on behalf of, but without the consent or interest of, my town of Bisbee, Arizona.

As this will be my first venture being a foreign dignitary, I'd like to inquire as to what time of year is the best fit for your schedule, how you should be addressed (and should I do that thing where we kiss each other on both cheeks) as well as maybe the name of a good sushi place.

I feel that this meeting will be of paramount importance to the future of the world as we know it so I will bring my camera. I also feel that it would be good if we could sign a document (of your choosing) together at the end of my stay for historical sake.

Please contact me at your earliest convenience if this is in fact your correct email address. I found it on a page that was written in a foreign language but your photo was at the top so I'm taking a stab in the dark.

Yours,

stanhope

A roll of the dice. In short time, I received an email back.

Dear Stanhope

I was very pleased to receive your letter. I must say I was quite surprised, to say the least, because I just recently discovered your work and really enjoyed it. I have seen you on Charlie Brooker's Newswipe, bits on youtube and No Refunds. The weird thing is that I have been talking a lot about you lately and introducing your stuff to my friends. I believe in coincidence. (Hope that´s not a problem.)

Last week I was in NY. There I met a cab driver from Ghana who used to live on a remote island in Iceland. When I got to the hotel I googled your town and read about the gays and Paul Newman. I have only once been to Arizona. It was on my way from LA to Boston many years ago. I spent 3 hours at the airport and bought a lot of cactus candy. But I once was a pen pal with a girl who was doing time in the Arizona state prison for women. I lost contact with her after she got released and went back on the road with her friends in Hells Angels. Her name was Kathy Sparrow. I have not talked to her for over 20 years.

I would be more than happy to meet with you. Maybe we could have our meeting in Hofdi House where the Reagan and Gorbachev summit was held in 1986? Wouldn't that be appropriate? It's the 25 year anniversary this year and about time for something historical to happen again

I know my secretary has been in contact with you but here's my private email.

Best wishes

joN gnarR

This trip had been Shawnee's idea but fuck him. I was goddamned famous in Iceland, at least to the mayor. I couldn't wait until Christmas. I had to go as soon as was possible. You can call a comedian out for stealing your bit but you can't castigate your friend for ripping off your vacation idea.

I wrote back and told the mayor that we should indeed have an official meeting at Hofdi House and sign important documents, perhaps even officially declaring Bisbee and Reykjavik "Conjoined-Twin Sister Cities." I suggested that although Icelanders speak perfect English, I should still hire an interpreter for the event, only having him repeat the mayor's accented English into English without the accent. I told the mayor that I'd also been pen pals with a prisoner, mine having been on death row where they can never leave you. I misquoted Dostoyevsky and wrote: "Someone smarter than me once said that you can judge a society by the conditions of its prisons. I don't know if it's true but that could be a fun venture in Iceland. Anything besides eating that rotted shark's head surprise."

I signed off with "Let's Get Drunk and Go Whaling!"

Let me explain that this sign-off came from a tour of Norway, where I had made it our battle cry.

"Let's Get Drunk and Go Whaling!"

I would continuously bellow this on- and offstage like an insane Viking until one night when it went a bit too far. I'd made the mistake of drinking Asahi beer at lunch with sushi, where we did coincidently eat whale. The mistake was drinking at lunch. You get a taste for continuing to drink all day. By showtime I was space debris. I was so confidently drunk that people viewed me more as an exhibit from an exotic faraway land than a comedian.

Nonplussed, I continued to cry out my catchphrase at the bar after the Trondheim show until I actually convinced myself that this was the right course of action. Now I only had to convince the others. I finally pressured the opening act, Dag Soras, and some fan to go out with me to try and steal a boat from across the street at the marina. I leapt up and over the chain-link fence with such amazing athleticism that Dag and I had to stop and talk about it. If there is retard strength, there is also drunken prowess. It was that well executed that it is still vivid in an otherwise mostly blacked-out night.

Now that we'd made it inside the marina, it was just a question of which vessel was the most attractive. Like going to a car lot with an unlimited budget. I knew nothing about boats or how to drive them. Those were things we'd figure out afterwards. What I had not considered is that a people as kind and civilized as the Norwegians would see any reason to lock things. I assumed every one of these yachts must have the keys in the ignition, but you couldn't even get inside of them. What do these people have to hide? I should have figured that out by asking why they had that fence that I vaulted so magnificently.

Fortunately we failed at my whaling adventure. I don't know anything about boats or whaling so it wouldn't have ended well for anyone save for the whales.

When I signed off with "Let's Get Drunk and Go Whaling!" to the mayor of Iceland, he responded that he was a vegan and against whaling. I told him that Bingo was a vegan as well, that she would never kill a whale unless it was in self-defense and that I hoped our journey wouldn't come to that. But he did say he had made arrangements to not only have us tour but also perform at Iceland's only maximum-security prison. I hadn't wanted to muddy up the vacation with doing gigs but a prison gig had always been on my career bucket list and if it sucked, I wouldn't have to worry about running into any of the audience afterwards at the bar.

I announced the show on my website and that since the show was just for prison inmates, the only way you could gain admittance is if you found a way to get sentenced to it. The intention was to create what would become known as the "Doug Stanhope defense" where defendants claim they only committed the crime in order to get into my gig.

The Honorable Jon Gnarr met us coming off the plane at arrivals in Iceland. He was with his elder son, Frosti, and they wore monkey masks, holding a sign with our name. We only had time for a few breakfast cocktails, a shower and a few more beers on the hour-long drive to the prison. Thank fuck Frosti let us smoke in his car. I was nervous, not because I was going into a prison but because I'd have to do a show without drinking.

The Litla-Hraun prison only houses eighty prisoners out in the middle of some endless, rolling lava-tundra and seems more like a summer camp for underprivileged teens in a place where summer sucks anyway. Some of the gates that were opened for us couldn't hold my dog Henry if he saw a rabbit on the other side.

Before the show we got a guided tour—not until later did we find out that our guide was a prisoner himself—and got to hang out with a lot of the guys in one of the cell blocks.

When I say cell and cell block, think dorm and dorm room. I'm writing this now from a Motel 6 in Sierra Vista, Arizona, that is far more decrepit and certainly more dangerous.

At the front of the cell block there was a rec room of some sort with a small Asian kid on a couch playing Tiger Woods golf on a PlayStation and a full kitchen to the left where the inmates made their own food from scratch—just like Mama used to make when she did hard time in Iceland.

There was a metal culinary table in the middle of the kitchen where large knives stuck magnetically to the edges. The knives were on wire cords like a bank pen; if you wanted to stab a fellow inmate in an Icelandic prison, you had to wait until he's rolling out the fresh pasta. At this Motel 6, I'm surprised the remote control isn't similarly fashioned.

Everyone was cool as shit. One guy saw me fumbling with a cigarette, looking for a door to go outside to smoke.

"You want to smoke? Come with me!" and we went into his cell. You couldn't smoke in the common area but you could smoke in your room. All the doors to the dozen or so rooms on the wing were open. He showed me his books and pictures and told me how he—as well as many other inmates—was working on a university degree online. A few more smokers came in and we shot the shit while Bingo made best friends of everyone outside.

Then I had to do the show.

The show was in a small, half-court gymnasium with folding chairs—again better than a lot of the venues I choose to play—with I'd guess thirty or forty inmates. His Highness Mr. Jon Gnarr opened in Icelandic for ten or fifteen minutes while I waited in the wings wishing I'd actually put some thought into what the fuck I was going to say. I'd planned on just throwing out the greatest hits—it's not like they would know it's all old material—but I was having a hard time placing exactly what those hits were anymore.

My show sucked but nobody seemed to be bothered by it but me. I figured I could just riff every easily consumed dick joke I'd ever written but turns out I forgot how most of them go, so there was a lot of me staring at my shoes in between bits or ending them midway when I couldn't remember the payoff. You know . . . that place I get to when I usually scream at the bar for more alcohol.

Afterwards while Bingo was getting email addresses, the inmates presented us with gifts including T-shirts—the prison has their own T-shirt which is cool as fuck—and a large card handwritten in perfect calligraphy that said:

Dear Doug Stanhope
    Our initial idea of showing you our gratitude for you
    visiting us prisoners at Litla-Hraun was to give you a

t-shirt with the inscription "I went to prison in Iceland and all they gave me was this lousy t-shirt which they gagged me with while f***ing me in the a**." This was deemed inappropriate so you get this nice card instead.

I still haven't gotten around to getting it framed. But it's on the very long list of things I have to do.

I wish I'd had more time to hang out and find out more about the guys and how the whole system works. Prison fascinates and repulses me. Prison on any level sucks shit but Iceland—like a lot of Scandinavian countries—seems to have a way to make it rehabilitative instead of just cruel and even more damaging to society at large. Next time maybe I'll stay a while, have some pasta and fuck the Asian kid with the PlayStation.

We left the prison and went back to Reykjavik to His Majesty Jon Gnarr's home for sushi with his lovely wife, Joga, and family—including his small redheaded child who, although he was only about six years old, may very well be in Litla-Hraun today in Hannibal Lecter restraints. We ate and went through most of the vodka we'd brought before we'd even taken a nap. I probably said the wrong thing more than once but hoped it would be chalked up to the very slight language barrier. Thank goodness we could smoke in the house.

The next day we met up at city hall and were given the full tour and were introduced to some of the other members of the Best Party including Einar Benediktsson, formerly of the Sugarcubes, who thankfully smoked cigarettes and thankfully was with the Sugarcubes so I could google the spelling of his name. I forget everybody's name anyway, but when they have Icelandic names I never really got 'em to begin with.

We then held our Official Meeting at the Hofdi House where twenty-five years previously Reagan and Gorbachev held their famous summit meeting in 1986. We posed for pictures in the same chairs they had posed.

The woman who ran the place greeted us and commented on how much she liked Bingo's shoes, a pair of knee-high black Converse Chuck Taylors. Of course Bingo immediately demanded that the woman have them. She took them off, put them on the woman and laced them up for her. Bingo happily went home in a pair of plastic shoe-condoms given out to tourists so they don't muddy up the carpet.

In return, the woman gave Bingo a gift basket of things from the house to take home with her, one that kinda took us both off guard. Wrapped in tin foil and palmed to Bingo with a smirk was a large bundle of dried mushroom stems.

"You know what this is?" asked the woman.

"Ooooh yeah!" said Bingo.

And with a wink and a nod we were off.

It was mushroom season in Iceland. On the drive to the prison they pointed out people on the side of the road and in the median picking them like dandelions. They'd told us we could get psilocybin anywhere like they were bored with it, like the cab driver in Vegas who is tired of people amazed that you can walk down the street with an open container. But to be given narcotics here during an Official Meeting at the Hofdi House? Fuck, it's too bad Reagan and Gorbachev didn't go tripping during their failed attempt at working shit out.

We spent the next few days just hitting bars and meeting folks in town. Everything in Reykjavik is in walking distance, a beautiful village of a city with great sushi and unassuming folks and lots of things on menus that I didn't dare eat. We also spent a lot of time curled up in bed the way a vacation is supposed to be.

On the last night we still had the mushrooms and still had to meet up with Frosti and his friends. We weren't really in the mood to trip but sometimes you have to push yourself. How often will we have the opportunity to tell a story like this?

Bingo crushed them up and wrapped them into moist bread balls—saying we could just swallow them like a pill, as though you could eat a pill the size of a fat man's thumb. I chewed it down gagging the whole way like I was eating a cricket on a dare. We waited for both Frosti and that first seasick agonizing wave of the mushrooms.

We saved some for Frosti. We aren't animals. When he showed up, they were crushed up on a plate and Bingo offered it to him.

"There's not much left but if you want some mushrooms . . ."

Frosti looked at it oddly, touched it and smelled it.

"That's sage."

"What?"

"That is sage, not mushrooms."

"What the fuck is sage?" I ask.

"Sage. It's like uh, you know . . . like potpourri."

We had just choked down bread balls full of potpourri thinking that the mayor's office had given us hallucinogens as an Official Welcome Gift.

We had a fantastic night. Frosti and I made drunken plans to get gay-married to obtain dual citizenship. I called his father the mayor to ask for his permission and it was so granted. We would make it a grand affair with a parade in Reykjavik in fashion with the British royals.

We never got around to it.

Bingo and I shit potpourri the whole way home and nobody seated near the airplane bathroom complained at all.

BREAKDOWN LANE

ingo gets a glazed, dead-fish look in her eyes when she's going under the weather of a mental break. It can come on quick, even before the waitress has time to bring her the Pancake Puppies or whatever the fuck she ordered.

She'd gone shitty the night before after a show in Omaha where we had to carry her out of the van in a pink princess gown at some shit-box motel with construction crew guys still grilling and drinking beer in the parking lot. Four of us hoisting a seemingly passed-out chick into a motel room. They looked on like they might be able to overpower us for the carrion.

Rock Island is one of the "Quad Cities," a quadrant of the worst possible places to be that all share a city border. I always try to eat before I drink and I always drink before a show, no matter how much that show means to me. I am professionally unprofessional in that way. Somewhere in between Bingo ordering her food and it being brought to the table, her eyes went charcoal black with her lids fluttering like a silent-film projector. I knew where we were going.

It was still light outside when she was gone and her meal lay untouched in front of her. I knew the drill but still went into my futile default of trying to preach logic at insanity.

These spinouts didn't happen on a regular basis but were not uncommon over a course of years. In a Denny's in some hayseed town, hours before showtime, her timing sucked. We'd been traveling together for enough years that I thought she should have some professionalism with her mental illness the same way I did with my alcoholism. Go full-retard on our day off.

It was probably two hours that I spent trying to talk, reason and beg Bingo into coming out of her state. The entire time she was thinking that I and everything else around her was an invented offshoot of her imagination, daring her to die. I can't explain it nor understood it when she explained it to me later. But I understand "bad trip." Same rules apply.

As showtime came closer I called Chaille, told him the problem and explained that the problem didn't seem like it was going to end anytime soon. There was no way I would risk having her put into an institution in the Quad Cities—not any of them under any circumstances. We were a group of fuckup comedians but we were more equipped to take care of Bingo than anyone in these bum-fuck towns.

We were renting a white-panel van at the time, the kind that work-release prisoner crews use when picking up trash on the side of the highway. Brett Erickson and Geoff Tate were on the tour and in the van, along with Brett's gal Kerry and a local friend of theirs. I told the Denny's manager what was about to happen only minutes ahead of time. I didn't want to give him any time to panic and call the authorities. I believe he would have, based on his reaction. Too late. Chaille swung the rape van in front of the Denny's. Geoff and Brett rushed in and picked up Bingo out of our corner booth by her legs and underarms, carried her through a now crowded restaurant and chucked her into the back of a white van, engine running in front of the entrance. I feebly announced, "Fraternity prank!" to nobody listening.

Nobody looked. Nobody cared. This catatonic woman who had clogged up a corner booth for hours had just been physically removed by a mob of street urchins and nobody sees a thing. Like white-trash mafia. After Bingo was heaved into the van, someone noticed that her coat was left behind in the Denny's booth and ran back in to grab it. The people in the booth beside ours were leaning in to eat her dinner that she'd been ignoring for hours in a psychological failure. I keep forgetting to never play there again.

She started to come around a bit on the way to the show. She noticed and pointed out someone in the van that she did not recognize, the local friend of Erickson's. Then she asked if other people could see him as well. We were too wiped to see the funny in saying that we didn't. We didn't find the gag until it was too late.

My show sucked. I can't not open with what just happened and what just happened didn't even yet make sense to me. And then I get angry when people are waiting for the payoff. The tour continued. It probably never came up onstage again. We all had our own problems to deal with on a daily basis. We triage situations and then get back to our own garbage once the present problem has been solved. The next night may have been Geoff Tate being jumped for playing too much Bob Seger on the jukebox or Erickson nearly losing a finger trying to break it up. Or maybe that was the night before. It's always something.

● ○ ◉

Even without psychological breakdowns, Bingo doesn't travel well. Especially through customs.

I've said it onstage and I'll say here again, I'd be more confident crossing through customs at an international border with bricks of hashish taped to my body than simply getting through innocently with my Bingo. For someone who has flown about half a million miles with me to twenty-some countries on four different continents, I still wouldn't be surprised to catch her using her passport as a coaster or forgetting to take off a metal jousting helmet before passing through the scanner at airport security. (This not something she has actually worn on an airplane but something that wouldn't be out of the question.)

The idea of her traveling by herself is even more distressing.

I stood at the international arrivals gate at London's Heathrow Airport. Bingo was coming to join me in the middle of a run at the Soho Theatre. It was her first time flying alone internationally and even though I'd given her a thorough woodshedding on the dos and don'ts, I wasn't at all confident. And with every planeload of people that washed through without her, I became even more agitated.

Eventually a woman's voice came across the PA system with that calm British accent.

"Would the party meeting Amy Bingaman on Delta flight from Atlanta please pick up a courtesy phone and dial . . ."

Fuck. I was not calm.

The first thing they said when I reached them was "Yes, Mr. Stanhope. First of all, don't panic. The paramedics are looking at her right now."

Panic.

Bingo had evidently piled way too much Xanax on top of her usual buffet of psyche meds, which alone already knock her out and make her goofy. This, lubricated with plenty of free in-flight cocktails, left Bingo unable to get out of her seat on the plane or make words that made much sense. The paramedics of course didn't know what the hell she was on nor could she function well enough to explain. They told me to sit tight.

I sat tight as fuck for an endless amount of time, myself still not knowing what had happened.

Finally the voice came back on the loudspeaker and I was back at the courtesy phone. They'd gotten her off the plane and I explained that she was on medication that could be the culprit.

The problem now was that she wasn't able to fill out the immigration forms. How long would she be there? Where would she be staying? These were questions she probably wouldn't know how to answer on a lucid day. All she knew was to meet me at baggage claim. They let me answer the questions over the phone to fill in the form and she evidently could manage to scrawl her signature.

Shortly afterwards, she was trucked out in a wheelchair by three flight attendants. Her eyes looked in every direction away from each other and focused on nothing while she laughed like an idiot. She was wearing an absurd green-and-white-striped poodle skirt with a T-shirt that our comedian friend Brendon Walsh made depicting a crude cartoon of a man defecating in a trail whilst exclaiming, "No problem!" The flight attendants were laughing as well, seemingly with her and not at her. She must have created an adorable scene. At her worst she still finds a way into your heart.

I'd come to the airport with Hennigan, who'd scheduled his exit with Bingo's arrival. Hennigan is always at my side when I'm in Europe. Without him I am lost and terrified and still don't know how to dial a cell phone internationally. He'd had me put up in an apartment walking distance to the theater so I didn't have to think. But I'd agreed that I would figure out the "tube" to get Bingo and myself back to central London from the airport. He gave me simple directions that did not factor in Bingo being a swaying, jabbering half zombie. You can only take the wheelchair to the airport door. Then you're on your own. Next I was pulling her bags and trying to keep her up on her feet while I navigated my way to this unfamiliar subway fucking thing that was so simple. I would've broken down and taken a cab but the thought of London traffic even on a Sunday gave me the shit-shivers even worse.

Once on the train or the tube or the subway or whatever those cunts call it, I sat opposite Bingo, who sprang up somewhat upright and told me she was hungry. I told her we'd be home soon but she insisted that she had food in her backpack. And indeed she did. She'd packed some cheese sandwiches for the trip, like she was going to the park for a picnic. Accounting for the time she'd had to drive from Bisbee to the airport, wait for flights during layovers, be detained by immigration and now on a train, the sandwiches had to have been sitting in a hot backpack for at least twenty hours.

I was wearing the one black suit I'd packed for the entire three-week run in London. I looked like a proper person on a noontime train. Bingo looked like Courtney Love spiraling into the abyss. People stared like I was some kind of interventionist, counselor or perverted opportunist. Bingo had a wet sandwich that her vacant eyes strained to focus on but failed. The sandwich would ebb and flow, flip and flop with each jerk of the train as though the train itself had comic timing, zigging to make the sandwich fold backwards over itself just as her mouth fell in to zag.

Before you tell someone to take a Xanax on a long flight, explain the difference between a bar (2 mg) and a peach (.5 mg).

●　●　●

Bingo's fucked-up arrival came towards the end of an already miserable time in London. I'd been doing quite well on my tours of the UK in the early and mid-2000s but that didn't mean I liked being there. The more the audiences liked me, the worse I felt for hating being in their country. Or countries, however it works. I'd take sleepers right after the show to fall right down and in the morning I'd take another with more vodka and a nice citrus to sleep again through the day. There is no reason to be awake in London.

At some point Hennigan came back and by then my whole day and probably my entire act consisted of how much I hated London and was terrified of dying on that horrible island. Everything sucked, from the food to television to the bars and mostly the bars. The years I've put into drinking have made me very particular, a snotty cunt if you will. I could give a shit about a brand name; the more plastic the jug, the better. I just want to sit there with my cocktail, mind my own business and get drunk. Pubs in the UK rarely have stools at the bar. You stand. For hours. They rarely have a proper rocks glass. The glass is very important. I don't want a vodka-soda in a tulip glass. They almost never have cocktail straws. I like cocktail straws. I have big ugly teeth and I don't like ice cubes bashing against 'em when I drink. Not a problem, Doug, because in the UK they dole out ice like it's caviar and the few cubes they'll part with are hollow and melt in seconds. Then they have the audacity to charge you separately for both the booze and the mixer, both insanely overpriced.

I now travel with my own cocktail straws and my own glass. Next time, my own ice maker.

On a previous UK tour, we showed up just days after the death of our good friend Russ Dunn. I'd had a lot of friends and family die by then but Russ hit especially hard because he lived in Bisbee and was part of our daily lives. One day he sat down on his couch, had a rum and coke and an aneurysm and then he was dead. Landing in London already depressed amplified the misery by ten. Bingo and I shuffled onto the train, wedged our bags into the always too small shelves and put our duty-free liquor and cartons of cigarettes under our table, fighting off the leftover drink and downers still in our blood from the long flight.

We finally unloaded our shit into the aparthotel near Leicester Square, thinking we'd finally made it there safely, when a wash of horror came over me. We'd left the duty-free on the train. In a city where you can pay seventeen dollars for a single, measured screwdriver. Where you pay fifteen dollars for a pack of cigarettes. All left behind on public transit underneath a table like an Easter egg for a vagrant. I never thought of Russ Dunn again the entire tour. I still mourn the loss of those bags to this day.

On this next trip I'd nursed all the duty-free I'd brought and then the duty-free that Hennigan and Bingo brought until I finally had to buy the UK local overpriced shit vodka a few days before I left. Brian and Bingo left before me and my meltdown was happening alone in a small apartment I'd been sitting in for far too long.

Coming home after the show I pulled the vodka out of the freezer to drink myself down only to pour an icy vodka slushie. It was half frozen. It was the final kick in the pants, a cocktail of insult with a splash of injury. I didn't know whether to blame the veracity of their shitty booze or their archaic appliances, a freezer so ridiculously cold that it froze the bottom-shelf antifreeze I'd purchased. I had to run the bottle under hot water to thaw it because the microwave—like the dishwasher and laundry machines—employed undecipherable characters instead of words. A Star of David, a rainbow, an ankh. Nothing that is obvious. You shouldn't microwave vodka anyway. It removes a lot of the nutrients.

Many months later at dinner with people, I recounted this tale of frozen vodka in one of my many diatribes on why I loathe the UK. Hennigan was there and burst into his hideous, soprano squeal of a laugh and it was minutes before he could get out the fact that he'd watered down that vodka before he'd left London, concerned I was drinking too much.

THE GRASS IS ALWAYS BROWNER

For all the traction I was gaining in the UK audiences, I was at the same time slipping in my own wet piles at home.

Joe Rogan and I had taken over the hosting duties for the jock-popular, feeble-tainment Comedy Central series *The Man Show*. In short, Joe and my sense of humor didn't fit the mold for the show's ingrained audience.

I'd already been protested at a stand-up show in Madison, Wisconsin, just before the airing of our first *Man Show* episode but still while it was being heavily advertised. Not for being a shitty replacement, but for being on the show at all. An agent had booked me in a theater and they had great expectations of a big turnout based on those ads alone.

I'd come in early to sound check—always an unnecessary obligation unless you're working with a guitar act—when the booker told me we were going to be protested. I never considered him to be serious. We'd only sold about 150 tickets for a place that held at least six hundred. The only person I could imagine protesting was the guy who gave me an inordinate guaranteed fee.

But sure enough, as the first trickle of audience started coming in, a dozen or less protesters showed up with signs. They were calm, almost complacent. Maybe they were, like the booker, expecting more people to be there.

Regardless, I was staining my pants with excitement. I couldn't ever imagine having anyone care enough about me to take the time to picket, much less for some dumb show they considered sexist. The protest was the result of a post on a campus feminist newsgroup. I was touched by their sentiment. I ran out with my camera and sheepishly asked if they would mind if I took some pictures. I was braced for a verbal barrage of hatred and didn't care. In the words of Steve Martin in *The Jerk* after finding his name in the phone book—"I'm somebody now!"

Nobody gave a shit about me taking pictures. No one said a word to me. They just stood there bored with their signs.

"Sexism Is So Funny . . . Says the Bigot!"

"Keep Your Jokes Off My Body"

"Doug Stanhope Is a Dope!"

It was funnier still in that, like my shows, it was more dudes than women. Yet nobody would engage me. The more pictures I took, the more I laughed until one of them told me that this wasn't a joke. They told me that they were serious, that sexism wasn't funny and that I shouldn't go watch this garbage.

They had no idea I was the guy they were protesting. I had to break it to them gently and then give them a moment to get their game faces on to give me shit. It's tough to look that foolish and then jump straight into your original game plan. We had a civil discourse where they rode their preplanned bullet points that *The Man Show* leads to rape, eating disorders and every other problem women endure. I wanted to explain to them that *The Man Show* wasn't even really that good to have such effect. If that shitty TV show could ruin the lives of women, the protesters certainly would have had far more problems had they seen my live show. They'd still have problems.

I hung out with them for half an hour or so and I tried to be a diplomat. We found common ground on other shit that sucked in the world. They were nice enough kids and if misguided, they were still just kids. I'm sure that when I was twenty I believed things I was taught rather than things I'd experienced or had grown to conclude on my own. Still, they were my first and to this day only protesters of my career. I wanted to hug them all and buy them all a beer but they weren't even old enough to drink, much less have a coherent argument.

The capper to the whole event came towards the end of my interlude with the picketers. While we engaged in a harmonious discourse, one of my "fans" coming into the show walked into the group, staggering and stumble-footed, and asked the protester next to me what his problem was. I stepped in and asked the drunky-fuck if he was going to the show. He told me that yes indeed he was going to the show. He told me that it was just comedy and if I didn't like it, I should just go fucking home.

Both my protesters and my audience had no idea who I was. Even the feminists had to laugh, including the few ladies amongst them.

Some ladies don't like the media portraying unattainable body images as much as I don't like the fact that I will never have "Abs of Steel" or whatever the most recent infomercial might be. The people who fall for that bullshit—the guys taking human–growth hormones and the girls upchucking cheesecake—are people who think they have nothing more to offer society than being fuckable. Nobody jerks off picturing somebody's sense of decency or superior intellect. Fuckability gives people without better qualities an achievable goal. Don't protest their last resort.

BROWNER PASTURES

The herpes on my dick are not nearly as disconcerting as the herpes on my resume. Before the stink of *The Man Show* could even blemish my nameless profile, I went one step deeper.

I hosted an episode of *Girls Gone Wild* just on a goof in the same way I pretended to be a traveling salesman on *Jerry Springer* years before. It seemed funny at the time—another discounted but worthy title for this book.

I was sitting home alone in Venice, California, on one of those empty nights where you think you might just drink a little bit and take care of yourself. Then Paulie from the bar pounded at my door with a friend in tow. They had to inform me of the genius idea they'd concocted down at O'Brien's. This is one of those moments that reminds you why sober people bitch about how irritating it is to be around drunkards, while still understanding that the opposite is also true.

Paulie's friend ran the *Girls Gone Wild* website. Their previous host was Snoop Dogg. If I spelled Snoop Dogg incorrectly, don't fix it. It's fucking stupid. They were looking for a new host for the next DVD and, with me being the new host of *The Man Show*, it was a slam dunk in their eyes. I told them to set it up and call me just to get them out of my house. I'm a drunk too so I assumed they would forget.

They called the next day and had arranged a meeting with the smarmy, barnacle-to-the-stars owner of *GGW*—Joe

Francis—who wanted me to be the new host. I went to his office and we spent a few obligatory minutes of trying to be cordial. The connection was weak and the bullshit was strained. In short time, a reeking silence draped the office.

It turned out that while they'd told me that Joe Francis wanted to pitch me on being the new host, they'd told him that I wanted to pitch him on me being the new host. We drummed our fingers on the desk, each of us waiting for the pitch to start.

Finally he asked me what my idea was. I told him I was under the impression I was there to hear his idea. The fake laugh we shared when the puzzle was finally put together was the most genuine laugh we'd fake for the rest of our short relationship. I told him I'd put some thought into it and get back to him.

Paulie and I went to my apartment and instead of putting thought into it, we put beer into it. We got drunk and wrote up a proposal that held little or no substance other than over-the-top braggadocio as to why I was the perfect host for the show and that with my new position as host of *The Man Show* and the inherent cross-promotion, they would be insane not to hire me at once. The email was jammed with every industry jargon cliché I could come up with and weeping with all the groundless self-confidence that is the foundation of Hollywood. It was a spoof of a proposal. We were crying by the time it was done and for good measure at the end I added: "PS. Don't Fuck This Up."

Hit "Send"!

This must have been the exact kind of moxie they were looking for in a new, unknown host and I was hired. We went out to seven or eight college towns in Georgia, Texas and Arizona—those are the ones I vaguely remember anyway. They all blended together like an *MTV Spring Break* montage of drunken idiots. All I had to do was be funny. But my brand of humor wasn't copacetic with what dumb chicks who'd show their tits on camera for a free trucker's hat would find funny. And I don't find dumb chicks attractive.

Maybe the word "dumb" is inaccurate. I don't mean that they'd be any more attractive if they could find Canada on a map, or didn't dot their *i*'s with hearts. I'm talking about a complete lack of soul, desire for knowledge, curiosity or original thought. Girls who parrot television sexuality as a replacement for anything interesting to say and don't really mean it. Girls who confuse name brands for style and money with joy. Girls who just don't get it. Dumb chicks. And the rolling cameras were like a bug light drawing them in.

My cracking wise did anything but make these girls go wild. In fact, it could make a girl who was in the midst of going wild stop immediately on her heels and leave. There were times I wasn't allowed on the bus during tapings so I didn't ruin the wildness in progress. The only girls who ever seemed like they wanted anything to do with me were the ones nobody wanted going even the least bit giddy, much less wild. They were mutants like myself and were always the first to show up.

"Okay, I'm gonna take my top off! Are you ready???"

"Ah sure. Go right ahead."

"Are you filming?"

"Of course. Go ahead and show us."

Tits or something like them appear.

"Did you get it?"

"Yep, we got it."

"But the red light wasn't on."

"Don't worry, we got it. Here's your free T-shirt. A large, I'm guessing?"

"Do you know when it's going to air???" in desperation as the crew quickly disappears.

The whole thing was sad and abusive on every level, starting and ballooning at the top. Joe Francis is such a boorish, vile and megalomaniacal person that at times I even skipped his private jet in favor of taking the bus with the crew. Imagine Donald Trump if he were young and could get an erection. A frat boy worth fifty million who'd still bang a girl in the hotel suite toilet and come out saying, "Smell my fingers." Not in the funny way like a comedian would. Like some guy who would fuck girls at after-parties and then immediately throw them out just to make them cry. Like some dude who would brag about it and collect his high-fives.

Nobody said shit to Joe until he left the room. Everybody hated him. But his pig teats were lactating cash and everybody continued to nurse. I wish I had said something. He is fucking disgusting. I tried my best to avoid him but that doesn't excuse what I'd become part of and still doesn't.

All the while Eric—the "vice president of production" whose real title should have been "flunky"—followed behind me with his tail wagging. He was the one who pulled the trigger on hiring me and now I was his liability.

"I'll never forget what you said in that first email! 'Don't Fuck This Up'!"

Remember that I was only hired to do one single video in an endless series of soft-core titty flicks for semi-hard men. But that one video would be the one they advertised. The ploy was to get you to buy the one video advertised on TV and that started you on a perpetual subscription you could cancel anytime. On one of my first tours of the *GGW* offices we passed an empty bank of desks with ringing phones. Eric said, "That's the cancellation lines. Our running joke is that anyone who answers them gets fired."

My video came out and every late-night cable viewer was bludgeoned with it every fifteen minutes for seemingly years. I'd done it as a joke and for the money but the commercials still aired long after that money was gone and the joke had turned embarrassing.

But I wasn't out of the woods yet, contractually or morally. Whatever I thought about Joe Francis as a subhuman being, I bit one more time. Not long after we'd finished filming, I was asked if I'd host their upcoming Super Bowl pay-per-view halftime special on the fictional Girls Gone Wild Island, which is just a large estate on a beach in Mexico. To be fair, it was fucking huge and beautiful but that wasn't enough for Joe Francis. He had to lie and call it an island.

The halftime special would pay twenty-five thousand dollars for a day's work. My concern for how many girls could get harmed in the making of the show got lost in my periphery and I signed on the dotted line.

But as the original commercial continued to run and become a growing source of embarrassment, I asked my then-manager to get me out of the halftime contract. She said she would and by the time it was supposed to be taping, I was comfortably on vacation in Costa Rica with at least a dozen friends including Becker and the Alaska contingent. There, my manager tracked me down with word that Joe Francis was still expecting me and was threatening to sue if I broke the contract and didn't show up. Becker and I had been going to Costa Rica for a few years by then—before I had any problems in that country—and had always talked about buying a place there over too many Pilsen beers. Lesser men drink Imperial in Costa Rica. Becker and I are Pilsen men through and through.

We decided that it was best I leave the party and go do the *GGW* bullshit and that I would put the money towards whatever property Becker could find. Becker did find property and has since built a house on it so that I have a place to hide if I'm ever on the lam. I know you won't find it. I've been there and I know I couldn't find it again.

Leaving Costa Rica to GGW island meant flying back through US customs in Houston and then back through Mexico City, where I can still smell the rotting sewage outside the airport while I smoked, and then to Puerto Vallarta before a ten-mile drive to the *GGW* campsite. I made the production well aware that I didn't want to be there and that I would be drunk for as much of it as was possible. I did not disappoint.

I have three memories. I had a lady co-host who took too long getting ready and we were late for rehearsals that night before the filming. Joe told our driver he'd be fired if he didn't get us there ten minutes ago. Thank fuck I was already potato-faced because the ensuing race at a hundred miles per hour on winding twenty-five-mile-per-hour roads would have surely had me in a high-pitch squeal. Instead, I was happy to die. I'd noticed during the day that cops drove pickup trucks with tall roll-bars holding spotlights. On that insane, roller-coaster suicide drive, I spotted headlights coming towards us and cringed. When I saw the spotlights flash from above a police vehicle, I was happy that we were about to be pulled over. When I saw our driver respond in kind by flashing his own high beams, I thought we'd die in a shoot-out. When the police didn't even turn around, I was perplexed.

We finally arrived at the rehearsal and I asked the driver how he pulled that off. He explained that when you drive an expensive car that looks official—in that case a black Suburban with tinted windows—the show of aggression he'd displayed makes the local cops think you're someone of higher authority. That's some fucking balls. And money. Years later I did a private show for American time-share salespeople in Cancun. The guy who booked me said he could never go back to living in the States because the corruption in Mexico made living too easy. He told me about a time he'd been pulled over on a Christmas Eve in an otherwise total blackout and simply gave the cop fifty bucks to continue on his way home.

I did that show on a slowly revolving dance floor to a nightclub in the round. It was horrible and I couldn't bribe my way out of it.

After the Death Race 2000 to the *GGW* rehearsal, I went into a banquet room of a hotel where thirty-some women sat in four different team uniforms. Joe Francis stood at the front and shouted directions for what was to happen the next day. The special was a series of sports-meets-titty-dancing-related obstacles, a low-budget *American Gladiators* with tits on a beach. I don't remember a single one of them, nor would anybody else who watched it. At the end of the rehearsal, one girl said she wanted to change back into her street clothes to go out on the town. Francis went into a fit of madness and told her she could not. It was suggested that she be put on a bus back home. She burst into tears. This was some Hitler-level power tripping and we all looked at our feet. We knew it was all bluster but she didn't. I would have flown her home myself. I didn't need the money this bad. Nobody did.

I spent the next day filming so drunk I'm amazed I could make words. The only snapshot memory I have is of them filming me crawling on all fours to my room. I was that drunk that crawling was probably all I could accomplish but somehow I sold them that it would be funny for the show.

The next morning I took the same insidious flight back to Costa Rica. I knew what the expression "blood money" meant but now I "got" what it meant. I never went back to ask about the supposed residual checks. I was happy not to have them.

It ain't over.

The worst part was that I still had to promote it. I think of this every time I hear an actor promoting a film they know is a plate of slop. Porn chicks and prostitutes who have to promote—like those from the Bunny Ranch HBO reality show *Cathouse* are in the most unenviable spots. They could never come clean and say, "I fucking hate it. It's humiliating but once I got into it, I couldn't find a way out." Nobody wants to jerk off to a girl you know is crying on the inside, save for maybe Joe Francis. I'm sure there are a few who love what they do or at least prefer it to answering phones in a cubicle with the same fake smile for pennies on the dollar.

As I had with *The Man Show*, I now had to put on the face and sell this porn-sploitation to any media outlet that would have me. *Girls Gone Wild* was worse in that I had to go on *Howard Stern* with Joe Francis and a handful of girls and dishonestly encourage people to buy this dreck, which I purposely did poorly.

Stern has a reputation for making you say shit you might never tell a close friend, much less divulge on the air. I have a reputation for saying it anyway. More than once Howard has actually told me not to say things that were true but might get me in trouble. Stern was my hero and my "I've made it!" moment the first time he had me on. To have to sell some *Girls Gone Wild* bullshit out of contractual obligation on *Stern* was dishonorable at best. Fortunately for me, Howard likes to focus on the fucking and there were girls there. That took the focus off of me.

At some point during the show, Stern asked me how much pussy I got filming *GGW*. I told him honestly that I got none. I added that it wasn't only because I was married at the time. I told him that I didn't want my DNA anywhere within a hundred yards or miles of Joe Francis.

Even after the money was spent and the commercials stopped airing, the herpes scar of *GGW* still haunted me. A few years later

Joe Francis—*GGW* megalo-patriarch and predator, not new to being locked up—got arrested again for some financial or moral malfeasance.

Fox News ran the story on the hour and every time they ran the same footage; the graphic "Girls Gone Wild Owner Under Arrest" ran with commentary over an endless, silent loop of footage of my drunken face from the infomercial, making it look like I was the one who'd been busted.

They say no press is bad press. I would have preferred no press.

ACTUAL PORN

When I was asked to host the annual Adult Video News (AVN) Awards in Vegas, I thought I'd finally been recognized by my own people. The AVNs are what are commonly referred to as the Oscars of porn. I felt like I was their perfect Billy Crystal. Like porn people, I put out DVDs that guys would have to hide under their mattresses too.

I had no idea that porn people took their careers seriously. Porn is a go-to, always funny topic for comedians, maybe the number one topic. I assumed that porn people had the same point of view. I know that porn is far more popular than comedy in the amount of views but I couldn't imagine there was any ego there. I assumed the awards would all be pillow fights, Ecstasy and inside jokes.

I'd played the Acme Comedy Club in Minneapolis where usually the crowd looked like they were there for something out of *Lake Wobegon Days* rather than my fist-fuck comedy. One weekend night there was a couple in sweaters in the front row center that looked like in-laws who only faked the smiles because it was Thanksgiving. I kept ribbing them for being offended, for not putting any effort into what kind of production they were coming to see, making them out to be prudes.

Joke was on me. After the show, the gentleman approached me at the bar and told me that he was also from Los Angeles and in fact a producer of porn. He invited me to watch a shoot when we were both back home. I gladly accepted. I showed up at a castle-styled home in Chatsworth—the Hollywood of porn—at some hour that seemed very inappropriate for this type of enterprise. Daylight, to be specific.

None of what happened was anything I'd expected. There were only five people there aside from me. The producer, a cameraman, a makeup girl and the two actors. The chick I don't remember her name. The dude was an actor named Erik Everhard. It's a difficult name to forget. In my heart of hearts, I knew that the porn industry exploits and feeds on women who are damaged. You ignore that heart when you are jacking off. But that day I knew I wouldn't be jerking off and expected to eye-witness what I knew to be true.

It was all the opposite. Erik showed up with the flu and made it clear that the last thing he wanted to be doing was fucking a really hot chick. The lady on the other hand was there to get fucked and fucked well. She was very vocal about it.

"What the Fuck??? Why did you yell 'CUT' when I was just about to come???"

Erik would come over near me during breaks in the shoot and I'd try to make funny. He looked at me like I was a fucking asshole for even being there before walking away to cough up snot. You'll tell me that this was an anomaly where the girl loves doing porn and the guy seems the victim, or at least like he deserves more sick days. I would tend to agree even in an uneducated assumption, even though my only firsthand experience was the complete opposite.

What I took away from it all was that no matter how glorious or enviable your career might seem to the general public, once it becomes something you have to do, it will one day suck.

Kinda sad.

Yes, even having to do porn might suck but the AVNs was an awards show. I assumed that it would be different and that drunken frivolity was certain to ensue. I was glad to be invited to the party.

You've seen less tension and backstage jitters at an Italian wedding. Everyone at the AVNs was on edge and snapping at each other. Nobody was having fun. They actually cared about winning. And for the most part, they were assholes. If I watched any one of them getting corn-piped in a film afterwards, it was out of spite and with a reticent boner.

Nina Hartley, a true porn star with porn name recognition from the days when such a thing existed, was introduced to me on the afternoon of the awards. She told me like a general would tell a front-line troop who was sure to die: "Good luck, have fun." Then she told me to stay away from sex jokes—that although you'd think they'd work in this audience, they wouldn't.

Talk about a pre-show head fuck. That'd be like me telling her before her first-ever porn shoot: "Have fun, be yourself. Just don't take off your clothes." I had already front-loaded all the sex jokes I could find for my set list and it was too late to rethink and rewrite.

The Venetian banquet hall where it was being held was over-full at about thirty-five hundred people. I'd been told upon hiring that I could not drink before or during the show. I had a reputation for getting plastered and fucking up shows, evidently. So I had to keep my drinking undercover by drinking openly and a lot, once I could see that everybody was too caught up in the moment to care.

I opened the show to almost nobody out of the thirty-five hundred in attendance paying attention and the few who were, hating me. What I didn't know until afterwards was that, all the while I was onstage telling jokes, they had giant screens hanging from the ceiling away from me and towards the crowd with a roaming cameraman shooting live shots of porn chicks in the audience showing their tits and pussies at their banquet tables, all hoping to be crowned the queen of jizz flicks. Why would anyone look at the dude onstage talking? I could have read baking tips off a Ritz cracker box or blown my head off and no one would have noticed. Porn stars would have stood on my corpse, blood leaking from my skull as our spoiled dreams coagulated, tearfully accepting their award for "Most Believable MILF in Teen Porn" or "Least Likely to Be Otherwise Employable."

The worst part was knowing that my part wasn't even close to over. I would have to keep going up after each award and be disliked again and again. It lasted for well over three hours.

People call it the Oscars of porn but it isn't. I wish the Oscars could be so honest in their vanity. At the AVNs, once a category or film had been awarded and the actors in question had nothing left to win or lose, their entire banquet table entourage would leave en masse in the middle of the show, either celebrating or indignant at the slight, and loudly blow out of the showroom. I'd love to see that at the Oscars. I'd love to see Meryl Streep lose on her Best Supporting nomination and get up during the winner's speech, waving her entourage to grab their coats and head up the aisle towards the exits, stealing the bottles off the table as they leave. Fuck who wins Best Picture, our business here is done.

Again, like the porn I saw filmed, kinda sad.

I thought we were kindred spirits, you and me, porn.

Once it becomes a business, I guess it can take all the fun out of it.

We can all take it all too seriously.

And if there was ever an award for "Worst Ever Host of the AVNs," I have no doubt I'd be a winner.

● ● ●

The only time I've had the opportunity to smoosh my penis up against a porn star's private parts came years later. I'll get to it in a roundabout way, as seems to be my "style" in this book.

The Office in Chattanooga, Tennessee, is one of my all-time favorite day-drinking bars in the world. For me the criteria is stumbling distance to the hotel and proximity to food. The Office is attached to a clumsy Days Inn that also houses a twenty-four-hour diner. The bar is tiny, has about six stools, three tables with a jukebox and as of this writing, it still allows smoking. Valhalla. I've never had a bartender there that I didn't fall in love with and I've never had a show in that city afterwards that I wasn't too shitfaced because of it.

The reason I bring this bar up is that I tend to have a Jekyll and Hyde memory. Sometimes I will remember things from when I was drunk only when I'm drunk again. I spent an afternoon before a gig at the Office bullshitting with one of the regulars, slowly imagining my show going in the toilet and not caring. As the small talk ran into the usual grandiose—that sweet spot in the indulgence where everyone is interesting and everything begins to look beautiful in life—I asked him more about his backstory. It almost felt like I gave a shit. He said he'd recently moved to the area after having been a doorman at a strip club in South Florida. Then it came up that I was a comedian, probably when I wanted to seem more interesting myself.

One drink leads to another and wouldn't you know. Turns out we'd been old friends for a minute back in a day. The titty bar he'd worked in was owned by my old friend Scott, who'd once roped Bingo and me into playing in a charity poker event at that same strip joint with celebrities (of my caliber) and porn stars, one being an actual star of 1980s porn—again, back when porn actually had stars.

My drinking buddy here in Chattanooga had been working the door that night of the poker party.

Scott the owner was friends with this porn star and I'd actually performed at her porn retirement party at his other club in Colorado Springs not long before. I'd even been removed from the stage at that show. I was doing a bit about how girls like her would never fuck me. It went on graphically into how one day she'd be old and ugly, carrying her tits in her pants pockets, rolling over her labia with the wheels of her walker, etc. And it went on and on, each detail of her hideous future spelled out so distinctly that you could almost smell it.

The payoff was that at the end of the bit where I'd say, "Oh yeah, that day will come! And *THEN* you'll fuck me!" Sure, you have to hear it in its entirety to get the full effect. The point is that one of her friends backstage knew I was drunk and thought it was just a run-on trashing of what she would look like, just me being a rambling asshole. He didn't know that there was a payoff. He came out and grabbed the mic out of my hand before I could get to the punch line, without which everybody thinks I'm just a rambling asshole. I wanted to go person to person in the audience and explain where the bit was going. Instead I hid in plain sight, people avoiding me like a wet cough.

Fortunately at the poker event, the porn star didn't remember any of that. She was one of the only really cool people there who, like us, was more interested in the bar than the cameras. She was probably the only one who hung out with me and Bingo at all. The rest of the new-porn gals were giggling hollow shells who'd proudly wear a dunce cap as a crown, wearing makeup like it was done by a mortician trying to mask a violent death. Our girl was a human being, a fun, intelligent human being and, in this crowd, that made her an outcast like us.

Scott knew her well and told us to keep her away from co-caine as though that was possible in South Florida. But he didn't tell Bingo and me to keep away from cocaine. And nobody told him that we were neighbors in the same hotel.

I'm not bragging when I tell you that I have been involved in too many threesomes and they are always awkward. Invariably everyone involved had to be incredibly fucked up just to make it happen. Usually the girls knew each other and repeatedly fell into giggle fits of "OMG I can't believe we're really doing this!" Not sexy. I had one fivesome where I was so drunk that I could only focus on squeezing enough blood into my pud to achieve penetration with all four of the ladies so that the story was tech-nically accurate. There is no doubt that they would have pre-ferred it had just been an all-girl drunken foursome had I not been there. They let me in out of pity. I have the Tony Romo of dicks. It can squeak out a win on the road in Buffalo but when you put it in the big game under pressure, it fumbles.

This was no different in Florida with Bingo and the porn star.

Several lines and cocktails later back at the hotel, I was twist-ing my coke-dick like I was wringing out a wet towel trying to get it workable so I might add my third into the Porn Star–Bingo two-some that had kicked off. I tried and failed. But on the positive side, I was scheduled to go on *The Howard Stern Show* in a matter of days. Knowing he'd always lead off with talk about fucking, I needed a good story. And the short version of my story was this.

If you're gonna have sex with your favorite porn star from the gilded age of XXX video—do it in 1985, when boners were easier to come by and the porn star wasn't post-retirement.

The upswing and the karma of the story is that, in real life but tacitly, I finally managed to get that punch line out.

"Oh yeah, *THEN* you'll fuck me!"

STILL, NOBODY KNOWS YOU

I am happy to say that I have paid to see myself live several times. From the early days when some thick-neck doorman would half slap me with a backhand at the entrance to tell me that it was a five-dollar cover charge, I would gladly pay just to watch him apologize after he saw me onstage. It was also a great out for when jokes didn't work. I could tell the audience that I was no different than them. I paid the same as them and I was also hoping I would be funnier. We were all on the same page. It still happens occasionally only now it costs more.

Artie Lange asked me to open for him at the Palms in Las Vegas after he was already ensconced as the new co-host on *Stern* and I was always forgotten as a guest. I knew the gig was going to be an inevitable death. The bill was full of Wack Packers and mainstays of the show. I think I was scheduled to follow Yucko the Clown. And I was the last guy before Artie.

Morning radio audiences are always the worst. Assholes who live their lives stuck in morning-drive traffic listening to radio on the way to a job they loathe, who sit on hold for hours hoping to get on the air to say something pointless. Now they are here live and still have all those pointless things to yell but there is no longer a call screener to hold them back. All of those unanswered calls are blurted out like an endless rain of dull-pointed arrows throughout the show.

I was almost happy when they wouldn't let me onto the show to begin with. Although I was on the bill and brought by a phalanx of security all the way from Artie's suite through the back hallways to the artists' entrance, the drunk-with-power backstage doorman said I needed my necklace-laminate to gain entry. I had assumed that the Secret Service delivery through Frank Sinatra tunnels would have given this guy a clue that maybe I wasn't a door crasher. I was wrong.

"I don't give a fuck. You need your pass." As he turned his back. You don't need a pass, you ape. You needed better knees. That way maybe you coulda gone pro out of college ball instead of being here all bitter and an asshole, stuck in a back hallway flicking me shit. I didn't say it but I wrote it down in my head. The Palms is one of those hotels where the beautiful people tend to go and rave and have unwanted pregnancies or whatever the fuck they do. It is something in nature that the more attractive the clientele a place draws, the more angry and shitty the doormen become.

Then I noticed that right beside the door next to us was a huge poster for the show with my name and picture right underneath Artie's. I pointed this out to the simian and my smug look only made him pissier.

"Don't give a fuck. They told me everyone needs their pass."

I'd taken the gig out of respect for Artie Lange, in that he'd asked me to do it at all. The money was good but it was a fact that Artie was offering it to me only because he liked me. He certainly didn't need me. And with this manatee door-plumber being an overt fuckhead, I decided I didn't need to be there for any reason at all. I'd had enough times in my life where I had to kowtow to some overzealous bar-muscle who was more concerned with his own waning power than the job with which he was entrusted. So I just quit. I was in Vegas and would be just as happy to gamble.

At some point somebody from the show found me at a black-jack table, apologized for the lack of courtesy and brought me back to the greenroom. As expected, by the time I got to the stage the crowd was too exhausted by the amount of opening acts and I was too exhausted by all the bullshit and hating the dance-club-nation vibe of the whole place. The show was an exchange of me shitting on the club and specifically all those notes about the doorman I'd jotted down in my gray matter, followed by the au-dience shitting on me and shouting me down for not being Artie, and then me shitting on the audience for being rubes who sit in traffic listening to radio on their way to jobs they hate and taking it out on these performers.

And with that, is everybody ready for your headliner?

Artie, to his extreme credit, followed this wail of me being booed by opening with: "For the record, I agree with everything that Doug Stanhope just said."

And to the extreme credit of the doorman whose many con-cussions on the college gridiron had left him without the ability for discretionary reasoning, he probably wouldn't have let Artie in without a pass either, regardless of his face and name being on the side of the building.

THANK YOU FOR YOUR FEEDBACK. YOUR OPINION IS VERY IMPORTANT TO US.

The only show other than Iceland that I can remember doing sober in the last two decades was years before at Ohio University. It was coming off the heels of *The Man Show*. It was called the No Class Tour but it failed to meet my standards of "classlessness."

I was headlining with Christian Finnegan, at that time known for the priceless "Real World" sketch from *Chappelle's Show*, and Ed Helms, then a correspondent for *The Daily Show* and now known from *The Hangover* movies and probably a lot more.

There are a few invariables when it comes to working college gigs and the main one is that it is going to suck. There is a difference between playing a college bar in a college town versus playing at a college on campus that the college itself is paying for—out of tuitions the students will never be able to pay back. Student activities are for the kids too stupid to get a fake ID or for those who don't find it amusing to watch a frat pledge drink himself into a coma chugging beer out of an enema bag. If you don't find that funny, then you will not like even the lightest parts of my show.

Campus comedy was always a sad sack of downers, some with blank picket signs and a Sharpie waiting for you to say the wrong buzzword so they can tell you and the world why you're an asshole. I've heard that it's gotten far worse since I last did one.

The Ohio University show was doomed from the start. The show had been accidently listed under "Family-Oriented Events" on parents' weekend, where parents were there to send their freshman sons and daughters into adulthood.

And since they weren't serving alcohol at the show and I only had to do twenty or twenty-five minutes, I figured I'd do it without drinking. It would have gone even worse if I had.

I'll give you a post that showed up online the next day.

From Ohio University's website.

Family-oriented events offered by OU, Athens • University Programming Council welcomes Comedy Central's "No Class" Tour to Athens. Comedians Doug Stanhope, of "The Man Show," Ed Helms, a "Daily Show" correspondent, and Christian Finnegan, a stand-up comic, will share the stage at 8 p.m. at the Templeton-Blackburn Alumni Memorial Auditorium.

Audience Member Posting

(whoever didn't do their research at OU is going to get shit on so hard . . .)

Hol-y fucking shit . . . that's what I was saying to myself tonight.

Ok, picture this. Ohio University . . . Sold Out Comedy Central Show, about 3,000 people . . . It was 99% Freshman, and it was mom and dad weekend, where mom and dad came to visit their newly released into the college world kids.. It was mom and dad and kid every 3 seats.

I was thinking oh Doug MUST have a clean set, no way he would ever do his regular shit to these fragile people..

I was SOOO very wrong.

There was 3 comedians . . .

ED HELMS, from the Daily Show

CHRISTIAN FINNEGAN, His most recent thing I knew him from was Dave Chappelle's Show..he was the dude from the "real World" skit that brought his girlfriend home and everyone fucked her.. Funny guy.

And DOUG.

We'll when Chris went on and the first time he said "fuck" I saw about 50 people's head flinch. oh yeh, this was going to be brutal.

Chris was very funny, but I could tell he held alot in..while not 100% clean, I still think he was censoring himself a bit..

Then Ed came on, he is VERY funny on the *Daily Show,* his set was good in parts but I think he was either not a frequent stand up, or he just had a off night . . . but still good stuff..

Doug was GOLD . . . . his best show I have seen yet, not because he did anything new, but because his balls grew 10 folds today..

HE WAS BRUTAL.. talking shit about college, scaring the parents, he was being as dirty as possible. But then he got into religion . . . .

It was hard to watch, seriously.. it was like watching someone you knew get raped. About 1/3 of the people (about 1000 people) stood up and left, people were yelling, people were screaming . . . . it was awesome!

Parents wanted to leave, the kids begged to stay. After I saw a woman trying to get people to sign a petition to get a refund, security was worried for Doug's safety, religious people were crying.. oh my god, what just happened . . .

We drove back to Columbus, and got wasted at their hotel bar, and talked about everything from cell phone plans to midgets, my lungs hurt from laughing and smoking. Doug was paranoid that he is going to get kicked off the tour from tonight. Anyways, I have some poor quality media at . . .

●   ●   ●

The university responded to the post that the ticket count was actually about sixteen hundred and only about three hundred walked out. The video I saw showed several but one old stooge was close enough to be heard shouting loudly from the back at the exit, saying something to the effect of "This man is a sick fuck and any of you that stay and watch him are sick fucks too!" Nice way to talk in front of the children, sir.

The link is no longer there but I'm sure you can find it if you search hard enough. Or you could just ask Redban. He was the kid who wrote the post and made the flip phone–era video. He is the one who eventually became Joe Rogan's videographer flunky and has now come into his own as the comedian Brian Redban. He is the creator of DeathSquad. They are like the Killer Termites only far more POWERFUL!

●   ●   ●

I'd tell you a story about a night that I killed, where I got a standing ovation in a sold-out theater. A night where everything went perfectly and made me feel strong and confident. But nobody wants to hear those stories. Those stories, like recounting dreams, are only interesting to oneself at best. I don't even take pleasure in remembering them. My brother is a cook and I remember him telling me that, with meat, the fat is where the flavor is. I am a comedian and I will tell you that the suck is where the funny is, and the funny is the meat.

Let's get back to sucking.

● ● ●

Hate mail is nothing out of the ordinary. I have a folderful. They were far more prevalent before people knew who they were coming to see. I used to sometimes fight with them. Then I'd just ignore them. Now I miss them. They were always fun when you had time to be creative with them.

From: "f*****" <*****@hotmail.com>
To: <doug@dougstanhope.com>
Subject: APPLETON WISC
Date: Sat, 8 Apr 2006 16:20:12 -0500
I JUST WANTED OT TAKE A FEW MINUTES OF YOUR TIME TO LET YOU KNOW HOW UNHAPPY I WAS AT YOUR SHOW AT SKYLINE ON THE 7TH OF APRIL. YOU GUYS WERE TERRIBLE. I NEVER EVEN LAUGHED (NOT EVEN SMILED TO MYSELF)
I DONT KNOW HOW YOU GUYS THINK YOU ARE FUNNY. I THINK YOU WERE GETTING LAUGHS FROM THE DRUNKS THAT WOULD LAUGH AT ANYTHING. YOU ALL HAD GOOD DELIVERY, TIMING AND GOOD CHARISMA ON STAGE. (EXCEPT THE CHICK) SO I DO THINK YOU WILL GO PLACES BUT YOUR ACT NEEDS WORK.
THERE IS NOTHING FUNNY ABOUT 911. THE TSUNAMIE, ETC.
THANKS FOR LISTENING,
F

From: "doug stanhope" <dougstanhope@hotmail.com>
To: *****@hotmail.com
Subject: RE: APPLETON WISC
Date: Sat, 08 Apr 2006 22:11:22 +0000

Dear F-

Thank you very much for your email. Your comments are taken very seriously and we happen to strongly agree with you on this matter.

As you are probably aware, The Skyline Comedy Club provides us with scripts each time we perform to insure that we present a new "act" every show. We were shocked to see some of the material we were asked to recite last night and argued fruitlessly with management to change or completely remove some of the more offensive and risque parts of the monologues. We also do not like the fact that we are forced to act as though we are intoxicated just to increase alcohol sales, a practice implemented by many comedy clubs.

I hope that you forward your thoughts onto the Skyline upper-echelon so as to bolster our own arguments. The fact that I am asked to poke fun even indirectly at 9/11 knowing that my friend Lynn Shawcroft, also on the bill, lost her brother-in-law in those tragic events - is insulting to me as an actor.

Please call Cliff or Pat at Skyline - 920 734 5653 and ask that we be allowed to go back to Thursdays script that dealt more with difficulties in relationships, Brokeback Mountain and Hooters restaurants - subject matter that is more palatable to the audience as well as ourselves.

Your friend,

Doug Stanhope

From: <f*****@hotmail.com>

Sent: Monday, April 10, 2006 12:14 PM

To: dougstanhope@hotmail.com

Subject: RE: APPLETON WISC

I AM SO SUPRISED TO RECEIVE SUCH A WELL WRITTEN RESPONSE. I THOUGHT YOU WERE AN DRUNKEN IDIOT. (HA-HA) I CANNOT BELIEVE YOUR COMMENTS. IS THIS TRUE?? IS THIS THE CASE WITH ALL COMEDIENS/COMEDY CLUBS???

I KNOW PAT AND CLIFF AND I WILL CALL THEM.

THANK YOU FOR NOT CALLING ME A C**T. I THOUGHT I WOULD GET THAT KIND OF RESPONSE. BECAUSE YOU ANSWERED SO ELOQUENTLY AND PROFESSIONALLY, THEN I CAN ASSUME YOUR WORDS AND THOUGHTS ARE TRUE.

THANKS FOR YOU TIME AND GOOD LUCK

F

What a cunt.

SUCKING ABROAD

I didn't exactly *say* that Irishwomen are too ugly to rape but what I did say couldn't have fit in such a beautifully succinct tabloid headline. And if what I had said onstage were that concise, the audience wouldn't have had the time to boo me and shout me down like they did before I got to the point.

Kilkenny, Ireland, is a quaint village that, to my understanding, is somewhere in Ireland. Perhaps it is even the most quaint town in Ireland. I was there for five days and I will tell you that quaint turns into boring faster than lust turns into shame once you've ejaculated.

Quaint is good for writing a romance novel that is going to suck and nothing else. They say that if you're bored, it's because you are boring and I have no reason to say they are wrong. I realize on a daily basis that I have very few interests at all. In Kilkenny I found myself consciously trying to stop from complaining but I failed and it seemed that every utterance was straight from the mouth of Mother.

Ireland, as luck would have it, couldn't stop complaining at the time either. They were what us city folk like to call "gone apeshit." It seems the news of the day, which turned into the news of the week, had to do with a supreme court ruling that made for a small change in the statutory rape laws of the country.

As I understood it, it had been the law in Ireland that if you were convicted of banging someone under seventeen, you went directly to jail, no questions asked, even if you believed the person to be of legal age at the time. Upon my arrival, the courts had ruled that it was unfair not to let a defendant claim that it was an "honest mistake."

Being that the drinking age was eighteen and that it is very common to have pubs serve those underage, this all seemed logical to me.

Problem was that—due to the court ruling—a convicted pedophile was released from prison pending a new trial and a few others were attempting to do the same. At the time there were only seventeen people in the entire country in prison whose cases could be affected by the new ruling.

They called the released pedo "Mr. A," a pseudonym given so they might protect the identity of the accuser. Mr. A was on the cover of all the papers shown with a sport coat over his head and face as he was led from the courthouse. The cover stories of those newspapers sent you to the five or eight inside pages that covered the story or related stories until you thought that all of Ireland was under a siege of kid-fucking.

Mass protests in the streets and not just where this Mr. A had been let out on appeal. Across the entire country and even in quaint Kilkenny. They were all putting down their bottles and picking up their pitchforks—and then of course realizing they could hold their pitchfork in one hand and still bring the bottle. Idiots with bottles and pitchforks, not a one wondering why there was still cobblestone under their twentieth-century feet.

I do not in any way distort or embellish the level of frothing histrionics that had enveloped this country. From the moment I stepped off the plane, you would have thought rogue pedophile sleeper cells had flown hijacked planes into the asses of Ireland's innocent youth.

People are easily swept into this brand of hysteria in almost equal line with their own boredom and how much their own lives suck. They need an enemy when the real enemy is their own poor choices. You didn't even want to have that baby in the first place and now that child has got you anchored in this idyllic little hamlet, glued into a *Groundhog Day* existence. The only escape from your per diem reality of production and predictability is the newspaper, shot under your door daily like a prison kite.

The media gives them an outlet for their boredom and regret the way the lottery gives them their only hope. Today this paper encourages you to believe that one single guy—wearing a sport coat over his head whilst being trailed by a throng of paparazzi, no less—is a DEFCON 1–level risk of slipping into your shrubbery and cornholing your kid. That misplaced anger makes you feel adrenaline for the first time since you initially finger-thumped your now–old lady when you were both roller-skating and drinking pints at fifteen years old. Or however old she *said* she was. You take that anger to the streets with a cardboard sign, sure in your own head that this is making so much more of a difference in the world than you packing the bananas at whatever Irish version of the Piggly Wiggly.

I'd come to do the Kilkenny comedy festival and to my great fortune, this headline news segued perfectly into my favorite new material at the time. I'd already been developing a routine about all the Myspace/child predator fear-mongering in the US so it didn't take too much coffee to rework the two into one long rant about people's overreactions and delusions to the risk of their child taking unwanted cock.

I never actually said that Irishwomen are too ugly to rape. I did say in confidence to Hennigan as we walked down a quaint street from breakfast and looked at the ladies—that I'd be surprised if women this ugly get fucked at any age. But I never said it onstage. Too easy, not enough explanation.

I'd touched on the subject in the first show in Kilkenny, just using the current national crisis as a segue to previously written material. The audience fell stunned and silent so I went back to the drawing board and wrote even more about their specific situation.

The next night was where it really went downhill. Understand that this was before I had any following to speak of in Ireland and was working mixed-bill shows, several comedians of any genre on one show.

Comedy night. Like music night. Must all be the same.

The second night I was going up in front of beloved Irish comedian Dara O'Briain. I'd say that he was the Jay Leno of Ireland except for the fact that Dara is funny. I just mean that he was that well known from television and most everyone in the audience that night was there to see him. I'd once done a television show of stand-up comedy that he hosted in the UK, opening my set by admitting that I was blown out of my undershorts on Ecstasy. Anyone who'd ever been tripping in that fashion could tell by my eyes that I wasn't kidding. By the time I got to the interview portion at the end of the show, I had to repeat to Dara that I wasn't joking. I didn't actually have to repeat it. I felt compelled to repeat it. Dara had to cut me off. Of course I was kidding, he told the audience. Doug is a comedian. Comedians make jokes. I didn't begrudge him for trying to cover his own ass.

That night in Kilkenny, Dara was the main attraction. Not my problem. I started in on the rape issue, on the point of someone making an "honest mistake" and having intercourse with someone they believed—or were misled to believe—to be of legal age. I ventured the idea that, as most of the women in Kilkenny were such misshapen pigs, if you were to actually fuck them, you would be more concerned the next morning about what species they were rather than what age. I proffered that one wouldn't ever consider how old they were until days later when—still staring at it slumbering in the bed—you'd wonder, "How long can one of these things live?"

Now, maybe you'd think that's just the same as saying that the Irish are too ugly to rape and perhaps it is, but I like my version better. The crowd did not and before I could segue into my own Myspace pedophile chunk, they were shouting me down in some unintelligible dialect where, although I couldn't make out the words, I was aware of the intent. Impending violence is an international language.

On a brief aside, every time I've worked the UK and Ireland, the farther you get from the major cities or sometimes even in the heart of them, the harder it becomes to figure out what people are saying to you. Even though it's the same language. Their common refrain is always: "We don't have an accent! Yooooou have the accent!" I see your point. My point is that nobody on that block of misery has ever had to say to me: "I didn't understand one fucking word that just came out of your mouth." As I have to do all too often when people talk to me after shows.

You always understand what I am saying. I understand maybe a few words you say to me. Who doesn't understand whose accent? Maybe you should adopt or at least mimic my accent. It seems to work more consistently. I mean, if you really want to communicate. The angry mob in Kilkenny did not.

The uproar at that show rose to a level where me having a microphone still gave me no advantage but I plowed on until a producer gave me the throat-slit hand gesture from the wings to shut it down. I was escorted out a back door for my safety and to the audience's great delight.

From the laughs I heard while I was out back smoking, I'm pretty sure Dara had a pretty decent show.

To say I was booed off stage sounds exciting but it was the guy who paid me that got me off stage. I was merely booed onstage. As my comedian friend Basil White used to tell audiences when a joke invoked their wrath—"I bathe in your hate!" I'd created a Jacuzzi of hate and could have exfoliated all night. So long as they kept bringing the beer it would have seemed like fun to me. The only person that can boo me off stage is the paymaster and he has to use a murder hand signal to inform me that I've fulfilled my contractual obligation.

History is written by the winners or just as easily by the alcohol.

The press started calling only because Hennigan started calling the press. "Unknown Comedian Has Shitty Show That Nobody Knew Was Happening" would not make the headlines without PR people making it happen. One journalist called my hotel and asked if it was true that I'd said that Irishwomen are too ugly to rape. I laughed and replied, "Yes, I guess I did say that . . . in a way . . . but what I really said was . . ." and then explained the entire bit. In her article she only quoted the part where I said, "Yes, I guess I did say that."

I was pulled from the two remaining showcase shows— shows featuring multiple comics—yet had an extra solo show added. Those shows sold out quickly due to all the hubbub and went fantastically.

I kept with the bit, ironed it out and it eventually, down the road, it became one of my most viewed bits ever on the Internet. I'd long since ditched the part about the Irish as by then nobody anywhere else knew about that news story or cared about Irish people. But at the time, as I left Ireland, the tabloid headline at the airport read: "Irish Women Are Too Ugly to Rape: Fury at Comic's Outburst!"

No press is bad press—unless you're the pedophile with the sport coat over your head being lead from the courthouse.

● ● ●

Sucking overseas is different in that you don't always know why they hate you or even if they really hate you at all. Sometimes they are simply being polite. Sometimes they are screaming words of approval that you don't understand and assume are an assault. Sometimes you just stop caring when you realize that you'll never understand. Serenity prayer. Accept the things you cannot change.

I was never a good comedy host. I think that is what got me bumped up to a middle act early on in my career. The host is supposed to make people feel at home, welcome. Just like at a dinner party. My act was the guy who got drunk too early and jumped into the pool naked. But I learned how to fake it long enough to be pushed up from host to weird naked guy. I learned a few tricks to get me through but forgot them as soon as they were no longer necessary. I still suck at hosting.

The Edinburgh Festival Fringe in Scotland is a month-long cluster-fucked jubilee of a million acts that you don't want to see and a million people who come to get drunk and not want to see them. But they come to the shows anyway. Comedians will do shows literally anywhere. I was there once when a comedian did shows on a cab ride to the three people in the back. And I'm sure that even he had shows that weren't sold out.

I was asked to host a late-night show in a small bar called the Tron, the same bar that I'd done on my first Fringe fest. Late-night shows usually have the "dirty" or "X-rated" theme so I'm your guy. But I'm a shitty host. By this point I treated all crowds like they were my own audience and these were not. Opening the show by telling everyone that they're "an assembly of idiots" who should "just shut the fuck up and drink" would work at my own show. Here it only made folks a bit tense and agitated.

There is no way to know how long I'd been awake at that point or how many shows I'd done. The truth is that most likely I'd been shut in my apartment all day, done my own show and was reasonably drunk enough to host this late show. In hindsight it feels like every Edinburgh show was one wobbling binge meeting another. Regardless, I was in no mood to be dealing with after-hours drunks as is the job description at this gig.

In between acts, I did a bit about Ecstasy when some girl started screaming, "That's not funny! My sister died from Ecstasy!" I was out of time and patience and began railing on her, saying, "Nobody dies from doing Ecstasy! You die from garbage that was sold to you as Ecstasy that was shit that some dude made in his toilet. And your sister should have known to drink more water if she's going to dance all night like an asshole." As I went on and ranted about how her story was the reason drugs should be legalized and regulated, she ran out of the room crying in a fit of histrionics. Well, there's a good break to bring up the next comedian! And now that I had 'em all fired up . . .

"Ladies and gentlemen, your next act coming to the stage, all the way from America . . . Scott Capurro!"

Scott Capurro, a flamingly gay American comic, is very funny. But he isn't better than cigarettes so I went to my usual spot out on the back stairwell to smoke. Evidently the crying girl had gone upstairs to her two thug friends or brothers or husbands and told them that the American comic downstairs was making fun of her dead sister! So these two fucking knot-headed hooligans came down and walked onto the stage on either side of

Scott, thinking that this must be the American comedian who'd talked shit about the sister. And they were going to kick the eyeballs out of him.

Scott, having no idea why he was being flanked onstage, got even more gay and asked, "Whoooo *are you*???" I wasn't in the room but I imagine him twirling his hand and snapping his fingers. Regardless, by all accounts he was not intimidated in the least. There were no bouncers and the ladies who were running the door somehow calmed and eventually removed the savage beasts from the stage. I was out back oblivious to the whole event until someone ran out and said, "You've got to get out of here NOW! We've got to get you to another bar!" We ran for our lives before they could even explain to me why we had to run.

I used to defend my usage of the word "faggot" in that I only used it as a word meaning weakness, without stapling it to any type of sexuality. If I were in Scott Capurro's shoes that night, I would have been the bottom with no place to run. Scott was a queer who saved my ass and stared adversity in its ugliest ranks while I ran like a faggot.

I'd feel like I owe him a blow job but I'm not that attractive and my giant teeth don't suit the experience. And I'm not that good of a host.

JUST FOR SPITE:
A FESTIVAL

This reminds me of the reason I went into rehab."

Those were the last words Greg Giraldo said to me.

It was July of 2008 after I'd been removed from the greenroom at the *Dirty Show* at Montreal's Just for Laughs comedy festival. I'd had an argument with the nerd who ran the event or, rather, he had an argument with me. He'd taken exception to a scathing update on my website about the fest and I calmly—if drunkenly—stood my ground that essentially he treated comics like migrant lettuce pickers. Imagine him as Bill Gates if Bill Gates didn't know shit about computers but stumbled blindly into a place where he was in charge of it all and then got all swelled up in the front of his baby pants because of it.

Just for Laughs held a lot of sway in the eighties and nineties when comedians were landing huge deals for sitcoms and networks were throwing panic money like confetti at everybody. Those deals started to drop off by the late nineties but the festival still ran strong and the best of the best comedians still attended. I'd performed there in 1997 and 1998 when I was living in LA, when there was still some vague hope of scoring free network scratch. By the time I performed there again in 2005, I'd already given LA the finger and moved to Bisbee. The lure of a big deal was of no consequence. I was just there for the paycheck and the party.

In 2008, the head weasel contacted my manager about me coming back. At this point, I no longer did mixed-bill shows. Like the Kilkenny festival, they didn't usually work out well for me. People who want to see Judy Tenuta or Jim Gaffigan don't necessarily want to see me on the same show. I'd also been booking my own shows on the road in rock-and-roll clubs so I could figure out the basic percentages of the ticket price versus the cut, usually now with me getting between 80–100 percent of the door.

Just for Laughs offered a ten-night run doing my own show for the amazingly insulting fee of eleven hundred dollars. A hundred and ten dollars a show. When I was brand new, doing hotel lounges and random dance clubs in the far reaches of Montana and Wyoming, I'd make a hundred twenty-five dollars as an opening act. Now that I was known enough to do ten nights at the biggest festival in North America, a hundred and ten seemed reasonable to them.

I don't remember what the ticket prices were supposed to be but it put my percentage down to single digits. They take a big chunk for themselves for the "prestige" factor.

This wasn't just a "no." It was a loud "Fuck No." I could book one Montreal show on my own on short notice with no advertising other than on my website and mailing list and make more in one night than they were offering for a full run. You can wipe your prestige on your sheets. The more the insult of their offer burned into my psyche, the more I knew I would have to do exactly that.

Thus was born my "Just for Spite" festival, booked at a tiny, rat-box punk venue. Every decent venue gets swallowed up by Just for Laughs during the two weeks it runs. My people wouldn't complain. It only held fifty people so I had to do two nights to prove my point and make more money than their ten-show run.

Also, I'd get to enjoy the JFL after-parties, the main reason comedians still go there. There is nothing more fun in the world than hanging out and getting blasted with fifty of your favorite comedians all in one place. One of the comedians in my show had some cocaine, which would help carry me through the night. He was only eighteen, the legal age to drink in Montreal, and looked far less. We were doing key bumps without discretion in the back stairwell of the club when a bouncer stumbled upon us. I hadn't considered that this might be an inappropriate location for doing drugs. It was Canada. I figured that it's all cool.

The bouncer just rolled his eyes and gave us some kind of "Ah, c'mon, man!" and we apologized and went elsewhere. So I was right. It's Canada. It's all cool. The kid was staying in a youth hostel across the street so we decided to move the party there, now with two more barely adolescent friends of his in tow. More pigs for the teat. One had never done cocaine.

"But fuck yeah, I'll try it! I just want to be able to say that I did blow with Doug fucking Stanhope!"

That's not really a story I wanted on his resume. One, because he looked thirteen and two, because I wanted that cocaine. For him it's a good story but for me it is medicine that will get me through a bunch of JFL parties without falling down. But it wasn't my cocaine to make that decision. As the key passed in a circle, my phone rang and I saw that it was Bingo. I answered in a theatrical cheer.

"I can't talk to you right now, honey! I'm in Canada doing Cocaine with Children!!!"

"Uuuh . . . okay," a voice said. "This is Evelyn your neighbor. I'm on Bingo's cell phone. She isn't doing very well."

Bingo was off her meds or on mushrooms or both and was having a very bad trip, the severity of which got me out of any questions regarding my "doing Cocaine with Children" declaration. Being a comedian, people often think you just say ridiculous stuff like that for no reason.

Now I was trying to calmly explain to my kindly sixty-year-old neighbor lady how to talk someone down from a bad trip, all the while watching the bindle dwindle as the key went around like a carousel without me. I got off the phone before the supply was spent and cleaned up the leftovers. The kid got his story and I got a cab to Club Soda.

That's where I was when I got ejected from the greenroom. Ron White, Nick Di Paolo, Brendon Walsh and a shitload more comedians were all at Club Soda in the greenroom between shows. Ron even gave me his laminate so I wouldn't have a problem getting into Henry Phillips and Mike O'Connell's show later that night.

A good time was being had by all.

Until the pus-wart that runs the festival showed up.

It was obvious from his face that he'd read my website post that shit on his offer and where I'd announced my Just for Spite fest, and he wasn't happy about it. I smiled and tried to avoid the topic. I knew it's always a bad idea to get into that kind of shit when I'm drinking but he didn't know that and he pressed the issue.

He questioned my basic arguments that (a) he paid shit to comedians when the festival was making a killing and (b) that he was outright insulting to comedians by telling them what material to do and how to do it. He'd done this to me after nearly every show I'd ever performed at the festival. I would just nod, smile and ignore his unsolicited and unqualified suggestions.

I told him that his offer to me was less than I made for my first-ever paid gigs in 1991. He responded by telling me how much money he was losing on some other comedian there that year, a point he repeated several times as though it had any bearing whatsoever.

"So you offered me basic cab-fare money to cover the costs of other poor decisions you make as a shit booker?"

As to him coming into the greenroom between shows and telling comics which bits to keep or drop—in the infuriating tones of a pandering camp counselor—he told me that it was necessary because I had not been doing well.

"What about Jim Jefferies?"—who I'd performed with at my previous JFL in 2005.

"Jim Jefferies did great," he said.

"Then why did you keep telling him what material he should use?"

"Well, obviously what I told him worked."

Why didn't he just do the comedy himself if he were this good? You could see where this was gonna go nowhere and the fewer points he could make, the more irritated he became. He then unwittingly painted himself into a corner by going on and on about how poorly I did the last time, that maybe I was drunk or maybe I just didn't care anymore but that I wasn't funny and how I sucked "nine out of sixteen shows," like he kept statistics, which I wouldn't doubt.

"If I was that bad, why did you make an offer to get me back this year?"

Pause.

Cartoon steam leaked from his ears.

As I dropped an imaginary mic, he grabbed my arm and almost cried: "It's time for you to leave." He pushed me as though I was resisting to make some show in front of the other comedians. He stopped momentarily. "And I'm taking this laminate because I know it's not yours!" pulling Ron White's pass off my neck. He said this exactly the way you'd say, "And it's my ball and I'm going home if you're not gonna play my way!" only he wasn't joking.

I said nothing more—mostly because the huge security guy showed up and I was undoubtedly hammered. You will never appear correct in an argument if you are the drunk one, no matter how factual you may actually be. Two plus two equals nothing if you're saying "four" with a tilt and a slur. Why bother. The bonehead who runs the Just for Laughs Festival is a condescending shit-baby who bought the nicest swimming pool so that every summer he can live in the illusion that people actually like him. I was stupid to even waste a minute talking to him at all with this many old friends around.

So I shut up and left with a lot of his free greenroom beer in my bloodstream and paid to see Henry Phillips and Mike O'Connell out of my pocket. Money works just like a laminate and the show was worth every penny. I just wish the performers would see nickels on the dollar for it.

By the time I ran into Giraldo and a couple other comics on the street, I was a stumbling wreck. The coke had worn off long before and now the drinks hit all too quickly. The kind of drunk that affects all of your motor skills while leaving your brain intact, a cerebral palsy–type of hammered, or the "Muhammad Ali" if you will.

My story about being ejected from the venue came out of the corner of my mouth with a stammering drool and that's when Giraldo made his rehab remark. I was a bit insulted as drunks tend to be when their point is overlooked because of their staggering.

I was quite relieved when someone emailed not long afterwards that they'd seen Greg perform so shitfaced that he barely made sentences. It's nice to know that you aren't the only comedian left with a cocktail in your hand. It was not satisfying at all when he died of a prescription drug overdose two years later. Cheers to you, you funny motherfucker.

• • •

Prescription drugs are also a constant for me—downers and only enough to sleep—and it's bothersome when people die from them because you are never given the specific dosages or combinations involved in the death. That is information that can really be useful to other users. A heroin overdose tells you nothing since the potency or purity of the heroin can vary wildly. Prescription drugs aren't cut with baby laxative. You know exactly what strength you are taking so you can regulate with far more accuracy.

I first took Xanax at an Ecstasy party in Alaska somewhere in the late 1990s. We were all coming down and someone gave me a blue (1 mg) and told me it would help me sleep. Shortly afterwards, somebody else gave me another blue making it a full bar of Xanax where a peach (.5 mg) would have been plenty.

Long story short, I pissed the couch I was sleeping on and woke up convinced in the moment that someone had pissed on me in my sleep. Those were the kind of friends I did drugs with and that'd be the kind of thing they might do. I scurried for any piece of mail that had the address on it and got a taxi as quickly as possible before anyone else woke up.

I can't count the number of times Chaille or Bingo has woken up in the middle of the night on the road to stop me from pissing in a hotel closet or on an air-conditioning unit. Maybe that's where the bathroom had been located in the hotel the night before and my reflex memory just guided me to that spot. What I do know is that for every time they woke up and caught me just in time, there had to be many nights they didn't wake up at all. I'll never know how many times I've sleep-pissed all over a hotel or even on my own stuff.

I take Xanax regularly to sleep: .5 mg. A peach. I have a prescription for flight anxiety. I didn't tell my doctor that a lot of that fear comes in the form of flying in my dreams, which is far scarier because you have no airplane when you fly in your dreams, just your body sailing through the air giving the finger to an angry mob of violent assholes chasing you on the ground. My regular flight anxiety as involved with traveling is mostly the fear of not being able to smoke or having some dullard next to me try to strike up a conversation. Xanax and ear plugs work for that as well.

One thing I've learned is that if you're only taking pills to sleep, over-the-counter sleeping pills are completely underrated. Basic store-brand Sominex will put you down quite well. It can stay with you the next day for longer than you like, longer than the prescription shit but nothing that smoking a little meth won't straighten out. I joke about the meth.

I used to have a prescription for Ambien, which I ditched because it can be dangerous when mixed with alcohol in that you can do really weird shit and not remember any of it. I can give you countless stories that I've heard from other people—taking Ambien with only a few whiskeys on his couch and waking up on someone's lawn in a strange neighborhood or my former manager's husband who took one on a flight with only a couple of drinks and almost had the plane grounded after a blackout tantrum over nothing. That's a lot different than pissing in your suitcase after a bender and a Xanax. That's where you wake up in your car in somebody's living room with their kid under the wheel. Last thing you remembered was having a nightcap and an

Ambien to fall asleep watching *Intervention* and now you're in prison for twenty-five years.

My only story was that I took an Ambien (6.25 mg, I believe) at home when Hennigan was at the house when I was relatively sober and went to bed. But not long after, I got back out of bed and had long business conversations with him. In the morning I brought up the same subject and he told me we'd already discussed it. He said that I was completely lucid and alert and was dumbstruck when I told him I had no recollection of it whatsoever. Not a fantastic story but enough to make me stop taking Ambien.

Scary, but not "die in your sleep" scary.

That's why it would be nice to know what kind of pills, dosages and combinations these scrip-heads were taking and what mixture killed them.

Greg Giraldo was—as someone pointed out to me on Facebook—smarter and funnier than I'll ever be. I didn't know him well but I was a huge fan.

The last time we spoke he said I looked like the reason he went to rehab. The last thing I would have said to him would have been: "Just take two of those. Two of those things is more than plenty."

The worst he'd have done is pissed the couch.

Rock and roll.

THE DYING OF
A LAST BREED

There was a moment where Dane Cook was referred to as a "rock and roll" comedian simply because of the amount of tickets he sold and the fervor of his mostly adolescent female audience. They could have called him the "British Invasion" if he were British. It was that kind of hype. I've never been jealous of his success but I will admit that it made me crazy when they called him rock and roll.

He was a bubblegum pop at its richest. I was rock and roll if only in comparison and in a time when rock and roll was no longer popular. It was a title that I only felt I deserved when I felt like he'd stolen it from me.

Dane Cook never drank alcohol much less did drugs. I had several bad shows from being pie-eyed and did drugs sporadically. Hardly Keith Moon but at the time, it was a rare occasion when you could find any comedian to do acid with after an ugly Sunday show, including kids who'd just want to do it with me for the story.

I doubt Dane ever left a hotel room untidy much less trashed. I trashed the same hotel twice, the first time so tamely that I was allowed back the second time. In Cincinnati, Ohio, they would put you up in some corporate mainstay that didn't allow smoking. But the club allowed you to be waaay too fucked up to the point where you didn't care about the rules when you got back to the room. And Cincy is fucking cold in the winter. I worked a week there and smoked every night in the room, trying to stay near the window. I was charged the two-hundred-fifty-dollar smoking fee and I fought it. The room smelled like smoke because I always smell like smoke. Take it up with American Express. It wasn't until the next stay that I was eighty-sixed.

The next time I was booked there, the same hotel was remodeling and reeked of fresh paint and chemicals so badly that it kept setting off the smoke detectors. That's how dense the fumes were. My cigarette smoke never did that. One morning, Bingo and I were woken up yet again to the fire alarm blaring at 6 a.m. My patience is thin in the morning. Very thin. I jumped up, grabbed the metal trash can and proceeded to smash the smoke detector off of the ceiling. I assumed it was the same removable type you have in your kitchen, the kind that goes off when the batteries are dying and wakes you up in the middle of the late morning. The reason you don't have smoke detectors when you know you should.

This smoke detector was hard-wired and wouldn't come off, only dangled like a piñata. It didn't matter since every other alarm was going off in every other room as well as the hallways. I called the front desk and used every obscenity that I could provide while I told them I'd just smashed their scream-machine off the ceiling due to their negligence. I reminded them about how they tried to charge me two hundred and fifty clams for smoking and now they were poisoning me with chemical smells. As though the poor fuck working the front desk at dawn was the person responsible for the years-old charge. Real rock-and-roll guys don't call the front desk to tell them they just trashed the room.

Shortly afterwards, there was a knock at the door. The fire department was followed by the police, followed by the front-desk person. I was informed of whatever severe penalty I could be facing for destroying fire safety equipment. Then they told me they were going to let us off easy by throwing us out of the hotel immediately. Bingo, who is always naked in any hotel room no matter who is present, asked me if she could have a moment to put on clothes in order to pack. I gave her the "no" sign with my eyes and a smile. She caught on and leapt out of bed, naked as can be and started arranging her luggage. All the authority figures spun into disarray, begging to step out and give her time to get dressed.

"No. You're fine," she said.

Fucking love that girl. We collected our shit and had to call a fan we knew locally as a last resort for a ride. We could have called a cab but we had no idea where we were going. She picked us up and drove us around until we found a Red Roof Inn one exit down. It was cheap and had smoking rooms. Sometimes trashing the room works out for everyone. It was very rock and roll.

I will never live up to my reputation as a comedy fuckup like my predecessors. I am only a strong horse in a weak field. There are no more Belushis, Farleys or Kinisons. For better or worse, that kind of lifestyle is no longer celebrated. It is pitied and intervened upon by people who die pious and boring. They now say comedians like Hedberg could have done so much more—if only—rather than acknowledge that they achieved what they had, at least in part, because of how they lived.

When the whole thing started it seemed like we were all drunk and ambivalent, ripping every moment into ridiculous affairs if only for the stories' sake. Some comedians focused solely on their craft and their career and I tended to avoid those types. Which wasn't difficult as they tended to leave right after the show to go back to their hotel and work on a screenplay or a television project or yell at their agent for allowing some vulgar miscreant like myself to be their opening act. By then I'd be wildly drunk with the fuckups and the staff, trying to talk a waitress into letting me beat off on her tits in a bar toilet. Or in her car in the parking garage. Wherever.

Then it all suddenly seemed to change. On some dime everyone turned sober. It wasn't like rock and roll where corpses started showing up in hotel rooms and pools of vomit. A few did but for the most part it seemed that everyone just stopped. Like someone yelled: "Last call." They became ambitious. They got tired or scared or just plain bored with it all. They started to take comedy seriously, which seemed such a deformed way of doing comedy.

Then you'd get stuck working with the sober guy who spent the whole week bragging about how much harder he partied than you. "Shit, I used to have twelve shots of tequila lined up on the stage and I'd do 'em all before I told my first joke. Oh and hey, can you not smoke in the minivan. My wife will get really pissed off if she smells it."

Everybody had their reasons. Some developed serious problems and had to quit. Others fell victim to kids or wives or a big opportunity to write gags for 3rd Rock from the Sun. Even in comedy there is a certain pressure that there is a time to grow up. I've ignored that for the most part. Others did not. They had aspirations to be better or bigger, prettier and healthier, to climb the ladder or hunker down and be decent husbands, wives or mothers or fathers. They wanted to become real adults, community people or captains of industry.

And at some point along the way, we all became the people we used to pretend to be.

Like when your mom said, "If you keep making that face, it's gonna stick like that."

Mine stuck.

Maybe smashing a smoke detector in a fit of anger misman-agement pales in comparison to Zeppelin hurling televisions through hotel windows down onto Sunset Boulevard. I'm only saying that it's alcohol that fuels that ridiculous morning rage, which in turn fuels my act. A bundle package.

I smoke in hotel rooms because I'm a rebel and I thumb my nose at authority! And because I have two hundred and fifty dollars now that I call "Fuck you" money. Or at least "Buzz off" money.

• • •

Nowadays when you have to initial on the hotel receipt at check-in that you agree not to smoke under penalty of a fine, I al-ways ask if I can pay that up front. This always causes a kerfuffle and I always keep the straight face.

"Can I just give you the two fifty right now?"

"No, no. It's because you're not allowed to smoke in the room."

"But you just said I could for two hundred and fifty dollars. Let me just give it to you now before I spend it on something silly."

"Um . . . let me get my manager."

Then I tell them that I was just kidding. I've found with non-smoking hotels or rental cars that if you leave a load of rotting shrimp or aged takeout Indian food inside overnight, they will never be able to detect any odor of cigarettes. Let them figure out how to make the symbol of a red circle with a line through it on a hotel door that translates into "No Old Curry."

Brendon Walsh and I trashed a comedy condo in Louisville, Kentucky. We left a dead bird crucified on a cross amongst other egregious filth for the cleaning lady to find. We heard about it from several different people who'd heard it from the club. We still hear it. The thing is that we never did it. Not anything even remotely close to it. But we let that rumor flow. Most of rock-and-roll lore is bullshit. Dane Cook had no rumors aside from being gay. Maybe that's because he didn't just fuck as many chicks as possible without any discretion or human decency. So mainstream. So pop culture.

THE 2012 UK TOUR

Partying Like a Rock Star, Losing Money Like a Rapper

The 2012 UK Tour made me quit stand-up comedy permanently, if only for a little while. The success of my previous visits there had given Hennigan and the promoter an extremely overblown optimism in what we could do on a really big tour. I didn't share their confidence but grudgingly went along with it. Either I'd make a lot of money like they were assuring me or I could rub the fact that I was right into Hennigan's face for eternity.

The first problem is that I'd already played the UK in 2011. Generally I turn over an act in about eighteen months. It's not written all at once by any means. It just evolves until I think it's time to record it and start building again. And generally there's a good percentage of any set that simply won't translate in the UK. I need at least two years between tours there to have enough fodder to warrant the ticket price. I prefer three years. I was going back eleven months after the last run.

Usually I'd work alone overseas but knowing my game was weak, I figured I'd bring my comedian friend Henry Phillips as an opening act to bolster the show and for moral support. Bad beats and shit luck are Henry's modus operandi and I could smell it on the horizon.

The next problem was the sheer scope and ambition of the expedition. Seven ugly weeks on that rock. I didn't know they had that many cities. But they do and a lot of 'em are close to each other. I'd play a theater to a half-full crowd and then a few days later we were back at a bigger theater in a city that's only ten minutes away from the first, wondering why there's far less people. I mean if we couldn't sell out the first one, why do you think booking across the river and upgrading the size of the box will pay off?

I didn't know who sold who on the amount of people they thought I could draw or what they based these projections on but I'd been comfortably playing three- to four-hundred seaters in London or Manchester and now I'm out in East Bushwhistle-by-the-Sea in a two thousand–seat hippodrome playing to 150 people, all sitting as far apart from each other as possible.

If you wanted someone to blame, you could point to any seat in the Sprinter limo van that was initially our form of transportation. It had six seats in the back, three facing three, with a table between you and a storage compartment in the back large enough to hang sides of beef. I always sat in a backwards-facing seat as I felt I had no future.

Somehow this big a rig was necessary. There was Henry and me accompanied by Hennigan and Bingo, as well as a separate tour manager driving with the promoter or the promoter's son riding shotgun on the wrong side up front. Henry and I should have done like Wiley Roberts and just found a sucker local comedian with a car.

Tensions rose with every unsold ticket. The tour manager hated Hennigan, Hennigan and the promoter hated each other and I assumed everyone hated me for not living up to the expectations I never had. It was all a very British hatred. Subtle and simmering, palpable while polite. Within the first few gigs we were already counting down the days like a prison sentence. I counted them in socks.

I'd packed my one black suit and an entire backpack with seven weeks' worth of black, ankle-high Walmart socks. I can go an eternity without showering—I wrote this entire book in less than five showers—but clean socks are a must. Knowing that doing laundry in Great Britain is as simple as making paper out of a log, I brought a pair of burner socks for each day of the trip. Every day I'd leave a used pair in a hotel and every day the bag got a little bit lighter and we were that much closer to home.

The excess of touring costs only got worse. For the Scotland leg of the tour, they'd made the obvious decision to go from the Sprinter van into a double-decker tour bus with fourteen sleeping berths as well as a master bedroom, previously used to house Lady Gaga's entire tour. Now it was available for our show with only two comedians and zero backup dancers or choreographers. So they grabbed it. It was more of an empty youth hostel than a bus. There was a viewing room at the front of the upper deck, past the coffinlike sleeping cavities, that had a tiny sliding glass window just big enough to allow one person at a time to smoke. Or perhaps the window was there to toss out any possible remaining profit after you added up the cost of this monstrosity. I've read enough rock-and-roll biographies to know that all the glitz and perks, every deli tray or bottle of booze in the greenroom, every comped ticket for a friend of a friend and every hotel room for every unnecessary head on the bus comes out of the bottom line. That's why rock-and-roll bands would sell out stadiums and still come home broke. We weren't selling out much of anything.

You don't need to be in show business to understand that you don't shit on a tour bus. You don't even piss in it unless you're trying to repel an alligator coming up through the toilet. Most shows we just parked at the loading dock of the venue and used their facilities. In Glasgow, there was no loading dock and no place near the venue to anchor the beast. Our only option was to rent a spot at the central Glasgow municipal bus station. If you've not had the experience of downtown Glasgow, imagine Detroit if people hadn't fled when the auto industry died, only because it had been replaced by a burgeoning heroin trade. Now picture the public transit hub that would be the epicenter of that imaginary Detroit. There we sat, hanging out in our luxury liner right beside the 502 to Kilkirkmouth and all points north, with all the nocturnal stumblebums and drifters who missed the last fare out. Close your eyes and let your imagination create a vision of the toilets at this smeg-mecca of that inner-city bus depot.

Now smell that vision.

Now imagine that you have to pay for this privilege. In the coins of a currency you don't understand.

Bus station pay toilets. The big time.

Henry was the first to find this out the hard way and kindly came back to our rolling chalet with a pocketful of coins, meting out correct dumpage change to each person on the bus with pity in his eyes. People were waiting in line for my show while I was waiting in line to take a shit. I should have scrawled "Lady Gaga Wuz Here" on the toilet stall door.

That show was part of a comedy festival and was actually packed. I distinctly remember a specific heckler. I had a rambling bit about how a lot of my material didn't work in the UK like it did at home and, reading off of my yellow legal pad, asked if I could try some of it out.

"Okay, here's one example. Um . . . Do you people 'dream' over here? I mean, like, at night? While you're sleeping? Or is that just an American thing?"

The heckler in the third balcony wasn't being a smart-ass. He was drunk and completely enraged.

"Are yeeeyoooo fookin serious, mate??? You think we dooont feckin dream over here????"

The joke was written about you, not for you, sir.

The fact that the third balcony was still within a hurler's toss of a pint glass was overshadowed by the glee that we'd sold enough tickets to have anyone up there at all.

We hung out with comedians Morgan Murphy and Greg Proops for a short while afterwards in the greenroom but couldn't sell anyone on the bus station after-party. That was a low-key affair.

Low key until late night when Hennigan said something fucky to a drunken vagrant while I was outside smoking. Neither Hennigan, Henry, Bingo nor I can remember exactly what Hennigan said or what precipitated it but Hennigan responded to the guy with something along the lines of "Fuck off, you homeless cunt."

This seemed to scrape up the gentleman's dander. He spun into a rage that only left us seconds to flee inside the bus and lock the door. The drunken fellow proceeded to pummel the bus with his fists, demanding an apology in his thick Glaswegian accent with a heavy lilt of Buckfast caffeinated wine.

Most of what I could understand and clearly remember was him screaming, "I'm noot fucken homeless!"

Although we outnumbered him three men and a lady to one, we hid like children. Glasgow has a well-earned reputation for violence as much as comedians have a reputation for the opposite. Pacifists by default. I'm sure most comedians, given the skill, would be out smashing skulls rather than writing gags.

The pounding and screaming continued all around the bus as though he were trying to make it sound like there were more of him than just one. We turned off all of the lights and would peek through the blinds when it became quiet and we thought he'd left. These were just the moments where he was catching his breath. He wasn't going anywhere. At some point, he'd evidently thrown his pizza at the bus and was demanding through every window to be compensated for the pie. Or else.

The bus had its own driver who we almost never saw. He was a brooding ogre who only came out of his closed front compartment sporadically to come back for coffee in the morning. On those rare and uncomfortable occasions he was always surly, complaining about previous acts that had been on the bus and what slobs they were. We knew these were indirect warnings to us. We never knew if he was even in the bus when it was parked. If he'd been on the bus that night, he wasn't getting out to protect his vessel from this raging mutant. We were equally scared of both of them.

This siege went on for seemingly an hour but maybe only thirty minutes, as memory tends to exaggerate. To us it was *Night of the Living Dead,* in this case the dead being singular. Eventually I had to make the call to go out and reason with the man and pay for his pizza. Everyone was against it but I felt it was necessary. Probably because I had to smoke again or use the pay toilet.

The vagrant was shaking. He looked like Aqualung and when he yelled you'd think he was Joe Cocker singing. I told him that I was just the driver and that everyone on the bus was piss drunk and meant no offense. He calmed down and I paid for his pizza. He eventually asked if our bus was for Daniel O'Donnell—a popular Irish folk singer who was playing in town the following night. He said that a lot of people were camped out to see him and that he assumed this was his bus.

I explained that this was not the case, that this was a comedian's bus.

He seemed let down that he'd spent all that time menacing a tour bus of someone he thought was famous. He wanted a story out of it as well.

The most enjoyable gig of that tour was in Inverness, Scotland. By the time we parked in the back of that city's "arts centre" (arts centers, however they're spelled, are always the worst places for comedy) all pretense of caring had gone. The venue was hosting a science-fiction convention during the day and the sight of miniature *Stars Wars* stormtroopers parading around and hanging out in the cafe bar only added to the sense of a mission gone wrong. I started drinking at breakfast. By the time the gig rolled around I was vehemently sideways. The show did not go well by the standards of the audience. I was having a hoot. By the time I got Henry back onstage to serenade the crowd with the theme song to *Welcome Back, Kotter* (a show that no one in the UK knows, let alone its theme music), many in the audience had left or were in the process of leaving. Not that I cared. As far as I was concerned this could be my last gig ever. They could never hate me as much as I hated myself but it was kind of them to be showing the effort.

I was melting down and enjoying every minute of it. I even saw Bingo dying laughing as the show was going up in flames and that only encouraged me to go weirder. I stopped any real attempt to do any prepared material as the show wore on—singing TV theme songs certainly wasn't on any set list ever—and I think I even lay down on the stage for a while, most likely threatening to keep rambling until everybody had left.

Eventually Hennigan came out and for the first and only time in my career, led me off stage to close the show.

Despite the indignant complaints of a number of ticket buyers, I'm pleased to say there were no refunds. The venue even tried demanding to be reimbursed for the debacle. Hennigan had to convince them that this was indeed my act and that we couldn't be held responsible if people didn't "get" it.

As the tour wore on, we were back in England, back in the Sprinter van. The paranoia was now at an all-time high because of my fear of being arrested for a Twitter war that I'd started at the beginning of the tour. I'll get to that story later on. But let's just say it was the icing on the cake—a cake that the British probably call pie and is cold and wet and probably cabbage flavored. The icing on a cake that was bleeding money, spiteful and now scared.

Hennigan left for part of the tour, immediately lightening the tension in the van that had become physically draining. We didn't like it when Mommy and Daddy fought. The shows still sucked for the most part but at least we could now laugh about it all. To be fair, a few shows were monsters. Everybody in other cities had warned us that Wolverhampton was a shithole so I knew it was probably gonna be fantastic. They weren't wrong about the condition of the town but the show was off the hook. Ridiculous high-energy crowd, roaring approval and a few violent ejections of rabble-rousers. That always brings the energy up. After the show, a massive brawl broke out in the front of the house. It was unrelated to the show but we didn't know that at the time. We were hustled by security to a back door where the van and a few dozen fans had anticipated our exit. They swarmed Henry and me like we were rock gods. A few tried to jump into the van, a girl telling me that she was with her boyfriend but was still willing to suck my cock. They pounded on the side of the van as we pulled away, cheering in approval. Not demanding pizza money. A rare bright spot on a floundering tour.

The last four nights were in and around London so we stayed at the same hotel and shuttled back and forth in the van to the shows. My sock bag was nearly empty. The parting cruelty— aside from the financial gutting—was that the hotel we stayed at for those last few nights was right next to a runway at Heath-row Airport with a view of 767s headed home every few minutes. Some people might complain about the noise. I would have complained about the fence. It was perhaps the only thing stopping me from running in a panic into a rolling wheel well to get the fuck out.

Selling out the last show at the Hammersmith Apollo—my biggest show ever—was pretty overwhelming but didn't make up for the dejection or the monetary squander. I'd have done better playing wormhole bars in piss-stop towns in middle America where they have A.1. Sauce and cocktail straws.

I'd told Hennigan weeks before the tour ended that I was done with doing stand-up comedy as soon as we got home. I meant it. I've told him from the plotting of my first book that I would never write another book as well. My word is worth the exchange rate of dog shit to bitcoin.

* * *

I've been compared to Bill Hicks quite often in the later years of my career, almost exclusively and repeatedly in the UK where he is revered. At first this didn't bother me. I was flattered and somewhat scared as though I had to somehow live up to and fill his big dead shoes.

It didn't start to annoy me until I'd see people online shitting on me for thinking I was the next Bill Hicks. A wannabe Bill Hicks. And I was no Bill Hicks to a lot of them.

These were people who read lazy UK journalists who compared me to Bill Hicks and showed up for a Bill Hicks show. And guess who wasn't there? Bill Hicks.

Don't get me wrong, most people use the comparison as a compliment. But like most comedians, I don't hear compliments.

I only hear the assholes. And when hating them didn't fill the gap, I started to hate Bill Hicks. It's hard to do but I found ways. I could start and end with the fact that he was an AA guy but that would be too easy.

This fucking guy had lots of opinions and could draw you into some seemingly obvious logic that you might have otherwise overlooked but he had no person. You can listen to everything he's ever recorded and there isn't one iota of any real, soul-baring part of himself personally, nothing about his life experiences or him as an individual.

The guy died at thirty-two and while he was a wise soul, there isn't a thing that drops his own pants. He had enough insight on the big issues that he might have kept Air America afloat for another year doing drive time but there was no person. Humanity but no human. There's no reason he needed to be. But that is exactly where the likening of me to him made me callous.

Bill Hicks died from terminal pancreatic cancer and never deemed it important to talk about it in his shows while it was happening, preferring to trash the plasticity of Los Angeles instead. And you compare me to that guy? I'm the Goatse guy of comedy! My personal life has been stretched wide and wart riddled onstage for a long, long time. If I was diagnosed with cancer I'd open with it save for the fact Tig Notaro already stole that thunder in a special so spectacular that the entire disease seems spent, comedywise. Still, I'd be googling things like whether Hodgkin's was cooler than non-Hodgkin's and the etcetera.

It's difficult for me to take compliments at all. Comparisons to the greats are much worse. The truth is that I didn't even listen to a lot of the greats or get the ones that I did. I'm no comedy historian.

I never really got the small amounts of Lenny Bruce that I've heard. I wasn't alive or cognizant when he was around. I tried to listen to him when I was older and well entrenched in comedy. He talked in a lingo that made the "jive" from the movie *Airplane* have clarity. I get that he went through a lot of bullshit arrests, court cases and eventually into poverty and that paved the way for future comics. I just didn't understand most of the words.

I loved Richard Pryor when I was thirteen or so but by the time I was a comedian, he had been stolen from and replicated (poorly) so often that to go back and listen to him, he seemed like a hack.

Carlin was someone I didn't much care for until I found his later stuff, when he was as bitter as I was trying to be. I was never a fan of the clever wordplay. "Why do we park in a driveway and drive on a parkway?" It wasn't until I heard *You Are All Diseased* that I stole off Napster that I fell in love. Fuck Metallica.

I didn't really get into Hicks until I was starting to become compared to him. Then, like Carlin, it was a guarded love where I was more concerned about not having the same bits as them than actually enjoying them. Then came the Internet and one too many comments about me not living up to the Hicks legend that moribund UK journalists were branding me with.

So I blame you and them. You ruined my love for a brilliant comedian, you Hicksophants. He was a slayer of sacred cows and then you turned him into one. Ultimate cunt move.

If I ever get famous after I'm dead—only because I am dead—please shit on the people who idolatrize me. Say that I was no Jim Jefferies.

If Hicks were actually available for children's parties and had actually shown up for the one that Becker and I did, I bet he would have done what we did and run like a scared woman fleeing the lava of Pompeii. In that way, we are very much alike.

FLORIDA SEX OFFENDERS, PART ONE

eople who say that I am trying to be like Bill Hicks have never heard Matt Becker or Andy Andrist. I've been trying to be both of them for too long to remember. I want Becker's speed and content with Andrist's style of wordsmithing. And if I lived either of their lives, I'd want a good lawyer.

Having done that private party at the lawyer Jay Kirschner's house years before—no matter how much of a shit-apple I ate—was a small retainer to pay for the constant late-night haunting for legal advice we'd be pestering him with in the years to follow.

"My buddy just got a DUI for weed. What should he do?"

"I think I found that lady I married drunk in the eighties. You know a private investigator in Florida?"

"My friend 'Danny's' wife is suing me for calling her a lying cunt. What are my options?"

When it came to needing legal help from Jay, nobody screamed "Pro Bono" as loud as comedian Andy Andrist. Andy is a touched individual who seems to be unable to stop himself fucking up. He is also one of the funniest people alive because of it. If even part of the reason that his insanity was due to being molested as a teenager, I call it collateral damage. If that old man fumbling around with his junk made him that hilarious on a daily basis, I say look at the big picture. And people think I'm always negative.

Andy and I have been best friends for years. When we'd tour together sometimes people would say that he's trying to be like me when all the time I'm trying to be like him. Like Becker, Andy is legitimately one of the funniest human beings alive, where I am simply better at making funny into a sellable product. I hope they hate me for that as much as I hate them for being naturally far more funny.

For the many years I've gone on the road with Andy, one name always fell into his jokes.

Bo Y. Fondler.

Bo Y. Fondler, a name that you can assume has been changed by the lawyers of this publishing company who are gun shy to a fault regarding liability issues. This bothers me because let's say I randomly change "Bo Y. Fondler" to "Frank Wheeler" for legal purposes. Now anyone named Frank Wheeler is under scrutiny. Couldn't any Frank Wheeler sue me now? I could just use "John Doe" but knowing how many names I had to change in my last book, you'd wonder how this John Doe guy could have been in so many places at the same time.

I'll refer to my publisher as "HarperCollins" or "Random House" from now on.

Just pseudonyms.

Fondler is the man that ALLEGEDLY molested Andy as a young teen. I have to say "allegedly" because I wasn't there. Yet I can't imagine such detailed memory of being coerced into sexual situations in trade for, amongst other things, some sweat suits that Andy favored as a kid. I won't mention the specific brand without an endorsement deal. I know that the man is a real person and if Andy can come up with bits that funny over imaginary transgressions, he should apply it to the rest of his act.

"The worst thing is that my molester had hand braces. I realized later on that I could have just walked away. I didn't even have to run. I don't know if I was queer or just like helping people."

It's funny because it's disturbing and disturbing because it is true. Allegedly.

One day, Andy called me to say that he'd actually found Bo Y. Fondler on the Internet—fortunately now living in the same state as our Florida lawyer—and Andy was formulating a plan to avenge Bo's transgressions. Each call afterwards was filled with impossible *Ocean's Eleven* details, none of which could possibly work but were hilarious in their retarded intricacy nonetheless.

All I know is that the plans in the final phone call included Andy swimming across the pond of a golf course to gain access to Bo's gated community with a waterproofed backpack to keep his disguise of a cable guy dry for whatever came next. I laughed until he mentioned the fact that he'd already bought plane tickets for him and a friend he'd talked into filming the whole thing. When I pictured Andy swimming across alligator-laden waters on a Florida golfing hamlet accompanied only by some clown trying to tread water with one hand while trying to film, I knew I had to cancel some plans.

Andy and his camera lummox were already there with an arsenal of gimmicks from boy scout uniforms to giant handmade signs saying "I WAS MOLESTED BY YOUR NEIGHBOR—ASK ME HOW!" that Andy planned to spin like a barker outside the entrance of the gated community. The plans were as harebrained and scattershot as Andy's always were. I had to dial them back. Andy was clear in that all he wanted was an explanation as to why this man had done this shit to him and if the guy even gave a fuck that it had affected Andy. If Andy could have a legitimate dialogue, all of his absurd b-plans for revenge could be ditched. It's trouble when I'm the rational guy in any given situation.

I found a hotel just outside of this douche's enclave. Among the other things aside from Bo's address and number that Andy had found in his Internet investigation was the fact that Bo had a daughter in college. I had a simple plan that didn't require aquatic gear or alligator repellent. We watched football at the hotel bar, lawyer in tow, and waited until the alcohol dampened our nerves. With the camera rolling, I finally made the phone call. There was no answer. We waited a bit and had more drinks. I called again and there is still no answer. We made random guesses that maybe he's not answering because of the blocked number or maybe they're at church on a Sunday, and all but gave up hope of doing this the easy way with my plan. Eventually Jay the lawyer left and Andy went back to the room. It was just me and the camera flunky when I made one last futile attempt and dialed the number.

If I'd been drinking my cocktail when he answered, I would have done a slapstick spit-take. I tried to focus and calm myself as I hysterically motioned for the video oaf to start rolling. I told Bo that my name was Tim Heidecker—for some reason the first name to pop into my head was the co-star of *Tim and Eric Awesome Show*—and I told Bo that I was a private investigator who had some sensitive information about his daughter in whatever university she was attending. A simple plan. No matter how rotten a person might be, their children are almost always their Achilles' heel. Even if they are fucking children. I was right. He asked what it was about and I told him that his daughter was not in any danger but that, as a parent myself, I'd prefer to give him the information in person. I said that I was at the hotel just outside his gates. I'd meet him in the lobby.

By this time we'd already told the bartender our whole scheme and he was as anxious for a payoff as we were. So as I hung up the phone shoving the film boy towards the door yelling to the bartender that we'd settle up later, he didn't have a qualm. A story was brewing. We sprinted to the room, filled Andy in that it is was a go, miced ourselves up and made for the lobby.

Through the front door of the hotel was the lobby and if you kept going directly through, there was another door going to a patio and a pool. We set Andy up at a center table and had our video gofer back in a corner table with his camera hidden in some clutter we'd created. We jabbered plans about what we'd do when he showed like we were coked up on nerves alone.

We waited a long time. Turned out that in Bo Y. Fondler's paranoia, he'd called the police for an escort to this suspicious meeting with a private investigator. I saw who I assumed was Bo Y. Fondler walking in followed by his assumedly mail-order wife and the cop. The cop blew my already panicked nerves into overdrive but the alcohol didn't let it show on my face.

I met him in the lobby and said with the smile of a cruise ship director: "Mr. Bo Y. Fondler? Come with me!" It was all very Chris Hansen *To Catch a Predator* style. The cop asked which of us was the private investigator. Not knowing if it was illegal to falsely represent yourself as such, I told him that I never said I was a private investigator, only that I was investigating the matter privately. He seemed to buy it.

I led the triumvirate out the back door to Andy, sitting calmly on the patio.

"Have a seat, Mr. Bo Y. Fondler. You remember Andy Andrist?

"Uh, yes. Yes I do."

Andy unleashed a jumbled load of pent-up memories in a caterwaul of accusations. Do you remember the Adidas track suit? Do you still have the videotapes? Then some references to Penn State coach Jerry Sandusky who'd just been busted for fucking kids. It came out in such a torrent that I was as confused as the wife and the cop who'd been in a prick intimidating-cop mode since he'd arrived. They had no idea what to make of any of this. Like an interpreter for the insane, I told them plainly that Bo Y. Fondler had molested Andy as a kid. I was dressed in a pale-blue 1970s leisure suit and Andy was still blathering incoherently so none of this looked legitimate. Andy pressed him harder and Bo Y. Fondler said he wouldn't comment as he had no lawyer present.

I caught a moment to create a pause and then Andy asked him, "Are you at least sorry for what you did to me?"

And then this feeble wreck of a man, rocked backwards in this moment that he knew would eventually catch up with him, said without thinking, "Yes. Yes, of course I'm sorry."

The moment brought a silence over all of us. To anyone there, it was like he just fucking admitted it. It was the ultimate "You can't handle the truth!" moment. The wife lost her breath and the cop jumped sides onto ours.

Andy reminded Bo of the time he promised to buy him a car if he graduated high school in an attempt to keep Andy's mouth shut. As Bo backtracked and denied it, Andy slid his high school diploma across the table.

"I want my car."

At this point, Bo Y. Fondler asked the cop if he was required to be there and if he could leave. The cop reluctantly told him that he was free to go. He quick-limped off with his cane, the hidden-camera blockhead hot on his heels. The perp hid his face as our cameraman barraged him with ambush-journalism questions. Bo answered none. He jumped into his car and left. Without his wife. There is footage showing the cop consoling her in the parking lot, her knees buckling.

We all went back to the hotel bar and celebrated. We ordered champagne, which the bartender put on the house tab after hearing the outcome. I even made a drunken phone call to console the wife who had by that time already been brainwashed into believing that it was all a ruse to scam money from them. Sometimes you believe what you want to believe. Other times you believe what you have to believe.

And this was what would follow us.

Bo Y. Fondler filed some kind of injunction or cease-and-desist to prevent us from talking about the event or showing the footage. He'd used Andy's demand for a car as proof he was being blackmailed. Not that Andy wouldn't have taken the car but he honestly just wanted to know why this guy did what he did and how he lived with himself afterwards. Andy wanted to know if this guy cared that it had ruined Andy's psyche ever since. I wanted to know how it made Andy so goddamned funny.

The best comedy comes when it's in the most horrible circumstances and the right people need to laugh. Jay Kirschner loves doing law in the same way, when it's for the right reasons. He's generally defending shit-brows who are guilty and don't deserve reasonable representation. He doesn't get these kinds of cases often where he can feel as though he is finally providing an actual benefit to society and that's the reason he defended us, not just as a courtesy but as a pleasure.

I've asked Jay to explain exactly what happened in court in the aftermath. He tells me in detail and then my eyes grow numb and glassy in the barrage of his legalese, the same as they had in the courtroom. I know three things. One, Andy and I had to fly back to go to court wearing some thrift-store suits that made us look poor but reverent. No polyester disco suits. Two, after a lot of court-speak, a judge told us he needed to sleep on it. I think he was sleeping in the moment. But in a short time, the injunction was shitcanned. Something about "prior restraint" and the First Amendment. Lastly, and it took more fighting from Kirschner, Bo Y. Fondler was forced to pay for Jay Kirschner's legal expenses.

I'd hoped that somehow this would bring some closure for Andy, that in this so-called victory, he would be able to let it all go and in the wake he would become less funny than I am. But the trauma can't be taken away with a simple court ruling and Andy remains one of the funniest people alive.

FLORIDA SEX OFFENDERS, PART TWO

ow to a joke that I've gotten a lot of emails about over the years. My opening softball joke on my album *From Across the Street* is titled "Funny Thing About Child Porn."

It starts with a question.

"You know the funny thing about child porn? Aside from the lack of *credits* at the end? No big egos in that part of Hollywood. 'Who was the editor on this? I wanna use 'em on my next big-budget studio movie!' But no names at the end. Not even a nom de plume. Some people are in it just for the art."

But then I meandered and forgot the answer to the question that wraps it all up, the tag to the joke. Hence the inquiring emails. Yes, Doug, tell us! What is the funny thing about child porn other than the Hollywood asides that you made so jocular?

The payoff to the bit I forgot was that it was funny that child porn is the only crime you can get arrested for being a witness. You can't call 911 and say, "Send someone quick! I've just seen child porn and I can describe the guy!"

Not gold by any means, I know. That's probably why I forgot to say it on the album. Now I've answered your question so you can stop asking. I only put it in because it becomes important to the story.

I got a handwritten letter from a fan via the old-fashioned snail mail. This happens from time to time, as I give out my address on my podcast and in interviews so that people can send stuff to me and Bingo. I love getting real mail. You'd think with some of the deranged people who are attracted to the delightful verbal tapestries I paint, I'd play more on the safe side. But I also know that my insane fans are also broke, lazy and drunk and that I live far, far away. And I really do like mail.

Here's a handwritten letter that I received. I got it somewhere in the midst of an eight-day Fourth of July party and had my friend Hack read it out loud—without us knowing the content—to a bunch of us getting drunk in the kitchen. I had to let everybody know that I get fan mail. Ego. We all laughed at the gushing, fanboy content as he read it. At least at first.

> Dear Doug . . . or should I say feloow drunk Doug,
>
> I was at your show last October or November down in Ft Lauderdale, I was the creepy kid in black among the crowd of creepy kids in black and I really enjoyed the show and I'm glad I got to see you live because I was beginning to think you weren't real; I was starting to think you were some form of CGI digital Santa Claus that was sent down by God to save us from this retarded society we live in. At least I got to see the philosopher Doug Stanhope do his magic and I'm talking real magic, the kind that makes you want to drink even when you really don't want to.
>
> Anyway, since you're reading this you should knw that I'm already dead by the time you get this. I'm no fan of the world and even less the way I live in it, and there are some good things but I've had 23 almost 24 years to do those things, and although I want to stay a little longer and get to see some more I can't, for the moral justice thinks I have to do 7 years in a prison for looking at the

wrong kind of porn even though that happened to me as a kid and I never complained about it.

Anyway, now that I'm completely out of hope, I'm leaving you my favorite book, which I think you will like and maybe give a few ideas for new material. It's not perfect but most of the concepts in the book are similar to your views, just a little less vulgar.

So Doug, thanks for giving me something to laugh at, that was almost impossible with my gloomy outlook and sick sense of humour.

Thanks for being the one person with the balls to speak out the truth. I hope you are much more successful in what's left of your career and save some worthy people before it's too late.

Thanks and good luck

Your fan and follower.

Liam S.V. Hughes

Oh and by the way, it's painless helium suicide in case you were wondering. At least I DIED LAUGHING!

Well, that took a turn for the worse. Someone broke out a smartphone and found the obituary. It actually affected me. It may have been that we were in the middle of mocking some kid who could have been any kid that I meet after a show who's all fucked up and somehow found some kind of solace in my angst. A kid sending out a sincere, final salvo while I was shitting upon him for starting his fan letter by likening me to a deity.

Or it could have been that my serotonin was so low after days of partying that I would have cried to a Carpenters' song.

Or it may have been that I never got to reach him in time to tell him that it's nitrous oxide, not helium, that makes you laugh. Stupid.

It still made me well up a bit.

The kid was in Florida so, of course, I called Jay Kirschner to check it out and see if was legit. Jay got back to me. Liam was indeed facing at least that much time and probably more for twenty counts of being in possession of photographs of children performing sexual acts. He killed himself on the day he was due in court. Kirschner went on to tell me of this kid's prospects in prison and of trying to make a life after prison should he survive. I concurred that he'd made the right decision.

The difference between Liam and Bo Y. Fondler, I guess, is a lot in perception but mostly in action. Fondler was a shuddersome ghoul who'd molested Andy as a child. He also took lewd pictures of Andy. Liam was nearly a child himself and his letter made him sound as much of a victim as a perpetrator. He'd only looked at pictures, so far as anyone knows. Fuck, he could have been looking at pictures of a young Andy for all we know. Kind of a funny thought right there. The problem with defending someone like Liam is that you're afraid of coming off as someone who must secretly like child porn yourself. But it raises serious arguments on thought police. I've jacked off thinking about some stuff that I'd never do in real life. Nothing illegal. I just know that in reality it would probably hurt a lot or smell bad. But it's still a matter of fantasy versus action. What person of any substance hasn't fantasized about murder? I've watched graphic murders on the Internet. If anything, it queered me off actually wanting to murder people. Like S&M porn, it'd make you feel real bad afterward.

I don't know the answer but I know that a kid who's been fucked up by being molested shouldn't have to choose between killing himself or being beaten or killed in prison. He needed help. Or maybe he couldn't be helped. I don't know. All I know is that his letter humanized him.

It also made me wonder if that's how old Liam found my act to begin with, googling "child porn" and finding that first track of that one album of mine. It's a funny thought but it's plausible. That is the same album that I close on a story about another fan, Clark Adams, who had delayed his planned suicide when he heard I was coming to town. I phoned in a slipshod, hung-over abortion of a show that night, not knowing that it was Clark's big Last Year's Eve countdown. I found out about it in an email from one of his friends after the fact. Clark killed himself with helium as well, which was the crux of my story. On the album, I close the Clark Adams story with a high-pitched Alvin and the Chipmunks rendition of Clark's final words.

"Goodbye, cruel world!"

There's no way of knowing if Liam was beyond help or if I could have told him with any honesty that suicide wasn't the answer. But I could have told him not to use helium. It doesn't make you laugh and I already used that story in an old bit.

FLORIDA SEX OFFENDERS, PART THREE

Treasure Island

Bingo, Chaille and I had just finished a tour in Florida and took a needed break from all the boozing by getting drunk at another of my favorite day-drinking spots, the Thunderbird Hotel in Treasure Island outside of St. Pete. The 1950s neon sign alone makes you want to put on your ugliest Hawaiian shirt, slather zinc oxide on your nose and order a Singapore sling at Ikki Woo Woo's Tiki Hut by the pool. You'd expect Don Draper to be sitting beside you. Throw on your short-sleeve leisure suit for sunset and you'll be sauced enough to enjoy the guy playing Don Ho songs for tips.

We'd started drinking before the kickoff of the early NFL games and by sunset, we were getting a bit too rowdy for the tastes of the aged lizards poolside by the tiki bar. This was not a youngish person's domain. The dirty looks rained down as I was yanking my jock strap up from my shorts and over my distended belly—which I can easily bloat out to late third-trimester proportions—with the leg straps wedged into my ass crack. My friends and nobody else were highly amused. One woman was particularly irritated by the sounds of frivolity and made sure through a series of "ughs" and eye-rolls that her displeasure was known.

As we watched the sunset from the strand on the beach just in front of the bar, some dude was racing a remote-control monster truck at high speeds across the beach. We were waiting for him to kill someone.

Just then a pair of Florida cops showed up. We assumed they were coming to stop the inevitable carnage that the virtual drunk driver was sure to cause with his toy. Then they came straight to me.

They stood on either side of me and asked if I had been exposing myself. I told them that I had not. I told them a truncated version of how I'd been pulling my jock strap up to my tits but they weren't convinced. They told me that they'd received a report of me exposing myself in front of children. One cop stayed with me while the other canvassed the people at the bar, including that weathered handbag of a woman—the one we knew unquestionably made the call—who stood by her story that I'd exposed my genitals.

When it looked like I was surely about to be arrested, Chaille stepped in. He remembered that he'd taken a plethora of pictures of my antics and told the cops as much. They asked to see his camera. There was a pause. Chaille realized the amount of incriminating pictures that were on that camera from earlier in the tour. He offered a bargain.

"How about this. I'll show you the pictures. But I get to hold the camera."

The cop agreed and Chaille scrolled slowly through each and every picture of my silly jock-strap gags until they were satisfied that I was nothing but a goofball who'd worn the lampshade on his drunken head and that the woman who reported me was a lying, rug-burned cunt. By the time they let me go, she was conveniently gone. I wanted to drown her in the Jacuzzi. Brendon

Walsh immortalized the woman in a bit where he talked about leathery Florida women who you know used to be attractive but now they just look like Robert Plant.

With the cops gone and the buzz killed, Chaille went back to the pictures. He realized that if he'd gone back just one more, the cops would have seen Walsh from the night before standing proudly on his hotel bed in his late-night delirium pissing on his own mattress.

I recently watched a documentary called *Pervert Park* about a trailer-park community in Florida that houses registered sex offenders where nowhere else would allow them. Had it not been for Chaille taking pictures like a Japanese tourist at the Mirage, I could have been listed as a registered sex offender for showing my junk to children. I could have been stuck there in Pervert Park living between Bo Y. Fondler and Liam Hughes. A perpetrator, a witness and me, the wrongly accused. And I probably would have killed myself too. Just having to live in a Florida trailer park would be reason enough.

WRONG AGAIN

Diana Hone thought that suicide would at minimum help her financially struggling family when they got her life insurance.

She was a beautiful and hopelessly shy girl that would come with her husband to my shows at Winstons in Ocean Beach, California. She was the type who would always apologize for being polite and think that she had overstepped her boundaries for simply offering a compliment. She'd even painted a portrait of Bingo and me that she brought to a show, saying she was sorry that it wasn't finished yet. She hated herself for being everything you wanted in a fan or a friend.

I remembered this about her because it was endearing and because she was hot. I'm sorry if the latter seems base or shallow but it's intrinsic to human nature. Really beautiful and extraordinarily ugly people stand out in one's memory. Congratulations to you if you fall into either camp. I'm far less likely to remember the middles.

Diana had heard me talk about my mother's suicide on a Netflix special and this was the email I got from her.

Hi Doug,

I was hoping you could help me out with a medical question, if possible. I don't have any cool doctor or lawyer friends, but given your experience, I thought you might know someone I could ask. I'm done and need to check out this week. I have 50 30mg OxyContin and I need to know if that will be enough. I'm fairly opioid tolerant (I usually take 5 at a time, up to twice a day so that's around 300mg), so I want to know how much will be enough, or if there is something else I should take with it to make sure I don't wake up. I'm sorry to bug you with this shit, and if you can help me, I'll ask my husband in my letter to donate some of my life insurance money to some charity you like or some bullshit. This has been a long time coming, and unfortunately it's really hard to find this information online. I'm a useless shit, but at least I'll be able to financially help my family when I kick it. I'm sorry I never finished your painting. Self loathing makes it difficult to accomplish much. I still have it because the delusional part of my brain keeps thinking I'll finish it tomorrow . . . tomorrow . . . tomorrow. Like everything else. But it never happens, and it never will. Anyway, thanks for bringing some laughs to us in OB. You're one of a kind man. Oh, your Netflix special was fucking great.

I only include it because I get suicide emails frequently. The detail and utter lack of emotion in this one made me sure that she wasn't bluffing for attention.

I wrote back a simple "Finish the painting."

Not much of a pep talk but you never know how famous you are in someone else's eyes. If nothing else, maybe it would give her some temporary purpose.

She came back with "It's not gonna happen. I have other shit to wrap up in the next couple days. Please let me know if you get any info. This is as far as I got btw. Bye."

My own mother's suicide had been planned and she'd been advised by a doctor on exactly how much morphine would be a minimum dosage to ensure success. Diana's wasn't the first email I'd received since talking about it on that Netflix special. Several people who were in the same position were asking for specific doses or what kind of drugs could be used. Diana made it clear that she wanted nothing but information. No sympathy, no talking down. Just the facts. I don't exactly remember Mother's dosages and surely wouldn't tell a stranger if I did. I was sure you could find it on the Internet and told her that. I did offer that she had to stay alive for the finale of *Breaking Bad* that was coming up that Sunday but that was just selfish. I myself was terrified of dying before the last episode.

She responded with the following.

Every forum on the net just ends up with a thousand people talking about how precious baby's farts are, therefore don't kill yourself. No real clear guidelines.

Oh well, thanks anyway. Enjoy your tv show.

After assuring her I would in no way try to interfere with her plans, she opened up.

I'm unfortunately one of those sorry fucks that used drugs to cope with life instead of for fun (oxy, that is ... the other ones were fun). It was manageable from 15-25/26 years old, but it got out of control and I made myself quit cold turkey because I couldn't stand how pathetic I was. I've been (oxy)sober since, I'm a few weeks shy of 29, and each year I hate being alive more than the last. I've tried shrinks and all the other nonsense to no avail. I have a wonderful family that is unbearable to be around because I feel either loathing, hate or nothing at all, but I don't want to make their life any more difficult so I put on my happy face (which worked for a while but is near impossible now). This has nothing to do with why I wanna off myself, but my whole family is financially fucked so they're constantly stressed and miserable which is awful because they're such good people and I'm worth $250k dead, so that's just icing on the cake.

She included a naked selfie taken in a bathroom mirror and wrote: "Now I have to kill myself because I'll never be able to see you in person after sending this picture for fear of dying of embarrassment."

Other comedians get naked pics from ladies who want to fuck them. I've even been sent nude photos from girls asking if I could forward them to my famous friends whose emails are not public. Me, I get naked pictures from suicidal girls so the shame keeps them on task. Even with poor lighting it was pretty fucking hot. I'm keen to believe that wasn't the only reason I began to question my promise not to interfere. She had it planned to do the next day so I didn't have a lot of time to ponder the moral dilemma.

I was the only person who knew about her plan. I was on tour but I told her that I'd even stay on the phone with her and have cocktails while she ate pills, à la Mother, so she wouldn't have to be alone. I told her to delete all of our text messages and emails so I couldn't be seen as complicit after the fact. If I was gonna lose one fan, I didn't want to lose a second when her husband checked her phone. She kept telling me what a good guy I was for not judging her or trying to stop her.

We kept in communication through phone calls, texts and emails throughout that day and the next. All the while, I'd be questioning Chaille, Bingo and Junior Stopka in the van as to what the proper move was. If I ratted her out and she killed herself anyway, she'd die alone being betrayed by the only person she trusted to tell. If I let her go through with it, it's on my head forever. She wasn't terminally ill or facing prison. She was twenty-nine, perpetually depressed and gorgeous. I KNOW HER LOOKS SHOULDN'T MATTER!

Bingo thought I needed to let her husband know what was going on. Chaille was of the mind that this was none of my business, should have never been put on my shoulders to begin with and reminded me to plug merch during my set. Junior likes pie. So I was the deciding vote and I reluctantly erred on the side of betrayal.

I found her husband on Facebook and left him a message to call me ASAP. I didn't say why. Shortly after he called. "Are you fucking serious? This is Doug Stanhope? I can't fucking believe Doug Stanhope is on my phone!" I told him to relax, that I was calling to tell him that his wife had been in contact with me and that she was planning to kill herself.

"Oh, is she doing that again?"

His demeanor was both encouraging and demoralizing. If it was that common an occurrence, then maybe it was just another bluff and I'd misread her determination. Or I was right and she was going to kill herself but he'd heard it too many times to take it seriously. He told me that she'd been having a rough time and had been telling him she was going to commit suicide quite often.

"But still, Holy Shit, I can't believe I'm talking to Doug Stanhope!"

He said he was leaving work to go check on her. He must have called her first because she texted me.

"Really wish you would have talked to me first. It's my own fault for opening my fat mouth."

I sent a few texts trying to explain my reasoning but she wasn't having it. I'd fucked her over. I told her I'd be there for her and then I stabbed her in the back. And then I didn't hear back from her.

Her husband and I had said that whoever heard from her first would notify the other. It wasn't until the next night after the show that he let me know she'd been found in a motel bathroom. She left a note that explained how she'd woken up after taking the pills. As she said she would in the note, she had to finish the job by cutting her wrists as well as stabbing herself.

To this day I still feel like a fucking rat traitor. I regret my decision as much as I know I'd probably repeat it. I also regret, like Liam Hughes and the helium, that I didn't think to tell Diana that your family can't collect insurance from a suicide. Stupid.

I don't try to talk anyone out of suicide. I don't know you and don't know what you're going through that has driven you to that brink. I've shared emails with a twenty-one-year-old kid in the UK who suffers from trigeminal neuralgia, also known as the "suicide disease," regarded as the most painful known medical condition and has a 25 percent suicide rate for those afflicted. He hasn't killed himself as of this writing but would you be the one to tell him that it's wrong to take your own life?

This brings us to the case of Tony Nicklinson, who in a roundabout way gave my most hardcore fans their title.

KILLER TERMITES

I had just started into that ill-fated seven-week tour of the UK when I read an article about a man named Tony Nicklinson. He made national news fighting with the high court for the right to die. Mr. Nicklinson was what they call a tetraplegic, or having "locked-in syndrome." He was fifty-three and his mind worked perfectly but he was trapped in a body that could only communicate by blinking his eyes at a computer screen. He'd been there for six years and was at that time suing to have the right to an assisted suicide. You know, because you can't blink yourself to death.

The Nicklinson story affected me because I'm an extreme claustrophobe. I get claustrophobic in my own body when I can't reach an itch on my back. Sometimes I'm afraid to take hallucinogens for fear of fixating on the fact that I'm buried alive in my own fat carcass. Buried alive is one of my biggest fears along with burning alive. And I think that it's fucked up that those are your two choices for what to do with your body when you die. Tony Nicklinson was living my biggest fear. Reading about him made me feel something that I was afraid might be an emotion and I sprinted for a bottle of vodka.

Allison Pearson was and is a gargoyle columnist for the UK newspaper *Daily Telegraph* who'd also written two romance novels, a feat as impressive as a songwriter landing a jingle for a douche commercial.

With the Nicklinson case in the headlines, Pearson scrawled out a half-assed, empty-calorie op-ed piece titled "Do Any of Us, No Matter How Ill, Have the Right to Die?"

The underlying text should have simply been "Yep."

Fill in the rest with ad space.

The piece was disparaging not just about the right to die but seemingly of Mr. Nicklinson himself. She had very little or nothing of any bolstered argument on the issue, only snide, condescending personal jabs at the expense of a man who could only communicate by blinking his eyelids.

She suggested he should just starve to death if it's so bad. She suggested he just go off his meds and hope for an infection, like some cruel version of Mother's home remedies. All in the most sarcastic, condescending tone. She said that other people in similar conditions were making the best of it.

"Stephen Hawking comes to mind."

Really? Name another. Maybe Tony Nicklinson didn't have a Stephen Hawking genius brain to keep him entertained in that condition, day after day, year after pressure-sored year. Maybe his wife should have offered him that kind of tough love.

"Honey, why can't you be more like Stephen Hawking? Quit your grousing and pick yourself up by your noodle-kneed bootstraps and come up with a quantum mathematical equation that solves the big bang theory!"

Vulgar.

So after reading the article I threw out a tweet that included a link as well as the word "cunt," of course, to share the story. I also followed up with a tweet to her that I'd turned to Christianity so that I could pray she got an ovarian cyst, just to pile on.

I could have known what the response from my fans might be.

Shortly before this tour had begun, someone sent me a tweet or an email or a smoke signal to a link to the blog of a guy named Troy who had been stealing me. Not stealing a joke or some other petty comedy politics bullshit. He was stealing me. He had a blog that was taking stories from my lifetime of recorded material, web posts and interviews and printing them as though they were his own. He maybe changed the city, the name of the friend involved, etc. Otherwise they were all the same full stories, verbatim. It would be the same as if you found someone had copied your entire Facebook page with the only difference being that they'd Photoshopped their own head onto all of your pictures.

Not only that, but he was on all social media promoting this blog like he was looking to try to sell himself as me. "Come read my stories of drinking, drugs and fucking!" or something that benign. If I couldn't make myself popular in those exact same words in this many years, good luck.

I tweeted a link to Troy's blog with a simple "Fuck with this guy." And they fucked with him so harshly that he no longer exists on the Internet.

Over the course of the next forty-eight hours, Troy's blog and every other social media account were taken down and if you were to google his full name, to this day it would still come up with his attempt to steal my life. He is now listed in the *Urban Dictionary* as an example of a "shit dick" for "self-promotion through plagiarism." It was overkill at minimum. He was a bonehead who did something stupid. I didn't know it would go that far.

It got so brutal I had to call off the troops. I ended up feeling kinda bad for the guy and for being the person who fired the starting pistol. Maybe I should have been flattered or even sympathetic that some dude wanted to steal the fame of a guy who wasn't even widely liked much less well known. But it made me aware that I had a bored and equally hateful band of idiots who, like me, needed an outlet for their impotent rage.

I felt no remorse when shortly thereafter, the brunt of their aimless rage fell on Allison Pearson.

My tweet about Pearson's column referred to her as a cunt and I left it at that . . . buuuut my Twitter followers didn't. They read this cold-blooded article she'd thoughtlessly dispatched and pounded her on Twitter. Again, a small cabal of fans but virulent and dogged. They drenched her Twitter feed with every repulsive obscenity imaginable and wished her and her children paralyzed or dead. Some not as articulately as others but all malicious. It got so brutal that, like Troy, I had to tell people to lay off. Hennigan even told me to put the brakes on it and he is an irrepressible sadist.

Allison Pearson responded with a series of head-scratching tweets threatening to report me to Twitter, investigate my employers and call the police.

Hang on. You're going to investigate my employers? Meaning you are going to try to get me *fired?* From *comedy?* I would have gone so far as to say that I am my own employer. But the truth is that my audience decides my status of being employed or otherwise and they are the ones bombarding her with wishes and hopes of her kids being paralyzed or deceased.

I don't think you really want to talk to my employers right now, Ally. They're pretty high strung, especially when they've been drinking.

She tweeted again, twisting the "pray you get an ovarian cyst" into "he threatened me with cancer." I tried to imagine a real-world application for this threat.

"I want two hundred thousand dollars in unmarked bills or all these hostages get small-cell carcinoma!"

I was never contacted about the "investigation" but I assume that Scotland Yard was either bogged down with other serious crimes or they just don't live up to their reputation. I'm not that hard to find.

She called me a "vile misogynist" simply for using the word "cunt." That had no legs. Especially in a country where "cunt" is a word used far more often for a man, usually a man who is your friend. "It's yoor fookin turn to buy a pint, you fookin cunt."

I only referred to Pearson as a cunt because "black-hearted vulture of a human being who uses the weakest of people as carrion for an easy meal just to fill space in a newspaper without so much as a cogent opinion" doesn't jibe with the 140-character Twitter parameters.

So I shortened it to "cunt." Probably tame compared to what Tony Nicklinson would have blinked about her.

Shortly afterwards, the whole affair seemed to die. I assumed that Allison Pearson had shut her ridiculous clown mouth, put on her dunce cap and slinked off into the corner. I thought that was the end of it until a few weeks later when I found a big, full-color picture of me in her new column right beside a picture of a guy who'd just been sentenced to prison for "inciting racial hatred" on Twitter. He had live-tweeted the on-field heart attack of a black soccer player with the most puerile invective and was for a moment the most hated man in the whole country. His initial tweets and arrest happened within days of my initial tweet about Pearson.

Our photos sat side by side atop her new column about cyberbullying titled "The Curse of the Internet Trolls." Of course, she put herself in as an equal victim to the soccer player who'd nearly died on the pitch. The article starts out with the fifty-six-day jail sentence Liam Stacey received for online taunting of Fabrice Muamba as he was lying on the field after having a heart attack that began with Liam tweeting "Fuck Muamba. He's dead!!!" Fabrice didn't die but came close. What made me curious was what exactly he said that had him sent to prison for this inciting racial hatred.

He was sentenced to prison for fifty-six days of which he served half. On a side note that is praise for the expediency of the justice system in England, he was arrested, convicted, sentenced, served and was out free all within the length of our seven-week tour. Yet in criticism of UK law and logic in general, I wondered how this specific breach of the law could stand.

After some digging I found screenshots of Liam Stacey's tweets in question. They were a string of idiot trolling tweets, each using as many trained-offensive buzzwords as any moron could plug into a sentence. After he sparked some outrage with his initial "Fuck Muamba, He's Dead!!!" tweet, he followed up and responded to detractors with more of the same.

"Suck that dead niggers cock you aids ridden cunt!" followed by "Go fuck your mother, you inbred twat" and then upped the ante with the eternally quotable Mark Twain quote "Go rape your dog you twat." They were all equally inane and only one contained the word "nigger" and another softened to "black."

With the litany of abuses he blurted in a row, I couldn't understand how you could possibly pull out one that is punishable with a prison term while all the others were deemed inconsequential. Someone is getting imaginary AIDS here! There is a hypothetical mother being made love to by her own offspring! And what about the dog that is being raped? Does no person on this wicked island care about the animals??? For the love of Pete! The only person here who seems to be faring well in these fantastical trolling scenarios is the so-called nigger. He's getting his dick sucked as he lies dying. AIDS be damned, who wouldn't want to go out like that? He is the hero in the whole played-out troll. If the kid had to go to prison for unimaginative tweets, my outrage lies with the imaginary dog being raped. I've seen what that can do to people. Dogs can't even go to therapy.

Now the cyberbully article switched from Liam to me, who victimized her by referring to her as a cunt. Once. On the Internet. Oh, the inhumanity.

"Stanhope turned out to be an American 'comedian': being horrible and offensive is his job description."

No, my job description is a person who seeks to entertain an audience, primarily by making them laugh. Horrible and offensive, if that's how you see it, is simply my style. It's your style as well, but you do it to incite, not to entertain.

"Doug invited his unmerry men to join in the fun. Stanhope has 83,000 followers on Twitter and he directed them to "read this—Allison Pearson's column."

In full, my first tweet on the matter read: "To fully understand my rage and upcoming vitriol you'll first need to read this cunt @allisonpearson's column . . ." with a link to the rubbish article. I posted it so that people would be familiar with the piece when I talked about it onstage that night. Allison failed to understand that my act is my "column." I use Twitter to promote it. I'm sure she'd have no problem fitting the entirety of her hollow and hobbled arguments into 140 characters and still leave room for a hashtag, but I try to flesh it out more and save it for the stage.

"Over the next 48 hours, I learned a lot about Stanhope fans as they swarmed over my Twitter timeline like killer ants."

No kidding. My followers can be fucking brutal. They even scare *me* sometimes. I sometimes feel like the leader of some sub-Saharan African nation that changes names every four months and never makes the Western news despite the constant bloodshed. Meaning I fear that the small populace who was once loyal to me could turn on a dime and necklace me in a burning tractor tire in the town square with the same fervor with which they'd once elected me.

Pearson had previously tweeted that they were like a swarm of locusts and in another article she called them "swarming killer termites," both of which are a bit more creative than "ants." I liked "killer termites" the best. Before that I called my fans the "Sausage Army" without much enthusiasm as I didn't want to exclude the ladies who already seemed to be excluding themselves.

The moniker "Killer Termites" has stuck ever since for my hardcore followers. She couldn't even understand the concept of an Internet troll. A troll is an anonymous person starting shit for the sake of it without fear of retribution. I am not a troll.

I stand up alone in front of people nightly, my exact location announced well in advance, and speak my opinions openly and publicly. I have no personal security team and the ones the venue employ sometimes charge me the ticket price or don't let me in at all. Sometimes my only security is luck, when I've stepped out to smoke and violent marauders go after the gay guy onstage instead.

People like Allison Pearson have always been the trolls, sitting hunched over with a finger sandwich hanging from their mouth, typing out whatever reckless pap they please for the daily news with impunity. They are quickly becoming moribund vaudeville acts. The shoe is on the other foot as we, the people, have columns and readers of our own. She wrote what I found to be loathsome, I gave her a bad review on Twitter and all of a sudden the flurry of email she got wasn't so pretty. And I'm not even famous.

Tony Nicklinson lost his case with the high court for his right to die that year. Shortly afterwards, he died of natural causes. I like to think that he died naturally like Mother. And I like to believe his last word was about Allison Pearson.

BLINK BLINK BLINK BLINK.

● ● ●

The Killer Termites went on to do things under the banner of good as well. Rebecca Vitsmun had her house blown to rubble in a tornado in Oklahoma. She barely escaped in time to save her own life as well as her child. Wolf Blitzer managed to corner her in the wreckage of what had been her house for an interview. He closed the interview by asking her if she thanked the Lord for her good fortune of leaving just in time. He was probably used to a lot of Lord-thanking in Oklahoma.

Rebecca shyly responded, "Actually, I'm an atheist."

It went briefly viral with Blitzer looking like a dick after a meth-jack.

I was drunk when I saw it and immediately had Hennigan set up a page on a fundraising site. We put it out on social media and within days, the Killer Termites and atheists everywhere raised over a hundred and twenty-five thousand dollars to rebuild her home. She didn't. She fled the Jesus mongers in Oklahoma and bought a house outside of Seattle.

The people who follow me aren't all mean. But they are for the most part all bored and angry and, good or bad, they need an outlet.

Sometimes I think I could start a cult. Sometimes I'm sure of it. It could be funny in a certain state of mind. Like when you're hammered and everything is hilarious. But in the morning, I'm sure I wouldn't want to.

● ● ●

Fame is something I've had a taste of only enough to show me that I wouldn't want any more. Like eating eggplant. If you don't like a little, you wouldn't like a lot. To a very small group of people, I'm very famous. It can be disconcerting to have a girl unable to speak and start crying at the merch table after a show when you've just played in some sweat-locker dive that wasn't even sold out and only a dozen people in line for a DVD or a T-shirt. But to that one girl, it's Beatlemania and I feel like it's my fault for not being more widely known. Especially because it's a girl, a rarity in my fan base.

I've had a lot of people get tattoos of either my face, my autograph or quotes from my act. Some are terrible and I don't know how to react when they show me. Google image search "doug stanhope tattoos" and see what I mean. If it's a tattoo of my head, well, you've seen my head. Unless it's a cartoon version or the artist in question took enough artistic license that he faced losing his license altogether, it's not gonna look good. The autograph tats are even worse. My signature is a lazy, indecipherable scrawl where you might be able to make out the *D* and possibly the *S* depending on the level of my booze tremors when I originally signed it. Skin is difficult to sign anyway and the oils fuck up your Sharpie. The looser the skin, the harder it is to sign, which has led to many embarrassing moments when a drunk gal thinks it'd be cool to ask me to sign her baby-drained cleavage. Dudes as well. I was out after some show when a guy asked me: "Will you sign my balls? Because last time you signed my dick." I don't doubt that I had.

"No problem. Pull 'em out and batwing 'em."

I like the tattoos of my quotes. My favorite might be one guy who had a dagger plunged downwards through the skull of a fetus with a ribbon around it that read: "Would You Know My Name." It's a nod to a bit I did about going to heaven only to be confronted by the angry abortion that I'd had. The bit trails off with those Eric Clapton lyrics written about his child who died crawling out of the window of a high-rise. I'm flattered but I wouldn't want to be that guy trying to do the entire bit in order to explain the ink.

I've had a standing request for friends who tell me they are going to have a child. I ask that if the baby is born disfigured or deformed enough that it could actually sell tickets in a freak show, they will give it the first and middle names "Doug Stanhope" regardless of gender. This hasn't happened yet but if it ever does, I will tattoo the names of the parents on my ass as my first tattoo. Quid pro quo.

· · ·

As I've said before, I'm only famous within a hundred yards of my show and only for an hour before and after. I rarely get recognized in general life so when it does happen, I usually find it pretty fucking cool. It's cool when you're sitting in first class dressed like an asshole (I find it important to always be dressed ridiculously if I fly in first. It upsets the people you are pretending you aren't one of) when some kid walks by boarding, stops and looks at you.

"Holy shit! You're Doug Stanhope!"

I will fist-bump him and smile, knowing that for the rest of the flight, all these stooges sitting around me will be wondering what a "Doug Stanhope" is other than a fashion god who just made some young man spatter his pants. I fly often enough that I have top-tier status on Delta and usually get bumped up to first. If I'm traveling with Bingo and I get bumped up without her, I'll keep the upgrade even if I plan on slumming back with her in coach. I'll drink my free pre-flight cocktail in first and wait until everyone is onboard before retreating back to Bingo before takeoff.

"Excuse me, fat uncomfortable guy holding in your own girth in a bear hug. Would you mind trading that middle seat for a seat up in first class?" which is always greeted with cacophony from every other middle seat in earshot. "I will! I will!" Of course I could have just told the airline at the counter that I wouldn't need the upgrade but fuck them. I want the credit for regifting that prime seat. I earned that seat by flying 125,000-plus miles a year. I want the accolades.

First-class and diamond status are addictive and if I find that I'm short of the required mileage towards the end of the year, I will start flying and I won't stop until I hit my mark. Tucson east to Boston, all the way west to Anchorage and then back home. Never leave the airport. That was an easy one. Others were through LAX and then fourteen hours to Sydney, Australia. Stretch your legs for a couple hours before getting right back for the same route home. The longest was Tucson through Atlanta and then fifteen hours—the longest nonstop commercial flight going at the time—to Johannesburg, South Africa, for a few hours where thankfully they have a smoking bar. Hit the gift shop to take in the culture before catching a plane to Amsterdam long enough to have some drinks and a few cigarettes in the Delta Sky Club that is also blessed with a smoking room. Then off to Detroit just in time to catch the flight to Las Vegas where I hit the smoking cubicle and napped on the floor before I headed to Salt Lake City where they had smoking cubicles (evidently they're getting rid of them) and then back to Tucson. Seventy-seven hours total, fifty-seven of them in the air. More than twenty-four thousand miles. Diamond status achieved. For twenty-two hundred dollars I'd get to skip the line and be bumped up to first class for another year. Plus, I got to see the world! If you find yourself flying Delta in any given December, check the hashtag #AirportPubCrawl on Twitter and maybe I'll see you in a smoking bar.

I enjoy telling people that I am flying to Africa without any follow-up or reason why. I want them to believe I have any interest in travel outside of getting airline status. I would feel far more intriguing. The truth is that I have zero interest in any country's culture, history or landmarks. I like their bars, prisons and mental institutions, the latter two not easily toured. I find no reverence in playing on the same stage that Buddy Holly or Bert Convy once performed. It's quite possible that Geronimo once squatted and shat on the very same earth where I set up a game of cornhole in the yard. That is nothing but random trivia and that poop is long gone, turned into soil and possibly even grown a tomato. It's way cooler to think that I may have eaten Geronimo in a BLT. It doesn't mean anything to me unless it's funny. Taking a dump on the same toilet that Elvis died on would be worth a tour of Graceland and the residual backlash from the security guard who chased me out. That story would have comedy mileage.

I don't need to see the Serengeti in person. I have the gift of cable television and I don't even look at the African plains on National Geographic channel unless I can pause it, get a fresh cocktail and not risk ebola or a violent government overthrow. I only needed to see one video of a botfly being pulled with tweezers out of some dude's eye to dismiss going on an African safari. Fuck Africa. Aside from the airport smoking lounge, an oddity as rare as the protected species in their wildlife refuges.

The one time I did leave an airport during one of my mileage grabs—this one Tucson through Seattle to Narita, Japan, to Honolulu and then back through LAX home to Tucson—was only due to the twelve-hour layover in Hawaii and the fact that Roseanne Barr was there. She lives on the Big Island but I texted her early on during the run on the off chance that maybe she was in Honolulu, and she was. We made plans to hook up at my second favorite day-drinking joint, Arnold's Beach Bar, well hidden in Waikiki. I got there before the bar opened and checked into the seedy yet still overpriced hotel next door just to leave my backpack and change from my garish polyester 1970s traveling suit into some khaki shorts.

I ate breakfast at the overcrowded egg joint out front with a balcony view of Arnold's below. I ate an egg and a piece of toast, nursed a coffee and newspaper while waiting for any signs of life at the bar that doesn't open until the ungodly hour of 9 a.m. As soon as I spotted the cute bartender hauling chairs outside, I paid my tab and went down to help arrange the patio. I'll do the chairs, lady. You have more important work to do. Like that bartending thing I've been waiting so patiently for. Her name was and probably still is Dawn and she's one of the best bartenders in the world who I can remember. "Remember" is a key word. Next I spent approximately forty phone calls trying to explain to Roseanne the name and address of the place repeatedly as well as instructions on how to call a cab.

Roseanne is one of the funniest human beings I have ever met. By the time she'd maneuvered her way through the odyssey of figuring out getting dressed and getting in a taxi, it was already 10:30 a.m. and I was getting a bit souped. Remember I'd already logged about ten thousand miles and the equivalent amounts of Xanax and cocktails. But I know that Roseanne can catch up with you in a single shot of dark tequila or Maker's Mark.

Dawn the bartender, Roseanne and I had this hole-in-the-wall tiki bar to ourselves and by 11 a.m. we were dancing to Chuck Berry on the jukebox. By noon I knew that I had to get food into Roseanne if she was going to stay upright any longer. We went down the street where we got an appetizer at a hotel bar as well as more cocktails. We sat on their patio alone and drank and smoked. You can't smoke on the patio and Roseanne doesn't really smoke but she was smoking and nobody said shit because she is Roseanne. So I smoked too.

The thing about Honolulu is that when you are shitfaced in the afternoon, you can decide to go swimming in the ocean to wake up. Unlike Costa Rica where the ocean freezes over ten months out of the year. We zigzagged our way to a beach grid-locked with people to jump in the ocean in our underwear. I told Roseanne that we could just leave our clothes and her bag with some kind folks on the beach. I pointed out a nearby couple that seemed ethical, who she rejected as untrustworthy based on the book he was reading. It wasn't *Mein Kampf* or *Fifty Shades of Grey*. Just something innocuous that queered her on some personal level. She'll be the first person to tell you "I'm batshit crazy and people don't even know the half of it!" We then meandered the beach while she profiled people worthy to keep an eye on our shit. Finding qualified candidates, we stripped to our skivvies and jumped into the ocean, laughing like children. It was one of the happiest afternoons of my life.

Nobody would have known that this was Roseanne Barr unless she opened her mouth to talk but all we did was laugh. We grabbed another drink on the way back and then I poured her back into a cab. As I wandered, trying to remember my way back to Arnold's, an urgent need to piss came up on me in a way that made me regret never getting a prostate exam. Honolulu is like walking the Las Vegas Strip without the conveniences. Giant buildings that seem close but would take you ten minutes to get from the sidewalk to the front door. And these aren't even casinos. These are mostly condos and time shares. I didn't have time to pass a credit check and sign a lease in order to take a crucial piss. Finally I saw one that seemed to have a sign for a lounge and was closer to the street. I raced in only to find that the lounge was only open on certain days for happy hour and only open to the residents. When your colon or bladder have heard the news from your brain that you are that close to a bathroom, there is no printing a retraction.

I ran out and spun the corner of the thirty- or forty-story superstructure looking for anything to piss behind. A tree, an electrical box. A heron or a hobo. There was nothing but open air and full views. I made the decision to try to pull my short dick down and out of the long legs of my shorts and surreptitiously piss while I walked towards the back of the building. This resulted in me pissing all over my leg, shorts, socks, shoes and my hand. Mid-piss, I thought I'd gone far enough around the building that I could turn around and finish pissing on the way back. I turned around just in time to see that I'd been being followed the entire time by an angry, retired DEA agent. I'm profiling here but that's what he looked like. There was no doubt about the angry part.

"What the fuck are you doing???" he said as though he had to eat dinner off of this same walkway.

I wanted to explain the whole story. The whole day, the whole crazy flight. Every reason this city sucked when you had to piss and the drunken bliss of fatty-dipping in the sea with Roseanne. Instead I just sped-walked past him without eye contact and finished pissing in my shorts. I got back to Arnold's with enough time to tell Dawn that I'd pissed my pants and to have a few more drinks before changing back into my suit, ditching said shorts in the hotel room and catching my next flight.

Tell me about one of the best days of your life. If pissing your pants at the end of it would have made any difference, you need to try harder. If your favorite bartender wouldn't serve you when you come in telling her that you are steeping in your own wet, you need to find a better bar.

I'm not famous but if you ever hit Arnold's Beach Bar in Waikiki and Dawn is working, mention my name and then mention the guy who was there with Roseanne that pissed his pants and she'll know exactly who I am.

• • •

Here's how to fly as a drunkard. The TSA rule is that you can carry liquids in a one quart–size bag with the liquids being travel size, no more than 3.4 ounces per item. That means you can ditch the shampoo and conditioner and pack mini-bottles of your liquor of choice. A one-quart Ziploc will hold ten mini-bottles of booze. The nomenclature for a ten-pack of minis is referred to as a "sleeve" if you wanna look cool at your liquor store. Next you carry on an empty travel mug. You can get it filled on the other side of security with ice and soda water at any bar or food concession for free unless they're dicks. I've found that the bull-shit vitamin supplements Emergen-C or Airborne—basically vitamin-fortified, fruit-flavored Alka-Seltzer—make for a good mixer with water. Mix your drinks on the sly and soon your middle seat on the plane will feel like you're in first class. For pennies on the airport-priced dollar.

Remember to be somewhat sneaky. Drinking your own booze is as illegal in an airport or on a plane as anywhere else. It's just wicked easy.

• • •

Here's another airline tip that will probably never come in handy for you but it did one night for us. My old gal Renee and I were leaving Anchorage after what was always a bender and the local crew had been coaxing us to extend our stay for one more party.

There's always one more party in Alaska. We'd been tempted but we were already so strung out from the last so many days of epic abuse and I didn't want to pay the hundred-fifty-dollar change fee per person to change the tickets. We showed up at the airport early and stinking for a late-night flight and killed the time in the bar directly across from our gate. Still somehow we didn't hear the final boarding announcement and only happened to wander out to find out they were about to leave without us. They were cranky about it and I was cranky back. Why wouldn't you have the announcement play in the bar? What civilized human being wouldn't be in the bar up until takeoff?

The counter lady told us that we were the last people on the plane so there might not be any room in the overhead for our carry-on luggage. She said it more like she was wishing it as opposed to a helpful heads-up. We were in coach but I immediately saw open space in overhead up in first class. As I wobbled my bag towards the opening, I was informed by some nelly flight attendant that this baggage space was reserved for first-class patrons. I made an attempt to explain how the gate agent had said that there might not be room for our bags and that since we were last onboard, it shouldn't be a problem. I collapsed under the look of derision, realizing that everybody already hated us for making the plane wait. We found other spaces for our bags in coach and sank into our seats on the sold-out flight. Shortly after, the same flight attendant who wouldn't let my lowly coach bag ride in first class approached me and asked if I would mind trading seats so some kid could sit across the aisle from his family.

"Oh. You wouldn't let my bag fly up front and now you want a favor from me?"

I was full cunty and not wrong. But I was drunk. Like I've said, you will never look right in an argument when you are the drunk one.

I watched him storm to the front of the plane and hold a team meeting with the other flight attendants. I leaned into Renee and said with resignation that we were not going to be on this flight. Like when you blow past a cop twenty miles over the speed limit with out-of-state plates. You know you're getting pulled over. I already had my carry-on ready like license and registration for getting tossed.

After a small ruckus back at the counter trying to argue my case, we were told that we appeared too intoxicated to fly and would be put on a flight the following day.

And it turned out—at least back then—this service of being removed from a flight for being intoxicated and moved to another flight the next day was absolutely free. No change fee. Their bad. Go enjoy the party.

We called our friends and had them pick us up for one more party in Anchorage and saved three hundred dollars in fees.

Let me know if this tactic ever works for you.

THE KINDNESS OF
STRANGERS

'd always had an "outie" belly button but it wasn't until I started getting old and fat that it became an eyesore. It stuck out like the butt end of a Vienna sausage. It was always the first part of my body to get smacked-ass red when I was out in the sun, glowing like a giant clown nose on my beer gut. People would recoil in disgust anytime I'd remove my shirt. Fuck 'em.

The medical terminology is "umbilical hernia." The fact is that it is your intestines pushing out through your navel. And that's pretty gross. You should only be able to feel your own intestines by going through your asshole. Feeling them straight through your navel completely bypasses your prostate altogether, making it not just uneventful but awful and yet another reason to kill yourself.

I showed it to my friends in Bisbee at one of their weekly poker games. I don't always know what to say in mixed company so the obvious default is to show your most disgusting body part. Someone suggested that my gut-lump was an umbilical hernia.

There's a clinic down the street where I'd get my prescriptions filled by Dr. Jack. He was great about not asking a lot of questions. So when I went to refill my Xanax for my "flight anxiety," I lifted my shirt as an aside and asked if it was indeed a hernia or simply an outie. He said it was definitely herniated and that I could get surgery but that if it didn't bother me, I shouldn't worry about it.

No, it doesn't bother me. It bothers other people when they are trying to play poker or make eye contact at the pool when my shirt is off. But it doesn't bother me.

Bear in mind that this was the same Dr. Jack who prescribed RID to our friend Father Luke to get rid of scabies.

Allow me to go off on a side note.

When we first moved to Bisbee in 2005, we had our old friend Father Luke living with us for a while. At one point he caught scabies, or so he thought. Anytime scabies or any bug bite is explained to you, you get phantom scabies. You start to itch as though you are rife with them just hearing about them. It's much worse for Bingo.

Bingo had been off her lithium for two days and was dealing with it as best she could. Bingo in those days was out of her tit. Same diagnosis as today but nowhere near under control. Bipolar, schizoaffective, OCD, manic. Off her banana. Fucked for lunch. A bit wacky to say the least. It would have been hard to convince her that bugs were not crawling under her skin at any given moment anyway. Now that we told her that there possibly were actual bugs under her skin it sorta made things worse but she kept it together in her own way. She'd scratch some holes in her skin like a tweaker but within a short time she'd be back to dancing to "Diamonds on the Soles of Her Shoes" and writing "Scabies" across the breakfast table in Cheez Whiz. I didn't even know why we had Cheez Whiz but it was good to know it wasn't wasted.

Father Luke shuffled down to Dr. Jack to get a prescription— or "subscription" as he called it—for scabies cream. They make you get a prescription so they know you're not abusing it. Or perhaps it's all just a scam.

Father Luke told the doc that he thought the bumps were scabies. The rummy doctor barely blinked and told Luke that he'd phone in a prescription. No test or swab, barely a cursory glance. After you've filled out all the paperwork to prove that you have no money to be felched dry of, the doc would just assume your own diagnosis was as good as any he could come up with and off you went.

We set off bug bombs to fumigate the house and took off to the pharmacy to pick up the Sca-Bee-Gone or whatever and planned to get a motel for the night. It was only after the Zyklon B had been released into our house that the pharmacist told us the prescription that had been phoned in was for RID.

RID is a medication for head lice that won't do a thing for scabies. And RID is an over-the-counter medicine. Like aspirin. Toothpaste. The old doctor had phoned in a prescription for a nonprescription product. That's like phoning in a prescription for a frozen pizza or corn syrup. We had a prescription for shampoo that would do nothing and we couldn't fix it because the clinic was now closed—as mites were working their way towards our genitals or wherever they wanted to party that night.

We couldn't go home because of the fumigation. And we would certainly pass on this affliction to some other poor slob if we went to the motel.

(pause for hack timing)

So we're at the motel . . .

There we made frantic attempts to reach the doctor through his service before the pharmacy closed. Finally we got the irritated and obviously drunk Dr. Jack calling on a bad connection. Father Luke had lost his sense of humor at this point, if only to make the whole escapade funnier. He had welts like he'd been shot at with thousand-pellet guns.

"I'm dying of smallpox and this doctor is drinking Ripple down at the creek!"

This made Bingo laugh but it was that kinda laugh that you get just before or after you have beaten a homeless lady to death because you were drunk and wanted her scarf. It wasn't healthy.

We got the proper cream called in just before the pharmacy shut the addict-proof glass. Father Luke it turned out had been the only one infected. Bingo and I only had sympathy itches. The motel went out of business and we will never know if it's because Luke passed on his contamination.

But back to the hernia.

I showed it to my friend Nurse Betty and she freaked out. I told her that Dr. Jack said I shouldn't worry about it. Betty informed me of all the possible doomsday scenarios involved with belly-button problems—it could prolapse or pinch off; the list went on and on but the one word she said that clung in my brain like a tumor was the word "necrotizing." That can lead to death, she said. Death doesn't bother me. "Necrotizing" bothered me long enough that I would at least consider surgery, something I said I'd never do. I've spent my life ignoring problems and they almost always go away. Being a comedian, I had no health insurance and didn't have the slightest idea how to just walk in off the street for surgery out of pocket. No fucking way I'm going back to Dr. Jack to ask.

So I explained my condition on my website and offered a free autographed DVD and CD along with a T-shirt to any surgeon who wanted to pony up a complimentary stabbing in the guts.

Turns out my fans aren't all bankrupt degenerates and lone gunmen. Doctors actually do come to my shows. Just so happened that a couple we'd recently met on the road—Drs. Mark and Suzie Bazzell—happened to be anesthesiologists and lived up the road in Tucson. They emailed me posthaste after the update and offered their services. Anesthesia is 99 percent of the game as far as I'm concerned. So long as I'm unconscious, I could have my dry cleaner do the alterations. But they had a surgeon friend that was game and who waived her fee as well.

Yes. *Her*. Thanks I assume to Obamacare and the comedy of Amy Schumer, gals too can be doctors now. This was a hot Japanese lady surgeon with ropey arms who probably mountain bikes and didn't laugh at my examination room jokes and could have been twenty-eight or seventy the way Asian women tend to go.

My immediate concern was that this selfless act of charity on her part might change my ingrained hatred of women and Asians. Like those movies where a Klansman gets the kidney transplant that saves his life from a carefree Negro and learns a lesson. Would this complimentary surgery make me finally see the weaker sex and the yellow plague of the Rising Sun as equals?

Okay, I don't actually harbor animosity towards ladies or Japaniards but I do think racism and sexism are hilarious when done tastefully and with good humor as I have just displayed.

My initial visit was the one where you get asked a lot of questions and you tell a lot of fibs. It's funny how you lie and say you only drink about twenty drinks a week and their jaw drops like that's a lot. I asked her what this procedure would normally cost for a cash-paying customer. She said that she didn't know exactly but estimated between seven and fifteen thousand dollars. I didn't and don't understand how she could possibly not know and why there was more than a 100 percent difference in her ballpark guess. All I knew was that on either end, it was a fuck-ton of money.

This made it very awkward in how the fuck I was supposed to say thank you. It wouldn't be sufficient to mail a Red Lobster gift certificate.

So I told the doctors that in return I'd do a benefit show in Tucson for whatever charitable cause they were behind. They discussed it and fortunately they don't like people as much as I don't and decided it was best to do the benefit for animals, something even my diseased fan base could get on board with.

Every time I've been asked to perform a charity function that I can remember, I've declined mostly because people who go to charity functions don't want to hear the kind of misery and outrage I have to deliver. Plus I think most of them are scams. I'd rather just give a dude with cancer the money than give it to some alleged nonprofit. But this benefit was for the Humane Society and you can't give cash to a homeless kitten.

I was lucky enough to get a bunch of my favorite comedians to fly out for no money. Brendon Walsh, Henry Phillips, Brody Stevens, Lynn Shawcroft and Neil Hamburger all flew in from LA for the show for one of the best lineups I've been part of. My friend Jimi edited together a pre-show montage video of animal porn with the ubiquitous Sarah McLachlan song "In the Arms of the Angel" from those sad puppy commercials playing in the background. It was only soft-core animal-on-animal porn. I fought to get the infamous video of the guy getting killed being fucked by a horse added but things like "disgusting" and "liquor license" kept coming up. I wanted a Humane Society benefit that PETA would protest.

We raised almost eighteen thousand dollars for the Humane Society and a permanent spot on their elite and repetitive mailing list. My navel no longer sticks out like a turkey timer and we remain good friends with the Bazzells who I give full credit for Bingo and me still being alive today. Needless to say there is no way I'll ever be able to thank them enough. Especially when you consider I never even gave them the free DVD and the T-shirt I'd promised for the initial surgery on my website.

REALITY OR OTHERWISE

To the best of my recollection—which is always suspect—there was a war that started in March of 2003. Joe Rogan and I drove out to the house of some of his friends far east of Los Angeles. San Bernardino? Riverside? I have no idea. I wasn't driving. It wasn't my problem. I was just Rogan's plus-one for the war party.

This war was evidently planned out for the US audience with a prime-time kick-off that worked for the home viewing audience. Nine p.m. EST/6 p.m. Pacific. We were going to pre-game the event by doing ayahuasca before settling in on the sofa for the big show.

Ayahuasca is almost as big a procedure as preparing for battle from what it seemed. Like making brauts in the parking lot of Lambeau Field before a Packers game. There was a lot of preparation, a ritual, boiling these psychedelic vines into some brew, some tea that would make the whole invasion seem even funnier. I felt out of place in that I'd only brought a small bag of mushrooms, the kind you just chew up and swallow while trying not to barf. I was even too embarrassed to tell anyone that I had them once I saw the production value of their culinary display. I'd brought Boone's Farm and Velveeta to a wine and cheese tasting. Or so I thought.

After all the legwork and pageantry of making this sewer brew, we took turns choking down the vulgar concoction and waited for the grand payoff. I can't tell you how long we waited but I could eventually tell in the disappointed eyes of these professional trippers that there would be no parade. A sadness crept over the group that no war could ever make right. The drugs were bunk or the recipe was off and there was no denying it.

This is where I stepped in and meekly unrolled my ludicrously negligible baggie of caps and stems. I had no brand name to tout. I didn't know if they were *Anamaria muscaria* or any other label. I knew that they were called mushrooms and that I'd had them before. And that they had worked. I doled them out like you would if you were trying to survive one more day on a deserted island. Prison rations.

In short time, we were tripping lightning on just my little satchel alone. I felt like Rudolph the Reindeer on some foggy wartime eve. We dissolved into our loveseats and recliners and watched what would be a Super Bowl countdown to carnage. The president had given Iraq a deadline to do something that they wouldn't and didn't do. I don't remember all of the details. I didn't even have money on the game. All I remember is that the show seemed to go off on time. Maybe there was a coin flip, perhaps a band scheduled for halftime. But we shat laughing at the fact that we were tailgating a war and that the war was punctual. Soon enough, we were watching grainy footage of missiles landing in Baghdad, which had home-field advantage but was losing early on in the match.

When the game is that much of a blowout, you tend to lose interest. Especially when you are bent off of your block on tiny little mushrooms. We left before the end of the war. Thank goodness there was no last-minute comeback. I always feel bad for the people who bailed early to beat the traffic only to miss out on the greatest comeback of all time.

How Joe Rogan could manage to drive us home is beyond me. These were before the days where KettleBells or Onnit were his sponsors or his addictions. I don't even think he drank much back then. I'd drunk as much as I ever did and wasn't even fit to ride much less drive. At some point on the drive home I had to piss. Rather than ask Rogan to pull over, I opened my passenger door, hung on to the overhead handle and swayed pissing down the freeway at sixty-five miles an hour.

You'd think that even a monster like Rogan would take pause and call for restraint. But the country was at war and we all had to man up. Rogan did not take pause. He took video. Somehow, under the intrusive glare of hallucinogens and the overhead dome light, whilst careening down the highway, Rogan managed to drive and film me pissing out the door, all over the road and his brand new SUV without ever losing his smile.

Rogan's fame was never his strength. Rogan wrestled fame to the ground and fucked it into submission. Rogan took fame's championship belt, held it over his head and then traded it in for something of value. Rogan is smart like that.

He was doing *Fear Factor* for NBC at the time and the network comped him high-dollar seats for a Lakers game, probably hoping that the cameras would stop on him during a break for a free plug. He asked me if I wanted to go to the game. I didn't really care for basketball. Rogan hated any sport where people don't get hurt or die. But we both liked getting shit for free and we hated to waste the seats.

As the game was about to begin, we grabbed some burritos from the VIP buffet and took our seats. We were hunched over our laps eating burritos when the national anthem started. There was no need to tell people to rise for the song. We were at war! People shot up like they'd been tased in the colon. But Rogan and I were eating burritos. I turned to Rogan as food fell from his face.

"Should we stand up for this?"

The stares of the attendees surrounding us still seated and eating were murderous. You could physically feel the hatred.

Rogan barely looked at me or found time to swallow.

Like I was stupid for even asking.

"Fuck these sheep."

And back to the burrito.

We left before the end of the first quarter.

There was no reason to watch the Lakers. We'd just watched a war on mushrooms, a war that somehow kicked off right on schedule, prime time, just as Joe and Mary Lunchbucket were sitting down to their Hungry-Man TV dinners.

We'd just witnessed reality television at it's most pure, from behind the curtain of Oz.

Ever since my experience with *Jerry Springer*, my obsession with the fraudulence of reality television has too often kept me glued to a couch if for no other reason than to cry "Bullshit!" And it's all bullshit, usually on a much deeper level than saying that wrestling is fake.

Early on in my career I did a pilot for a hidden camera show called *Hotel Hell*. The participants thought they were on their way to be on a *Survivor*-type show in the middle of the California nowhere. They were led to believe that their bus had broken down on the way to the set and they would have to spend two days at this hotel. The hotel out in the middle of the desert was—as the title states—"Hell." Meaning, we'd fuck with them on hidden camera. The show could have been funny on premise alone but like too many shows I've been part of, the people in charge take precedence over the ones who they've hired to make it funny.

They under- or overthink it and overwrite it and fuck it all up. When you have a dead mountain lion in a Jacuzzi and a kid who can vomit on command, why overthink the plot?

The pilot obviously sucked and didn't get picked up but the producers pressed on. They flew me out months later to film more gags we'd never even done to recut into the pilot. I'd be wheeled into a room underneath a room service cart and then roll out, doing something inappropriate and undoubtedly hilarious. To nobody. They could just cut in random reaction shots that we'd already filmed months before. You might know that wrestling is fake but what if you found out that those two guys weren't ever actually in the same ring together? The show was still never picked up but knowing that they had no problem selling that deep of outright lies made me not only doubt all reality television, it makes me doubt even the nightly news. Maybe Rogan and I weren't even watching a real war that night.

I still watch these stupid fucking shows, trying to find the deception like an unrequested expert witness without a jury that gives a fuck.

For a while I had a segment on the brilliant Charlie Brooker shows *Newswipe* and *Weekly Wipe* on the BBC in the UK. I was the "Voice of America" without the consent of the BBC or America. One of the segments had me shitting on reality TV. Trout meet barrel. In it, I closed the bit ripping the then upstart show *Bar Rescue*. It was another rip-off of the originator *Kitchen Nightmares* with the formulaic and ego-bound Gordon Ramsay who would somehow be shocked every week that he'd never before borne witness to the conditions of the restaurant he was there to save.

"This is the worst I have ever seen" or "I have never met someone so awful" or "Never before on this show have I . . ."

Bar Rescue had the same formula with some bloat-headed blowhard named Jon Taffer saving bars instead of restaurants.

In my BBC piece, I closed by calling Taffer the worst fraud on reality television in America in that he was a pretend-douche. He was merely a mimic of his predecessors. You could tell that Gordon Ramsay was a serious shit-bucket. Jon Taffer was merely a cheap impressionist of fake outrage.

Bar Rescue went on to be a success and I watched it out of spite and because of the fact that it was set in bars. If you're gonna get drunk and watch worthless TV, you might as well watch a TV show that is set in a bar. I'd get drunk and yell at Bingo, pointing out how they were cheating camera angles, and putting in voice-overs to create scenes of conflict that never happened.

Then one day an email came in or a phone rang. It was the *Bar Rescue* people wanting me to be on the show. Jon Taffer was so honored that he'd heard me call him the biggest douchebag on reality TV that he wanted me to be on an episode. If I'd called him the second biggest, I wouldn't have gotten the call.

I'd just returned from a tour in Australia but still caught the first flight to LA to be there. I sat for hours filming in the Chevy Suburban while we watched live feed of his "recon" team inside the bar. I had to duck out to piss several times where I'd refill my travel mug of vodka and soda, trying to think of something to say. All of my commentary was wasted. I like the kind of bars he ruins. Who would complain about their drink being overpoured or the barely dressed barmaid being drunk and dancing on a pool table? The *Bar Rescue* formula is to turn every bar that I love into some variation of a TGI Fridays.

Eventually there was a point where the recon duo were unable to get a reaction from the bar owner to make for some conflict. I was very drunk now and told Taffer that I would go in there and rile some shit up myself. He let me go in. I was immediately pegged as an interloper by one of the bar regulars on what I found to be an otherwise closed set. He noticed that I didn't have a wristband on, meaning I must be on the crew. I threw a fake fit while I got free drinks and ate uncooked chicken, which I complained about even more loudly. Then I went to play pool with some waitresses, forgetting I was doing a TV show.

In the end, the episode aired. At the beginning, I was in the Suburban and edited down to an occasional nod or "yessir." But the editing was so bad that they would cut from Taffer and me in the SUV watching the bar in action into shots of the bar where I was at the same time sitting. I spotted myself immediately because of the undeniable bald spot that I never see in a mirror.

I'd like to do a show called *Reality Show Rescue* where I teach people to make reality shows that can trick people like me who are just watching and waiting for them to fuck up. But people like me aren't their target audience. Or maybe we are, so long as we're watching.

Before *Bar Rescue*, my all-time favorite show to hate was *Celebrity Rehab with Dr. Drew*. When I hate a television show, I can taste the contempt in my mouth. Yet it makes me crave it more. If you love to hate, you understand. If you don't, you are probably a better person. This long-term fixation with *Celebrity Rehab* culminated in a nearly fourteen-minute routine trashing both Drew himself and the cult of Alcoholics Anonymous on my stand-up comedy special *Before Turning the Gun on Himself*. After going back to listen to it again, it may be the most brutal personal excoriation of any individual, living or dead, that I've ever recorded. Like any ambitious yet lazy takedown, it had to invoke the Nazis—calling Dr. Drew the "Joseph Goebbels propaganda minister in the war on drugs"—and imagining his tortuous death in a prolonged, inventive, if not meandering fashion.

Half measures avail us nothing.

I treat any performance, recorded or otherwise, with a blind trust that the content will remain within the confines of the room. Kind of like an AA meeting, ironically. Part of that mentality lies in the omnipresent self-deprecation of thinking that what you said will never travel far and that if it does, the person in question won't ever hear it anyway. In short, I know Dr. Drew ain't in the room. So fuck him.

I hope Dr. Drew still hasn't heard the bit. But like my trashing of Jon Taffer, shortly after the special with the *Celebrity Rehab* bit aired on Netflix, I was asked by his producer to come on Dr. Drew's podcast. Like Jon Gnarr, I also believe in coincidence. But not this time. I could only assume that it was a well-deserved ambush but there was no way I could refuse.

I sat outside Dr. Drew's studio that morning, smoking cigarettes and drinking from my travel mug, conceptualizing the trap I was about to walk into. I went through my head, working on defending my salient points like a politician going into a debate. A politician who'd forgotten the part where he'd wished loudly and publicly for the opponent to be dragged through the streets, tied shirtless to a light pole and . . . well it goes on from there. Once I got on the air, we exchanged some tentative pleasantries before I cut through the tension and to the quick.

"All right, you didn't invite me here for no reason."

I said it amicably, like archrivals from professional sports teams would long after retirement. Sitting in a studio, face to face and mic to mic, all of the hours I'd spent loathing *Celebrity Rehab* became as ridiculous as a Yankees–Red Sox quibble from the days of yore. Drew admitted that he had heard I had some beef with him but said he was not the type of person to look up negative things about himself on the Internet. We immediately found common ground on having egos too fragile for that nonsense. Fuck that Google ego-surfing yourself. Once you've gained a solid audience, there's no longer any reason to seek out detractors online. On that level, Drew was as frail as I was and it sucked me in. Turns out that even famous people can occasionally have feelings just like regular folk and are not impervious to having those feelings hurt. A common enemy brings people together and we found that enemy in everybody else. And then I hated him for making me realize that, and I hated the fact that I really liked him as a person.

I still defended my original stance on why his rehab show was a lot of exploiting people at their weakest. You don't take someone in the throes of the DTs and send them boating with Gary Busey for conflict. That isn't medicine. He agreed with me and blamed the producers, saying he was also aghast at the idea. I told him that was like Nazis—again, always fall back on the Third Reich—saying they were only following orders. But in this case he was Hitler saying it. It was his show. Then I had to remember that *The Man Show* would have been seen as *my* show when it was awful. Having my name on it didn't make me the person in control. I got it but didn't want to concede ground.

I asked Drew what advice he would give if he were hosting a *Celebrity Rehab* with a cast of Charles Bukowski, Hunter S. Thompson, William Burroughs, Keith Richards and Dean Martin, all legendary fuckups who thrived on booze. He stuttered and finally responded that he'd heard Dean Martin wasn't really as drunk as he pretended to be. I felt like I won that round solidly. But more so, I still liked Dr. Drew.

For the rest of the podcast, not only did he begin to agree with me, he seemed to be arguing against himself better than I was. I went in prepared for combat and somehow he made me feel like I'd lost using the same arguments, like he was beating me at my own game. I left feeling like I'd made a friend who'd just drugged and raped me—in a beautiful, selfless way that made me the prettiest princess in all of the land. More Bill Clinton than Bill Cosby.

At first I felt tricked but not long after, he asked me to be on an episode of his HLN show to do a point-counterpoint with another guest on the topic of legalized marijuana. I don't smoke weed but you can guess what side I was on. And I was probably a dick about it where he probably played the straight man. You fall into a groove.

Dr. Drew has evidently admitted to being a narcissist. He likes being a famous doctor. I'm a narcissist in that I sometimes like to believe I'm some sort of doctor suffering from fame. Whatever bullshit keeps you on point but I think that we understand each other. And oddly we have become friendly, a point that I undersell on purpose so I don't have to ever issue an apology for my personal attacks.

Drew has not only been a friend since but an ally in other personal shit that I wouldn't have known how to deal with otherwise. And I still give him shit about boating with Gary Busey. He takes it well. When I had the drunken moxie to ask him to write a foreword for this book, he asked me if he was being punked. I told him I was sincere and that I would let him read it first. If he has in fact read the book—or what I would do and just read the parts about me—I will guarantee that his foreword will be completely unedited and give him free range on returning the ball-busting I gave him on that special. I'll bet money that he's too much of a gentleman. Almost a dare.

Both Jon Taffer and Dr. Drew appearances were the direct result of me publicly shitting all over them. Let's see if the next story gets me booked as a late-night talk show guest.

● ● ●

When Jimmy Fallon first showed up on the LA scene he was a humble, sweet-faced, friendly young kid with absolutely no discernable jokes. And he killed. It was bewildering. His entire act consisted of him going onstage with a guitar and a troll doll. He set up the premise in a disturbing British accent that he was holding auditions for the jingle for the new commercial for the troll doll. Then he would go through a series of impressions of the hit songs of the day and to his credit, they were spot on. They just had no jokes.

"Okay, first up is U2!"

He'd then play U2's "Desire" and simply put "Troll Doll" in place of the chorus. "Desire" became "Troll Doll."

"Next up, the Counting Crows."

Their song "Mr. Jones (and Me)" was cleverly rephrased into "Troll Doll (and Me)."

Spot on.

People literally fell out of their chairs. It was like suburban comedy jam. Folks heaving in tears and burying their faces between their knees, unable to breathe. Becker and I would sit in the back of the room and stare blankly at each other wondering what the fuck we missed. I'd seen comedians do the gag where, after someone left the front row to use the bathroom, they would get the audience in on a prank.

"When she gets back from the bathroom, I'm going to tell a joke that ends with 'And that's why my grandma doesn't eat Laffy Taffy!' It won't make any sense but you guys will all fall apart laughing and she'll wonder what the hell is wrong with her for not getting it!"

That prank never failed to kill. That is what it felt like to watch Jimmy Fallon bring those rubes to their knees. Like we were being set up in an elaborate ruse where the joke was on us. Fallon didn't have a single punch line. Not even the troll doll made any sense. He could have done the exact same act with a pumpkin or a hacky sack. It didn't even have to follow any rhyming or syllabic structure. It was just bad and I'd never seen audiences laugh harder.

There was no question the kid had some talents and nobody was more affable or polite, no big ego whatsoever. You'd think he was just as confounded by the crowd's reaction to his lack of punch lines as every other comedian was.

Becker and I were having this same conversation after one of those shows with an industry gal we knew from the Improv named Randi. It was at some Hollywood party full of Hollywood types at some Hollywood upscale bistro that I believe was in Hollywood. Jimmy was there and his arrival was the impetus to our motherfucking him behind his back. We were all in agreement that he had zero substance and nothing resembling a joke in his stupid act and we collectively scratched our heads at the phenomenon.

We then split up to go see if there was anybody cooler to talk to as is the Hollywood party norm.

Later, we ran back into Randi.

"I just wanted to let you guys know that I told Jimmy what you guys said about him because I've been telling him the same thing, that he needs to really write more."

Noooooo! Why the fuck would she tell him that we said that? Especially knowing what a soft-hearted, meek little kid he is. Why would she be so cruel to us by ratting us out?

"Oh. You did know that I'm Jimmy's manager, didn't you?"

No, Randi. We did not know that. Now we'd have to avoid him not only at this party but in life in general. That lasted about ten minutes before Becker and I ran into him. I cleared it all up with a meandering, "Hey listen, man . . . sorry but . . . you know, I was just sayin' is all."

To which he responded with a shuffle-footed: "Oh yeah . . . don't worry . . . I get it I guess." It was a good heart to heart.

I still find Jimmy Fallon intolerably unfunny to the point where I have to fast-forward through even a short commercial for his show. I am still astonished as to why people laugh at him. I'm sure he is still a fantastic human being, which is far more important. I've heard gossip that he has substance abuse problems, some common ground that would make him more endearing to me. Personally, I have to drink in order to repeat material I'm too tired of saying. His material sucks the first time. I would understand if he had to abuse drugs or alcohol.

I checked his Wikipedia page and under the heading "Influences" I'd hoped to see "cocaine" or "Drambuie." It only mentioned *Saturday Night Live*.

Should my berating of his brand of comedy go the way of Dr. Drew and Jon Taffer and lead to an invite to be on *Late Night with Jimmy Fallon*, I'll decline in advance. But I'd drink and do blow with that kid anytime. Blow that is cut with pabulum, like his jokes.

•   •   •

I used to want to drink with Chelsea Handler. I don't even know where she came from. I never heard her name or crossed paths with her in the small world of stand-up comedy even when I was in the heart of it in Los Angeles. Then one day she was famous. And she was a drinker who celebrated it. I wanted to drink with her.

So it happened that I was invited to be a guest on her show, *Chelsea Lately*, which I agreed to only because she seemed like a cool broad. I had as much business appearing on a celebrity gossip roundtable as I would being on the *MacNeil/Lehrer Report*.

I rolled into LA straight out of a Death Valley party, dressed in a filthy 1970s baby-blue suede jacket and a tie because I wanted Chelsea to know that I was professional. I still had a pocket full of mushrooms of questionable integrity that someone had given me. I only traveled with them because they were ground up and put into capsules that I carried in a jar of psyllium husk capsules. I overthink things sometimes. My comedian friend Lynn Shawcroft was in tow and the perfect bad influence when I suggested that we eat these mushrooms posthaste before the taping. Lynn never thinks I have bad ideas. Lynn was also perfect to be with, as I was about to go on a gossip show knowing absolutely nothing about pop culture. Lynn reads any tabloid rag she can find and probably eats lots of psyllium husk just so she can shit more often in order read them on the toilet.

We drank our sneaky drinks in the greenroom waiting to see if the mushrooms would kick or if we'd even be able to tell based on the residuals we were already riding. Shawcroft was trying to fill me in on the claptrap that was the tabloid news of the day in a ridiculous attempt to prep me for a show where I was completely unqualified. She was teaching the tango to an amputee moments before *Dancing with the Stars*. Dave Navarro was on the show and came into the greenroom. I blame him for killing the buzz. Something is wrong when you feel out of line for being drunk and on drugs around someone else's rock-and-roll hero. By then he was doing a lot of reality television while keeping the rock-and-roll eyeliner. Maybe the buzzkill was just the fact that we were both doing a basic cable celebrity gossip show and only one of us was taking it seriously.

Chelsea stuck her head in at some point and thanked us for being there. Noticing my grotesque suit, she sneered: "Thanks for dressing up." I couldn't tell if she was being a funny cunt or just a cunt. Sometimes you have no choice but to trust your paranoia. I don't remember a word I said on the show but I know they were few and far between and inappropriate when they finally came. I left knowing that there was little chance the public would clamor for me to return to the show or that Chelsea and I would be going out for a drink.

I googled "doug stanhope chelsea handler" to try to find the date of that show. In the results I found a podcast featuring a comedian named Dustin Ybarra. The topics of the podcast included "Chelsea Handler" and "The time Doug Stanhope . . ." It didn't ring a bell. I fast-forwarded through the podcast waiting to hear my name, the same way most comedians listen to podcasts. When I got to it, I realized I'd already had the story in my notes for this book. I just couldn't remember his name.

Funny how shit works.

His name is Dustin Ybarra.

Please hold.

THE OPENING ACT SHOULD ALWAYS BE FUCKED WITH. TAKE IT WELL. IT MEANS YOU ARE ONE OF THE GROUP.

The only opening act that I ever remember fucking with because I *didn't* like him was in my early mullet days doing a rural one-nighter in Farmington, New Mexico. I was with an ex-girlfriend and I'd played this dump before. These were always live-or-die gigs where the only friend you could count on was the other comedian, who was rarely anyone you'd met beforehand. This night it was some fat kid who looked like any overweight gamer who, when you talked to him, acted like you were rudely interrupting him while he was staring at the carpet.

I made every overture to make him feel comfortable and let him know he could hang out with us, even after we both took the beating onstage and nobody else was fighting for our attention. I thought he was an asshole when he probably just had social anxiety issues. He didn't have the clout to be an actual asshole.

We were staying in some old U-shaped motor lodge in side-by-side rooms. When my lady and I pulled in late that night, I meticulously parked within a half inch of his driver's side door, a tiny Honda or something similar that would barely fit him much less his luggage. We giggled like drunken sailors. By that I mean that we giggled like our beloved veterans of the United States Navy who, while risking their lives for our freedom, snuck up under the woolen sheets of a sleeping berth in a submarine and sniffed Wite-Out from one another's ass-chambers. We giggled in the same fashion and it wasn't even Veterans Day.

In the morning, we got up early and called his room. I put on what would now be considered a very racist and stereotyped Indian accent but back then would have been just a very believable impression of the Patel-motel mafia front-desk people.

"Hello, will you be checking out today?"

He fumbled with his internal clock and then noticed the time.

"Huuuhhhm, whuuu? Wait a second . . . it's only nine o'clock in the morning???"

"Oh, yes. New policy. Nine a.m. checkout."

We could hear the blubber-flunky through the adjoining motel door as he went into fits, slam-packing his bags in frustration. We peeked through the curtains watching him come outside and realize in theatrical exasperation that he would have to plow his fat ass through the passenger-side door and lumber sideways, wiggling around to get into the driver's seat.

I got a call later on from the booker, chastising me for being mean to the opening act. I cried ignorance to any of it. Never heard his name again.

Snitches get day jobs.

Tim Mitchell was no snitch. He was a team player but a rookie nonetheless. He was a Minneapolis comedian back in the day when it was a scene. He could give as good as he could take and better. I was there on a night off for open-mic night at the Acme Comedy Club. The manager at the time was his roommate. He told me that Tim kept all of his joke notes on his computer. This was in the days before the Internet. Tim was the kind of guy who may have actually built his own computer from thrift-store electronics. For all I know, he may have built the Internet to go with it. He was that smart and that stupid for letting his roommate know how to gain access to all of his jokes.

His roommate went in and printed off everything that Tim Mitchell had ever thought of doing onstage. Not just his bits but all the premises he'd just noted as perhaps one day being funny. The manager made sure that on open-mic night he had to follow me. I went onstage and blew through all the bits that I'd already known of Tim's. Then I pulled out the sheets of paper that had been printed off and burned through every premise machine-gun style, preventing him from even riffing.

He followed me with an empty wallet. I'd bankrupted his entire vault. I did not find out until afterwards that he had old friends in the audience who were visiting from Ireland. This was the only time they were ever going to see him perform comedy live onstage.

In the moment he told me that, I felt kinda bad. But in the long run, that's the only reason I remember the story. For the deep-track fan, you may also remember Tim Mitchell's name from a bit called "Rubber Fuck-My-Face" on my obscure first DVD titled *Word of Mouth*. The story itself might sound more familiar still from an HBO special recorded years later by a comedian who wasn't me, who changed a few details and didn't have the courtesy to mention Tim Mitchell.

● ● ●

Dustin Ybarra could take a joke. Eventually.

Bingo and I were working a week at the Addison Improv with Brendon Walsh. I'll pause to tell you that a "week" in a comedy club generally means four days and that the Addison Improv is generally referred to as the "Dallas" Improv, much to the chagrin of neighboring Addison where it is located. I will also add that when I say Bingo and I were working that Bingo doesn't go onstage. She does a million other things like write down new bits or tags that I riffed and wouldn't otherwise remember, facilitate introductions with people I'm only pretending to remember and help sell merch, including one night at the Addison Improv where she followed a crying bachelorette party that had walked out of the show into the lobby. As the bride-to-be wailed and her friends demanded a refund, Bingo asked straight-faced if they'd like to purchase a DVD as a memento of their special evening.

By this time on the road we were generally dressed in ridiculous thrift-store garb during shows just to break up the monotony of doing comedy. Addison was no different. One night might be pajamas, the next night maybe Chinese waiter uniforms and we never addressed it onstage. It was only for our own amusement.

Our opener was a local kid, this Dustin Ybarra. On the penultimate night—big word, look it up—he asked us if we always dressed in ridiculous outfits. I told him that in fact we did. Every night. I told him that the next night—the final night—we would close out on "Depends Night" where we would all wear adult diapers onstage without ever making comment about it. We were gracious enough to invite him to participate and be part of the gang. Dustin was happy if not very nervous to be included in our reindeer games.

We all dressed up in our adult diapers pre-show in the greenroom and giggled. Dustin didn't know that we were giggling at him rather than with him. Or we were giggling *for* him since he was having such a hard time composing himself. This poor, tubby fuck had no chops for this. He was so new to comedy that he was lucky to remember all of his words in a row. Making him open the show in a diaper and expecting him to not mention it was preposterous. He muscled through and never made excuses despite the fact that it ruined his act. He never mentioned the adult diaper.

We missed a bit of his show while we were retreating back into the greenroom to change back into our regular clothes. We'd had no intention of doing "Depends Night." We just knew that he wouldn't say no. Dustin concluded his death-set and introduced the next act to the stage. The following act breached the blind zone of stage lights where Dustin could actually see the performer fully dressed and frowning at him for his silly diaper.

Dustin didn't take it well. He found me backstage laughing myself into an emphysema cough. And then he started to chase me with violence in his eyes, a violence that he could not have actually delivered were it not for the level of humiliation he'd faced. He was as fat as I was easily winded and the chase ended after a short sprint.

Eventually we talked him down and explained that our fuck-with made him part of the group. That made him happy. It wasn't until the Google search and listening to that podcast that I remembered that we hid his clothes while he was onstage floundering in a diaper. I'd forgotten that he still had to go up in between each comedian in the diaper. Without ever mentioning it. The kid had heart and those are the stories you remember.

At least parts of them.

SERIOUSLY FAMOUS

I had a new special, *Before Turning the Gun on Himself*, coming out on Netflix in 2012. It used to be that when you'd record any CD, DVD, TV special, etc. there would be at least six months or so downtime while they edited, where you could start working on new shit before the release. You can't put out a special and then go back on the road doing the same stuff. That is unprofessional, according to me, the only person who does my act and therefore the only person who can be the arbiter of what professionalism means in said job.

Problem was that technology had sped up and the special was put out before I had time to make new shit work. That August we booked two weeks in Canada with the new special due to drop near the start of the second week. This gave me a little over a week to stitch together a new hour. I don't mean a good hour. I mean any hour. I frantically cobbled together any bits that hadn't been included on the last recording with old bits that I'd never quite worked out, wrote anything I could about whatever current events were happening and added a heavy peppering of anything I could riff. Anything about the town, the hotel, the neighborhood or the venue. Anything short of pointing to the guy in the front row and saying, "Nice shirt." There wasn't a waking moment that I didn't have a notepad in my hand and the news or a newspaper in front of my face. Like your digestive tract, in comedy you have to feed your head a lot when you know you'll be having to pull things out of your ass later on.

If I had a lesion for every time I've heard a comic say, "The day that comedy starts to feel like work to me, I'll quit," I'd have no remaining skin. Comedy felt like a lot of fucking work to me that week and in similar circumstances a thousand times before and since.

The new/old pebble-stone amalgamation of material flew fine for the first two nights, as I spent my time writing and re-writing on yellow legal pads. Then I got an email from a big-dick LA agency saying that "one of our clients is trying to reach out to Doug Stanhope. What is the best way to go about this?"

I paid little mind to this and let Hennigan field it. He loves big-dick LA shit. And I had a notepad of jokes to remember. Just before the show as I was waiting in the wings—wings being the piss-caked alley of a rock venue—Hennigan texted me.

"Evidently Johnny Depp will be calling you. I have no further information."

I texted back: "Whaaaaaa?"

Hennigan replied.

"Evidently Johnny Depp will be calling you. I have no further information."

Funny cunt.

Eight minutes to showtime. I'm staring at my notes but all I could think was "Why the fuck would Johnny Depp need to talk to me?"

That night I went up and immediately addressed the Johnny Depp email. There was no joke and the bits that followed from the yellow legal pad suffered as a result. I didn't care. I was consumed by why the fuck Johnny Depp wanted to "reach out" to me.

Meanwhile, I had to keep my phone on. Johnny Depp might be calling at any minute. If he called in the middle of my show, I could take it on speaker phone and kill ten minutes of stage time.

However, he did not call during the show. But in the days afterwards, it seemed like everyone else did.

Like anybody that drinks and makes false promises in the heat of a forgotten moment, I don't answer unknown phone numbers. But now it was a whole new circumstance. Now I was compelled to answer any and all calls from blocked numbers or odd area codes, never knowing if it might be Johnny.

Ring-ring.

"Hello?

"Hey, this is Cousin Joe from the *Cousin Joe Podcast*! Can you do my podcast?"

Fuck me.

Days went by and still no call from Johnny Depp. What could he possibly want? If it were for some acting role, it would all go through agents. I suck at acting so I knew it couldn't be that. Maybe he has a role where he'll be playing a haggard and crouched alcoholic comedian and wants to do a ride-along with me to see what makes that character tick. Maybe he wants a ride to LAX. Nobody wants to do that.

I was a forty-five-year-old man, feeling the phantom pains of his own amputated last legs. I shouldn't be spending my time daydreaming about Johnny Depp like a fat teenage girl staring at his *21 Jump Street* poster over my bed. Especially then when I needed to concentrate on my show. Jokes. New shit. I'd like to think that I'm too cool to really care why Johnny Depp would want to talk to me but that wasn't the case.

You have to understand that Johnny Depp had as much reason to be calling me as he would have to be calling you. Imagine that you're at work—cutting hair or milking cats or whatever you do—and when you come back from your lunch break, Millicent at the front desk tells you that Tom Cruise stopped by to talk to you and said he'll come back.

Tom Cruise left no reason for the visit and no time when he'll return. How long would it be before you're gonna be able to concentrate on a crossword puzzle?

Days more and I started to get paranoid that maybe someone was just fucking with me, maybe payback from someone I'd pranked. Anyone can send off an email saying they're some fat-cocked Hollywood agent and get you all worked up and confused. It sounded like something Brendon Walsh would do to me. And then I thought that if it wasn't a Brendon Walsh hoax, then I would definitely remember the brilliant simplicity of the gag and do it to him. I imagined Walsh calling me to tell me how he'd gotten an email that Harrison Ford wanted to come to his birthday party, while me and my friends were trying hard not to laugh.

The only thing that made me consider that the whole thing might be legit was that Marilyn Manson had recently gotten a hold of me on Twitter. That led to some of the most indiscernible drunk phone calls you could ever try to transcribe. Maybe I was actually becoming known despite my own best efforts.

After a week had gone by I'd given up on getting this mystery Depp phone call. On the bright side I'd developed a decent five minutes of material about it all, culminating with me turning into an elderly crazed man shuffling the streets and picking up random, unringing phones answering them with "Johhhh-ny???"

Besides, the material was what I needed to begin with.

Chaille and I boarded some plane in the latter part of the tour. We sat down in our usual seventies loud, plaid polyester suits, broke out our reading glasses and dug into the *Economist* and *Reason* magazines and I laughed at the men we'd become at our half-century mark. I made comment to all the drugs we'd turned down from fans after the shows in my effort to get my act together, to be responsible. Turns out Chaille hadn't turned them all down. I have a hard rule against traveling with illegal substances but evidently Chaille ignored that rule as these drugs weren't anything dogs are trained to sniff.

We both decided that our abstinence might be the problem.

My stamina for hallucinogens is pretty frail, the recovery period too long, especially during a tour. Chaille pulled out his pocket notebook, found where we had two days back to back in Victoria with the club inside the hotel. I can swing that, Mr. Chaille. Pencil in "Do Drugs!" We are professional people. We can schedule drug use to cause the least burden on commerce and detriment to the paying customer.

By the time we hit Victoria I'd built at least a reasonable skeleton of a new set. We had acid for me and mushrooms for Chaille prepared for a well-earned post-show vacation. My phone rang that afternoon with an LA area code. I looked at Chaille and he looked at me. I was again transformed into a chubby teenage girl hoping against hope. I answered my cell phone delicately like it was attached to an improvised explosive device. On the other end, a stammering Hunter S. Thompson started to awkwardly tell me what a big fan he was. Johnny had made that Hunter face for too long and it stuck. Chaille leaned in to listen like an even chubbier teenage sister. I ran to the parking lot to smoke. I have a hard time talking to strangers without a cigarette.

Johnny went on and ear-raped me about what a genius he thought I was. I've learned to just say thank you. For me and for most of the comedians I know, you greet any compliment with self-deprecation. This can convince the person who is complimenting you that they are wrong, that you really aren't that good. Johnny repeated his favorite bits of mine that I humbly had to correct. Nothing will force a comedian's hand into repeating his own bit at the table than someone else doing it in front of him poorly.

Later I'd find out that Depp knew about me through Marilyn Manson making him watch my *No Refunds* special during a bender. When I eventually told Manson about the initial Depp phone call, I didn't know they were friends. I just thought it was weird that two famous people had called me in a short amount of time. Manson was rightfully wanting credit for Johnny knowing me at all. Fame and all that comes with it is like owning a boat. It isn't any fun if you don't bring people who don't have a boat along with you. But you secretly want them to know that it's your fucking boat and you're the reason they are there. I do that with Junior Stopka when I bring him on the road. And he bucks back the same way I do by not trying or wanting to be famous or even noticed. I get it.

After quite a while on that first phone call from Johnny, he mentioned a vaguely thought-through television project he'd thought of for me and humbly asked if I'd have any interest.

"Johnny? I'm standing in a Days Inn parking lot trying to smoke out of the rain, about to play in a sports bar to sixty-five people. I'm not going to say no."

It took him too long to laugh. Too long to realize that I wasn't kidding.

And as I hung up, I realized that this phone call had ruined my new five minutes of "Johnny Depp Never Called Me" material.

I really needed the material.

NAME DROPPINGS

I wouldn't consider myself a star fucker but I'm without question a name dropper. I try to be blatant about it. Sometimes I'll catch myself accidently dropping a name in an underhanded way and have to stop and apologize for not grandstanding it a bit more.

"Oh? Did I just say 'A. J. Hawk'? Did I not mention that he is my close personal friend A. J. Hawk whom I know?"

Okay, some of the names I drop may only hold weight with my football friends in Bisbee who are 80 percent Green Bay Packers fans and I may have only met A. J. Hawk briefly once after a show. And after becoming friends with Johnny Depp, the quality of my name dropping showed a decisive chasm. It goes from Depp and plummets down to A. J. Hawk level, no offense intended to the fine former linebacker. There aren't a lot of names in between. But dropping names always has to be blown up big so that you don't look like you really mean it. Even when you do. Famous people liking you is cool in the same way it is when black people like you. Somehow it's worth so much more.

Star fuckers are different than name droppers. I don't know if there is a Webster's definition for star fuckers but to me they are people who need to be around famous people so that in some way they become de facto celebrities themselves. Like Joe Francis from *Girls Gone Wild*. Being around famous people always makes me more self-conscious than I can stand and I tend to drink too much to compensate. In this case, drinking too much means being way more drunk than other people who tend to drink too little. If everyone is drunk on the same page, things tend to work out. Drinking too much around famous people gives me an unwarranted sense of regret in the morning. I never regret being too drunk around people I don't know. But if they're famous, the regret makes me hesitant to name drop as it just brings up bad anxiety, that rush of fear that you probably said something stupid. Like when I made a Bryan Adams joke to singer Ryan Adams that he'd only heard from every single tool who ever sat next to him at a party.

In 2008 I got an email from Justine Bateman. It said that she loved my Showtime special *No Refunds*, that she agreed with everything I said and that she wished me great success. I vetted that it was in fact the same Justine Bateman who played Mallory from the eighties show *Family Ties* and immediately dropped the name on Bingo. I referred to her from then on as "my new girlfriend Justine Bateman," just to send Bingo into her adorable fake temper tantrums. It still works.

Garrett Morris had just opened a comedy club in downtown LA and I was booked there. I invited Justine, who said she would put together an "army" to be at the show. She came with a group of people, from what I remember a lot of industry folks. Industry—meaning agents and producers—are far more uncomfortable to be around than famous people. They are trained to work the conversations around bullshit like what your goals are and how they maybe could facilitate your dreams. Barnacles with a pitch and a club soda while you're on your fifth Manhattan. And I didn't have any dreams.

The comedy club was in a fairly decent hotel with the showroom somehow situated around a sushi bar with a separate bar downstairs. In this hazy hindsight, the comedy room probably sucked and certainly doesn't exist anymore. All I know is that the plan was to meet Justine and her army at the downstairs bar after the show. I was accompanied by Bingo and Lynn Shawcroft, who'd held back to man the merch booth while I raced down to entertain my name-drop opportunity. I tried to maintain some decorum and hide my level of drunkenness. I'm well versed, or so I think.

Justine and her folk were casually casual, the polar opposite of my usual post-show audience of shitfaced roustabouts, high-fivers and their stumbling ilk. I tried my best at small talk. I'd evidently worked with one of the producers at the table on a television pilot. I pretended to remember. I desperately waited for Bingo and Shawcroft to catch up with me and even out the odds.

Shawcroft had announced earlier in the evening that she was on a new low-carb diet that required she no longer drink beer, instead moving to vodka. The problem that night was that she had been drinking vodka at the same rate and volume as she would normally drink beer. It couldn't have been later than 10:30 p.m. when Shawcroft shuffled sideways into the bar with purpose, like a 4 a.m. spiteful drunk with something to prove. Bingo was in tow, just as drunk if only a bit more timid and as always, adorable.

The finely tuned industry-speak was interrupted and turned into bar-brawl volume chaos. Shawcroft spread out in the middle of the long table and proceeded to tell everyone in an angry slur what was what in an unprovoked tirade that culminated with her go-to tell of "You don't even know what love is!"

She kept yelling into the black hole of the silence she'd created.

"What is love then? Tell me! You don't know what true caring about people is!"

She followed these outbursts by long swigs of vodka and soda.

The table maintained their stares and side talk, ignoring the time bomb that was slowly exploding in the midst of the benign chitchat. Justine started busting balls out of the corner of her mouth that showed me she'd been here before. You talk shit just quietly enough to go over the heads of your company that is un-amused, amuse the ones in the middle ground who will get the joke, all without inflaming the drunk who is the problem. It's a skill. A skill that Justine had mastered.

Leftover pizza—the thin-crust fancy kind they serve on a stand with a can of Sterno keeping it warm below—was the needed distraction for Shawcroft to quit her inane blather. She asked the table if people were done eating it and everyone was happy to offer it up, hoping it would make her stop yelling at everyone. Yet in her attempt to grab it, she knocked it onto the floor, nearly setting the table on fire with the canned heat. Some people might take this as a cue to leave, both the drunk and the people tolerating the drunk.

Nobody left.

As the table made curious eye contact as to what might happen next, Shawcroft made the only move that remained logical in her own cloudy head. She got on her hands and knees and crept underneath the table to eat the pizza she'd spilled. She ate it hunched up off the floor like a squirrel. Justine raised the level of shit talk like perfectly hurled curve balls of a hall of fame closing pitcher, just out of reach of Shawcroft's ears.

I was mortified on two levels. One, I hated the fact that I gave a fuck just because Justine was famous and I was distancing myself from Bingo and Shawcroft hideously plowed. Two, was that they hadn't stayed drinking with me at my own pace. I was certain to be that drunk myself later on and by then they'd be passed out and I'd be drinking alone.

The Bateman group finally decided it was time to go as Shaw-croft rolled under their feet, hitting her head on the bottom of the table as she tried to get up. We all made polite goodbyes as though nothing ever happened.

In the morning, Lynn Shawcroft called me from her hotel room.

"Oh my God! Did I make an asshole of myself in front of that Mallory girl?"

"Um . . . yeah?!? You ran into the bar doing that 'You don't know what love is' shit and then knocked their pizza off the table and then crawled around eating it off the carpet under their feet. I mean, if that's what you call being an asshole."

Shawcroft paused and, without the slightest bit of kidding said . . .

"Oh no! I ate *pizza?* I'm not supposed to have carbs!!!"

Fame also makes it much harder to obscure someone's iden-tity when you have a compromising story that includes them and you are writing a book. I can write about Andy's molester, Bo Y. Fondler, and the publisher makes me change it to Frank Wheeler. Again, somehow that's no problem.

Changing the name alone doesn't necessarily work with fa-mous people. It's tough to pull off a story that begins with "One afternoon I was huffing spray paint on the set of *Pirates of the Ca-ribbean* with the star of the movie . . . 'Danny.'"

For the record, "Danny" and I did not huff Krylon together. I'm just making a point. But still, I hate to have to bury a good story just because someone is well known. And usually they hate it as well. Most famous people have to keep their sordid antics on the down-low because they have an image to uphold or they can be fired. I don't have to hide anything. I have no network to answer to, no sponsorships to lose. Only you can fire me by not coming to my shows or buying this book, which is obviously too late.

Here's a couple interactions with mildly famous people that I will try to get out in front of the lawyers by making them as vague as possible namewise, although by now their names are as obscure as my own.

I walked out having finished a show in the Southeast ahead of the crowd still settling their tabs. I'd quit smoking at that time, meaning that I now only bummed a couple cigarettes from folks before and after shows. The first couple out of the showroom were already outside smoking and I bummed one with confidence. I felt I had that kind of star power in this situation and besides, smokers tend to take care of one another. The guy told me he was a big fan and started repeating old bits he remembered from before I remembered remembering anything. I was impressed.

As the rest of the crowd started pouring out, I ducked back in the fire exit to the greenroom. He and his gal tried to follow but Bingo stopped him and told him that this room was "comics only." I ran interference and told her these people were cool. They had cigarettes.

At some point he awkwardly dropped that he was an infamous professional athlete from the days of yore who had a reputation worse than my own. Only more well known.

"Holy shit! You're *that guy!*"

A drink leads to plenty more and at some point we're downstairs in an after-hours club in a public bathroom stall where he's handing me a key bump. He was sort of meandering with a passive-aggressive apology about the quality.

He half shrugs and tells me: "It's not really good shit. It's not meth. But it's not not meth."

I snorted it and then ran quickly out to Chaille to make him write down the quote before I blacked it out or died from ingesting it.

"It's not meth. But it's not NOT meth."

Inadvertently brilliant.

The next night in the next town I wanted to tell the story but I didn't want to rat out his identity. There was a cable comedy series that had recently run, loosely based on his career without giving him credit. So I told the story that night saying, "I won't say who it was . . . I'll just call him . . ." and I used the character's name from the TV series rather than his real name. A few people got it. At least one didn't.

The next day I got a tweet from someone from the previous night's audience saying: "Don't worry I won't say anything about you and [the actor that played the fictional version of the real guy who got no credit for a television version of himself] doing meth in a toilet!"

I then realized that I'd inadvertently implicated a famous actor while trying to hide the identity of the guy that the character was based on.

The analogy would be if Bert Kreischer gave me meth-not-meth and then I used "Van Wilder" as a not so subtle pseudonym when repeating the story and then had to apologize to Ryan Reynolds, the actor who played Bert Kreischer's character as Van Wilder in a movie. It must suck more to have someone be more famous for playing you than for you being you.

●　●　●

I played some other club many years earlier where the manager told us that the quarterback and kicker from that area's hometown NFL team would be coming to the early show on Friday.

In my youth and exuberance, I thought it would be funny to get a Nerf football to try to nail a field goal through the kicker's up-turned goalpost hands to close the show. By the time Friday arrived, I knew this was a bad idea, but I'd already found a Nerf football and I hated to waste it.

I announced that the kicker and quarterback were in the room in the back and set up my silly field-goal idea. The kicker reticently played his part, arms up while I teed up the football from the stage. There was no momentum going into this. The crowd felt like they were being put on the spot as much as the poor kicker. They iced me. I kicked the Nerf ball directly into the front row inches before me, blasting their drinks all over themselves and their neighbors.

"Thank you. Good night."

After the show, the kicker and the quarterback came back to the greenroom. They wanted to hang out for the late show. I was a nobody and they probably felt like nobodies too, being the worst team in the NFL at the time. They were probably familiar with poor fourth-quarter choices like mine that night.

The late show was different, as my only obligation was to do five minutes in front of the special event that night, Dr. Dirty: John Valby. This was a guy who'd been legend when I was a teenager in Worcester, Massachusetts, who did dirty songs with dirty words that rhymed. Spoiler alert: "suck" rhymes with "fuck," as does "cocksucker" with "motherfucker." But his crowd were more crazed than even mine have now become. This was a musical Andrew Dice Clay with a mob of fans that aggressively yelled "Fuck You! Fuck You! Fuck You!" at the guys who were only there to pull his piano onto the stage.

I was terrified. I watched this angry horde get more and more combative as they got seated and even more overserved. The quarterback loomed over me in the wings, his mouth just as agape as mine in fear for my immediate future.

"Man. I wouldn't wanna be you right now."

This from a man who was used to routinely getting booed for being the quarterback of the worst team in the NFL in one of the most brutal markets in America. I didn't wanna be me either.

He pulled me aside and asked me: "Hey, do you party?"

I was too young to understand the nomenclature of cocaine. Years later I remember a stranger giving me a simple half nod from across the bar after a show and knew it meant bumps in the men's room. But back then I just assumed that "party" was a term for drinking and said yes. Obviously I partied. I'd been drinking with him for hours.

He slipped me an envelope that I retreated with into the greenroom to find the surprise of powdered confidence.

The backstage announcement for me starting the show was barely audible over the vicious chants of the crowd.

"Fuck you! Fuck you! Fuck you!"

I told my opening joke and some woman yelled something back with bile spitting out of her neck.

I called her a cunt.

The crowd blew up in hives with laughter at my gifted ability to be so clever and I killed for the next four and a half minutes.

Thank you for that white-flaked burst of confidence, my one-night friend. I'll only refer to you as my Jewish grandmother. And when your kicker friend bemoaned being shit on by your head coach when he was "the best kicker in the NFL," it was your confidence that made me jokingly say, "Oh, wait. I didn't know you were Morten Andersen!" Zing!

BOURBON LEGENDS

Some things you just don't talk about. Especially when they aren't true.

You won't find anything in this book about me being in Grand Theft Auto. That's because I'm not. I never spent any time at all sweating my balls off in a CGI suit for the purposes of being a character performing at the comedy club in this game. For endless hours, only to never be used in the game. And if I did, I would have had to sign a nondisclosure agreement saying I couldn't talk about it anyway. So stop asking. Because that never happened.

Yes, I did mention in my first book that my brother and I missed our chance to snort my father's ashes mixed with cocaine. We'd had the idea but never got around to it before Keith Richards made news for doing that very same thing. If Bingo, Chaille and I later decided to do the same thing with my mother's ashes, I don't remember. If I don't remember that it's because we were supposed to be snorting those ashes mixed with the ashes of a famous person's mother's ashes, all mixed in the same amphetamine soup, well I can't really recall. Perhaps it turned out that a bevy of that famous guy's henchmen, stooges and apple polishers couldn't find an Allen wrench small enough to loosen his mother's ashes from the amulet he kept them in around his neck. Eventually, I don't remember us just bogarting my own mother and blow up into our sinuses.

I do, however, remember later that night being jacked up at the Comedy Store watching Marc Maron in the Original Room. I saw him in the hallway after his set and I was obviously gakked when I told him that I enjoyed his show. My face was contorting through a million emotions. He asked if I was okay. I considered trying to explain what had just happened but settled on just shaking my head and telling him that it had just been a weird night.

He stared at me more confounded than my own spinning head looked.

"Really? What's a *weird* night to *you??*"

I didn't try to explain. Because none of that happened.

THE INTERNET IS
FOREVER

mentioned earlier that you can find bad "doug stanhope tattoos" in a Google search. I see them and I hope that one day the poor bastard will get it removed or covered up. And then I realize that he really can't. Because he put it on the Internet. No laser or portrait of a screaming eagle will ever take it away.

Too often I have first-time comedians email me, asking me to look at their first open-mic set that they have put on YouTube. I cannot imagine the horror of any comedian from my pre-Internet era finding their open-mic days now available for anyone to see. Or perhaps I can, as someone posted gut-churning awful VHS-era video they'd found of me only six months into comedy. Don't post anything publicly without knowing that it's more permanent than a tattoo. You may have done well onstage in relation to your lack of experience, and your peers might recognize that, but the general Internet public will not.

Your gamble at fame may come back to ruin the day job that you never had the chance to quit. That old YouTube clip of you onstage, saying that women are nothing more than cum caskets isn't on your resume but it's on your permanent Internet record. The crowd might have laughed but not hard enough to keep you in comedy. The human resources department at Procter & Gamble didn't laugh at all and fired you for it. Only wager what you can afford to lose. Michael Richards had already cashed all of the checks before his incredibly flawed choice to repeatedly scream "nigger" at a heckler. He weighed his options. The Internet may be ever lasting but not as powerful as reruns of *Seinfeld*.

I had no choice in the matter. I started comedy before there was an Internet and I recorded material that I could not have known would be heard outside of where I thought it should be heard. Sometimes it worked in my favor, sometimes not.

● ● ●

Nobody will tell you that you have enough fame. If you actually found your fifteen minutes, you'll have a bank of people telling you that they can get you twenty more for a small percentage and that eventually they will get you a full hour of fame, so long as you put your trust in them. You can never be famous enough for people.

Your fans themselves will demand that they need you to be more famous and fuck you if you don't want it yourself. They want it for them. You are their vicarious dream of what they could have done had they only taken more chances. You are famous because they want to be you and they want to be more of it.

Never trust the fans.

Ricky Williams got famous because he ran around with a football and he did it pretty well. It made the fatheads in the stands very happy. He also liked to smoke pot and hated attention. That doesn't jibe well in the NFL. Or with the fans. After too many failed piss tests, subjugating to too many suspensions and having to answer too many questions, Ricky decided to just quit. The ire of the fans was that he'd quit right at the beginning of training camp for the Miami Dolphins.

He'd let down the team.

Dave Chappelle walked out on a multimillion-dollar contract because he felt that his personal mental stability and moral compass were more important than the money and empty accolades the rest of us are trained to strive for. Ricky walked out as well and became my hero. He wanted to enjoy his life more than he needed money and fame, a concept too inconceivable for people to fathom. He didn't need the posse, the Cristal in the over-hyped strip club and the fleet of Escalades that you wanted him to need. He didn't like the overbearing scrutiny from the press and the fans. He liked playing football but he also liked being at peace with himself in life—part of which was getting high—so he chose that over the grand expectations of a stadium full of drunken mastodons, each one using sport as a diversion from their own desolate existence and each one a coach and a critic.

What a dick Ricky Williams was.

He quit and then he disappeared. Several months later, a writer for *Esquire* tracked him down living in a tent in an Australian campground for seven dollars a night. He studied holistic medicine and found some peace. Whatever could be tested in his piss was his own business. The fans who barked for his hide for walking away from the game would be the same people who'd tell you that they'd quit their own jobs in a second if they ever hit the lottery. Ricky had won the equivalent of several. Like most lottery winners, he found that it made his life more problematic.

I remember when Ricky Williams walked away. I did a bit about it at the time—one of those painful pieces of material that you are so passionate about but that you know has a hospice shelf life—where I spelled all of this out. There is nothing more pleasing in comedy than going against the heavy stream of public opinion and winning them over. Not only did I take the side of Ricky Williams, I suggested that Ricky Williams should have waited until the regular season to retire. That he should have waited and then quit right there on the field in the middle of a play, if only to drive his point home even harder. He should have waited until the middle of a clutch fourth-and-one possession while the quarterback was milking his barked calls, trying to pull the defense off-side.

Hut one.

Hut two.

"I quit. I think I'd rather get high."

Then the announcers, astounded as Williams removed his helmet and his gentle stroll to the exit, would be confused and shouting, anticipating the penalty flag that would inevitably be thrown. Ricky would remain nonplussed.

"Nope. That's your flag now. I quit. I'm out of the penalty flag business. You'll have to mark off that loss of yardage at my house."

I suggested that Ricky should have kept his uniform and purchased season tickets, front row just behind the Dolphins bench and sit there every game, suited up and high as fuck. Every goal-line stand his team would look up at him, groveling for him to enter the game.

"Oh, shit. I can't, man. I am waaaay too high!"

At the same time I was doing this bit, I was juggling the same issues in my own head. I didn't know if what I was doing was based on what my handlers were telling me to do, what my few fans expected or what I really wanted. At that point in my life I really just wanted to walk off the field in the middle of the game. I'd felt like that before and I've felt like that since. I just never had the balls.

Recently the long-since-retired Ricky Williams found an old bootleg from a Sirius XM recording of that bit on the Internet. He thanked me that at least one person knew what he was going through at the time and had his back, even if he only found it twelve years later. It was one of the most career-confirming moments I've had. I felt validated.

When it was recorded, I couldn't imagine that it would ever be heard beyond the audience of eighty or so people that were in the room. At that point I didn't even believe anyone really listened to satellite radio, much less that it would one day be heard by Ricky Williams himself. All I remember from that night was that I drank ninety-seven dollars' worth of booze. I remember that because it was unheard of for a club to charge you for the booze that you, the comedian, were there to sell. It was like a football player getting charged for the Gatorade he dumped over the coach's head.

But Ricky Williams eventually heard that recording and that made my day. It still makes my day.

The flip side to that coin was when I was recording my second CD, *Something to Take the Edge Off*, in 1999, in front of sixty-some people in Houston. At the time there was a spate of premiere NFL quarterbacks who had children with disorders or diseases of varying degrees of gravity or neglect in funding. Boomer Esiason, Dan Marino, Jim Kelly. Mark Rypien. Football Sundays were chock-full of these athletes doing public awareness commercials for their respective causes. I was doing a bit about being terrified at the thought of what type of child I would produce given the amount of abuse and toxins I'd exposed my body to, given that these NFL guys were in prime physical condition and even they couldn't avoid kids with disabilities.

Writing it now in that way sounds so much less distasteful than the recorded version, where I'd list all of the players' names and mimic any given commercial with "Hi, My name is Doug Flutie and this is my boy Wacky! He was born without bones!"

The bit went on to address that I could never be the giving, dedicated parent these athletes were, and that I'd drop that baby at the closest church doorstep with a note in his little flipper hand.

"I couldn't be a responsible enough parent if my kid were born with a new suit and a full-time job, much less fish gills or an ingrown head."

There was no way of me knowing that one day this new Internet thing would take off and the audience of sixty people in Houston would one day become an audience of anyone with Google. YouTube didn't exist back then and I couldn't imagine elite NFL players stealing shit on Napster.

The Doug Flutie commercial at the time was raising awareness about the autism that afflicted his child. His boy did, in fact, have bones and did not have flipper hands or an ingrown head, not that there's anything wrong with either. Yet I wouldn't want him to come across that bit now on the Internet. Unlike Ricky Williams, I would definitely hide from Doug Flutie if I saw him in a bar. Just in case, I'll mention here that his www.flutiefoundation.org helps children with autism. I've found no charity for ingrown heads, but perhaps I'll start one when I'm famous and have to apologize for a lot.

• • ◦ • •

RETARDED

re·tard·ed
/rə'tärdəd/
adjective
adjective: retarded
dated offensive
less advanced in mental, physical, or social development than
    is usual for one's age.
Informal offensive
very foolish or stupid.
"in retrospect, it was a totally retarded idea"
    —*Google search*

Here, both descriptions apply. The first definition will be apparent in the story. The second applies to me posting it in the first place. I was searching my archives looking for a related story. I found this update that I put on my website in 2002. If a vague through line of this book is why I'm not famous, there couldn't be a better example than this. If I were to post this on my website today, I'd be assassinated, castigated or more likely, still be unnoticed.

Here it is unedited.

• • •

Here's a comedy rule that shouldn't have to be spelled out but evidently does. If you don't have any limbs—don't heckle. I'm with Andy Andrist, who is perhaps the funniest person on the top side of the earth, at the Acme Comedy club in Minneapolis last week. Andy tells me he's worried about his extensive "fat people getting handicapped parking/people in wheelchairs shouldn't get special privileges because a lot of them are in chairs because they are fuckups" bit due to a couple of patrons who are wheelchair bound in the crowd, one being little more than a torso.

The bit is absolutely ripping funny and can be worked so as not to offend, but it's still tricky to pull off. Andy is going to do it anyway because Andy doesn't give a fuck but before he can even venture into it, the torso starts blurting shit out and throwing the room into funeral-parlor silence. That's what happens when freaks heckle. If you—the regular drunk-off-the-street guy— starts bellowing out shit, trying to be the life of the party, then you know what to expect and will be verbally pummeled. But when a mop-top inebriate with ten-inch stubs for limbs decides to be the asshole for the evening it turns into a black hole of comedy because the comic can't say shit back without the crowd looking at him like he's gut punting a crack baby.

This has happened to me on many occasions. There was the time where the midget couple brought their retarded son to the front row of a show at Jokers in Dayton. The more I tried to fight out of the hole, the worse I made it. The worst was when I used to work at the other club in Minneapolis years back. There was a regular group of rubberheads who would be brought in now and then under what I assumed to be some kind of "laughter is the best medicine" program. I assume this because these people weren't just a little bit touched. They were full-blown butternoggins who hadn't a clue where they were or why they

were there. So you'd walk onto the stage, oblivious to their presence and right in the middle of a setup you hear a terrifying
"DAAAAAAAAAARFPH!" from the back of the room. You don't
know if you're being heckled or if you have one ball hanging out
of your pants.

If you're lucky, you spot the problem, give a shrug and a wink
to the audience and try to plow through. But good luck if they
happen to be behind the lights somewhere and you go into knee-
jerk heckler mode and spew out your best "Hey, Chico, why don't
you go eat a bag of dicks, you fucking retard!" Now you wonder
why the audience hasn't started yelping approval as they usually
would, so you cup your hand over your eyes and see that you've
just publicly berated a low-watt gurgler in a high-back chair who
begins to break the icy silence with guttural sobs.

Try pulling out of that hole. "Sorry, I didn't know you were
really a retard" won't get the audience back on your side. Skip
your closer and head for the farthest barroom.

Am I saying retards shouldn't be allowed in comedy clubs?
Yes. Yes I am.

I'm not saying it should be a law nor would I post a sign, but
use some common sense for fuck sake. The caretakers/handlers
who brought them would say that it was good therapy for them
to be around laughter and smiling people. Well, good for them.
Put 'em in a circle and throw a burning raccoon in the middle.
They'll all laugh and smile for hours. Instead you put them here
where they've turned laughter and smiling people into awkward
silence and people who wish they were at the movies instead.

I applaud the people who work with people afflicted with
these disabilities and can think of no job that is more selfless or
requires more patience and understanding. That's why I didn't
take that job and why I don't want you to put me in that position
against my will.

The case with Andy is different. This person had all of his mental faculties (save for what he drank away that night); he just didn't have arms or legs. And he was a belligerent asshole.

Andy played it perfectly and just gave benign jabs in return until he could feel that the audience had spent its full supply of empathy. Then, among other things, he challenged him to a race up stairs and closed by saying he now understood why God punishes some people.

●　●　●

I could still make the same argument using less derogatory language. But if I *had* been famous when I posted this, I would have lost my Disney contract, my Burger King commercials and all hopes of ever being president. Or at least the first two.

There is no logical argument against how Andy dealt with the Torso. Even the Torso loved it as all hecklers do, thinking their assholery made the show so much better. Torsos are no worse than the average legged person.

As for my argument that "retards" shouldn't be allowed at comedy shows, well, I guess I can see where that could come across as somewhat caustic. If I were stating that case in a court of law, I would have taken a less vitriolic and more eloquent approach. I would have simply stated that perhaps there were venues and activities that might be better suited and more enjoyable for these fine folks.

I searched my archives for that old post to tell a different story of a girl who had been a caretaker for a "low-watt gurgler in a high-back chair" and brought him to a show in Portland. He did the same discordant hollering out that I described in that original web posting. By this time, I was better equipped for dealing with the unforeseen at shows. I saw the girl at the bar later and we talked. She said that her charge—the guy in the chair—was unable to speak or hear. She explained that she brought him to the comedy club because he indeed liked to be around laughing people. When other people were laughing, he would laugh. I had no problem with that as, unlike those old Knuckleheads days, I'd now developed enough chops to deal with dicey situations like that. I understood and I felt some compassion. She and I spent the weekend together.

Back then her name was Amy Bingaman. Now we call her "Bingo." And she's a fucking retard.

You don't even know what love is!

• • •

I later used the term "low-watt gurgler in a high-back chair" in the film *The Aristocrats*. The term is now listed in the *Urban Dictionary*. I am not cited as a source. But I know and whoever made the entry knows. I'm happy to languish in the infamy.

• • •

When I die, there will be a small chorus of comedians who will say it was sad that I was underappreciated and could or should have been so much more recognized. And if they die before me, I will say it was sad that their own unquenchable desire to need more, get more, be more might have made them miss out on that one night that you had to cling to the driveway, out of your brain on psychedelics, to the point that you pissed your pants on purpose, leaving your wife to change you like a baby. You would have never taken the time to skip drunkenly into the ocean with Roseanne. You would have missed the time the girls from the band Birdcloud peed on you. And you would have slept through that vacuum cleaner salesman story in Alaska. It wouldn't have seemed believable even if you were awake. Some of the best nights in your life will never make it onto your Wikipedia page. Stop worrying about your credits and consider enjoying your day.

You die at the end.

* * *

I left Los Angeles in 2005 to live in Bisbee, Arizona, the hidden, eclectic cul-de-sac of the desert Southwest just at the border of a Mexican town that Mexicans have never heard of either. People asked me why I'd suddenly picked up roots of an arguably rising career to seemingly go on the lam in a place that was too remote for even a vigilant stalker to make time to visit.

I'd tell them that I moved here to make it big.

It used to be a joke but, using my own personal barometer of what it means to be successful, that is exactly what happened. There is no comedy scene here and I'm glad for that. I miss the comedians but I don't miss being around the business. Living in Bisbee made me love comedy again. Now when I have to go to LA or New York, I feel giddy like it's a high school reunion every time. I laugh at acts that I would have crucified under my breath in the back of the room, back when this business was my life instead of my living.

Nobody knows stand-up comedy here. When I come back from the road, at best my local friends will ask me "How was your trip?" No differently or in-depth than "How was your vacation?" Then we move on to football or who of our friends made it into the "Police Beat" back page of the weekly newspaper. I'm only famous here at Safeway. As a customer, not as a comedian.

We've had some legendary Super Bowl parties here at the house over the last ten years, some of them lasting as long as nine days. We would generally have a show in the yard with live bands on the Saturday night before Super Bowl but that trailed off after Nowhere Man and Whiskey Girl died. They were a married local musician duo and close friends who could be the foundation of any makeshift jam band that could be put together at the last minute. No matter how sloppy drunk or amateur the rest of the participants were, Nowhere and Whiskey could make them great. But then Whiskey died of a lupus-related blood infection just after turning forty. Nowhere Man followed her out later that day with a bullet through his head. Jam bands kinda fell off after that, without them as a cornerstone. The neighbors are probably happier because of it.

You need to know that the small neighborhood we live in is so quiet that you can hear someone's television at night a block away and six houses down. And it's usually something boring. So having a live band on your patio means that everyone in the entire neighborhood can't help but listen. The noise ordinance says it has to be shut down by 10 p.m. and we stick by it, but sometimes they call the cops anyway.

The first visit from the police was when, after the music, I thought it would be a good idea to put some comedians on the stage. We had quite a few top-notch comics who were drunk and ready to go. Kristine Levine went up first and I immediately saw the problems coming. I knew that our crowd would love her but I hadn't considered that my neighbors, who had never called the police about the music, might take exception to most of what we consider funny. I remembered Brandt Tobler who was evicted for having me play his backyard. I paced like a nervous club owner anticipating the bad comment cards. Kristine Levine, unnecessarily amplified, graphically detailed the condition of her obese undercarriage after having three children.

"My pussy looks like it swallowed a dog that chewed its way out!"

Imagine this kind of material and worse resounding through the walls of every house within three blocks in any direction. It wasn't after 10 p.m. but I still waited by the gate for the police to show up, which took all of about eight minutes. The way my house is situated on a downslope, you can't see the patio and yard from the street over the corrugated tin fence. I walked out to the cop car to try to circumvent the problem. As the cop and his partner came out of the car onto the street, I politely asked them if there was a noise complaint. He said that it was in fact a language complaint as he swung open the gate into the driveway. There he was greeted by about eighty people and a comedian onstage, all silent and staring at him. Like he'd inadvertently opened a side door of a live theater production and the entire play shut down because he'd accidently walked onto the stage. The pause lasted an eternity.

"Okay, first question. Why weren't we invited?"

That's a cool cop. Granted that it's easy to be the most popular guy at the party when you're the only one with a gun, but that's still pretty fucking cool. We told him that we'd move the comedy portion of the show indoors. I completely understood the complaints. I might be annoyed at hearing "Mustang Sally" at top levels on my Saturday night at home but comedy is different. If I had to listen to Jeff Dunham while I'm trying to watch TV, I'm calling the cops.

The next year on the same Saturday night before the Super Bowl, the cops came again. This time it was just party noise in general and well after the 10 p.m. ordinance. It was one of those fortuitous times where the party happened to break up in the minutes between the complaint and the arrival of the police. They walked into a few drunken conversations still chattering on in the yard and assumed that the complainant was just overly sensitive. I told him that I tried to be observant of the rules and was myself concerned about disturbing the neighbors. He said he was aware of that because he'd been called here the year before.

"Wait, are you the 'Why weren't we invited' guy?"

"Yeah! And why weren't we invited again?"

The next morning I called the police station and invited them all to the game. They didn't show but laughed and appreciated the offer. That was years ago.

As I write this, the Patriots just defeated the Atlanta Falcons in Super Bowl 51. It was the biggest comeback ever in Super Bowl history and the only one to ever go into overtime. And again, that same cop showed up. This time he came to watch the game with his wife and kids. I don't allow kids in my house but I make an exception for famous people. Officer Bob Friendly is famous to me and I love to drop his name.

FAME RETARDANT

When I was growing up, my elders would always judge the level of someone's success by how young they were when they could retire. They would tell you that Paul retired at thirty-eight with a sense of wonderment and envy, as though the man had been released early from prison. The implication is that working sucks and the implication wasn't subtle. Even if that was a baseless, ingrained belief, I still don't see how it's wrong. What evades me is how those people who do retire early allow themselves to actually relax and enjoy it. *Having* to work at any job is a loaf of shit but when I actually take the time to spend weeks or months slobbing on the couch, I never feel comfortable doing it. I'm constantly agitated. Always that gnawing restlessness that I should be getting something accomplished. I've always said that I could quit comedy and never look back and I'm certain I could do that. But I'd always feel like I should still be doing something else.

I've never been one of those comedians who says "The stage is my life" or the ubiquitous "I'm just so happy to have been given the gift of making people laugh." No comedian cares if you laugh. They care if you laugh at them. If that comedian kills and the rest of the show sends you home outraged and crying, that comedian doesn't give a fuck about you. He cares that he killed.

I'd like to be happy doing nothing at all. I have shiftless comedian friends who are my seniors who do nothing but play video games all day, have no money and still live on ramen noodles without a care in the world. I envy them while I remain dumbfounded by the rich and famous who don't just quit now when they never have to look back. I'm stuck somewhere in the middle.

I've gone on Netflix binges so epic that Netflix couldn't keep up with enough content to support them. I put as much effort into sloth as others do into achievement. But I never felt relaxed, even if there was nothing specific that I should be doing otherwise.

Howard Stern has seven hundred billion dollars that he keeps in cat carriers full of cash in a storage shed. I know. He made me count it. The reason that he still continues to get up at four in the morning to do a four-hour radio show when he's close to eighty years old mystifies me. Maybe he's like me and just can't handle the guilt of slack. Maybe society convinces you that it's wrong to not always want more, even if you don't really want it.

I live within my means and could probably just quit and live small here in Bisbee based on my life expectancy. Yet here I am writing another book. I blame it on the inability to say no. Or maybe it's a sadder version of ego where I'm just flattered to be asked. That's one of the problems with being a drunk. Your own personal version of what is the truth fluctuates over the course of a day. If this book had been written in one day, it would be in three chapters titled "Sober Regret," "Happy-Hour Enthusiasm" and "Drunken Who-Gives-a-Fuck."

It wasn't until I was engaged in a deeply emotional, impassioned relationship with my close personal friend Johnny Depp—who I've lain in bed with in our underpants while he tenderly held a knife to my throat—that I had the true and ugly upclose experience of what it is like to be hugely famous.

All the clichés of the loneliness, the lack of privacy, everybody wanting something from you and never being able to gauge people's intentions are probably true. By all accounts, that is Depp's reality. I have never seen that with him. Not only was I never destined to be famous, I have proven to be a fame repellent. Johnny, who can't leave his house without batteries of paparazzi rushing his heels, has never even been blinked at once while I have been with him.

He was going to bring his son Jack to my show at a comedy club in LA. He may as well have been the President of the United States. His phalanx of security came hours early to map every entry, exit and possible sniper's sight line like they were Secret Service. They did everything short of sample the appetizers for poison. When showtime came, Johnny came through a side door and hung out in the greenroom like anyone else. When I went onstage, Johnny sat in the sidelines of the crowd, dressed exactly like Johnny Depp. No baseball hat and sunglasses, no Hollywood incognito. He was a fucking gay pirate with his kid.

Nobody noticed.

The next day, Johnny asked if Bingo and I wanted to join him and his daughter to go to Target. He said that he'd never been to a Target store in his life. His kids needed back-to-school shit. Absolutely, we would like to go. It would certainly be chaos!

We wandered around Target with not a care in the world, like we were roaming a barren fiord looking for a quiet place to picnic. Johnny was still dressed as a gay pirate but now in the fluorescent lights of a crowded box store. Nobody save for a few foreign women even batted an eye. Johnny was just fascinated by the colors. Anywhere else, he would have had TMZ galore taking video.

At first I wrote it off as people thinking he was a Johnny Depp impersonator. Why else would he go out dressed like that? Yet it continued to happen every single time I was with him in public. Nobody ever noticed.

Ever.

I am sure it is because of me.

I am not simply unfamous, I cock-block fame. I am fame retardant.

• • •

I once asked Johnny while he was shooting a movie that he outwardly hated why he still did all this bullshit when he was worth megamillions. Why he didn't simply retire. He said that it was because he employed sixty-plus people who counted on him. There lay the trappings of fame. You can't quit because that would mean some Nicaraguan housekeeper who has worked for you for thirty-plus years would be out on the street. I understood. I only have Hennigan and Chaille to worry about. And our wives. I know that they could all survive on their own without me but I know it's so much easier for all of us the way we are doing it now. And so much more fun. It has been a jumble-fuck of fun.

Every time I catch myself in that mental rat trap of "I could have done more with my life," I realize I *have* done more with my life. I just don't remember a lot of it. You'd blame the years of alcohol but the years alone will do it. I know plenty a peer my age who hasn't soaked their head in booze for decades and they can't remember shit either.

People who tell you that you could have done more with your life typically mean that you could have done more with your career. They equate work with living.

Years back Dave Attell called me to ask about decent venues in New Orleans. At the time I had never worked New Orleans and I told him as much. In classic Attell he said, "Suuure you have! Remember the night when we did that show and you made the woman cry and then we ate beignets and you hopped a freight train???"

I laughed at his patented non sequitur silliness. But as he added more detail I realized that it wasn't a joke at all, as it slowly came back to me. Andy Andrist and I had road-tripped after a gig in Atlanta to see Dave, Mitch Hedberg and Louis Black doing a theater in New Orleans. Afterwards Andy, Attell and I had crashed an open mic and I had indeed sent a woman out crying with my post-9/11 vitriol and the ensuing argument. Later still, as Dave ate beignets at Café Du Monde next to the railroad tracks, I saw a slow-moving freighter and ran to it, hopping onboard and traveling all of a hundred yards or so when I got scared and jumped off. Andy remembers me peeing off it as well. It takes a village to piece together a solid bender.

Yes, I could have done more with my life. Like losing a leg to remind me of the night in New Orleans.

And as for my shit memory, it may be solely responsible for my saying I have no regrets.

When it all started, it was all a drunken goof. Most of my cohorts quit along the way and probably reflect fondly on the time that they at least gave it a shot. Some found an offshoot of the business where they were more adaptable. A few made it big and can't stop thinking about ways to make it bigger. Fewer still, a sliver of us looked at this life as an endless party, compelled to drive it until it ran out of gas. We all put on a face as kids and kept doing it until eventually it stuck like that.

At some point along the road, we all turned into the people we used to pretend to be.

*　*　*

"You're just hangin' out / At a local bar / And you're wonderin' / Who the hell you are / Are you a farmer? / Are you a star? . . .
　　Keep on smilin' through the rain."
　　　　—Wet Willie, "Keep on Smilin'"

ACKNOWLEDGMENTS

There are so many people I have to thank for this book that I can't even remember.

So let's just leave it at that.

Fuck you, then. I'll try. I'll do it drunk and refuse any type of editing.

If I could hire Tracey Wernet to just sit quietly for hours making me drinks, crocheting unstable drink coasters and then being my own living editor and thesaurus . . . well, she would probably be available without her dumb husband Greg Chaille making her do hump work. My favorite parts of writing this book were her company.

Alex O'Meara, as always, was a trusted ear even when I didn't take his notes, mostly because I forgot them. he also likes to give me grammar notes. That is why I am demanding to leave these acknowledgements as I write them, so you know that I write like I'm on Twitter and fighting a character limit yet ignoring unnecessary commas.

Brian Hennigan and Ben Schafer don't seem to have much concern about quality control over expedience. I am weak and tend to follow their lead. Hennigan is great at telling me that I should have included that one great story just after the deadline has passed. Fuck that guy too.

There are a bunch of agents and deal-makers and go-betweens that I don't know which deserve some thank yous. They also got a check. They can trade that in for the opportunity to see their name in the back of the book, the part that nobody reads.

I asked both Ricky Williams and Norm MacDonald if they would consider writing the foreword for this book. They both seemed amenable and both asked to read it first. I hadn't even finished when I had the booze-amplified courage to ask them—via Twitter at that.

Let me go back a bit.

Todd "Stupid-Face" Barry asked me to write the foreword for his book about a year ago. I swelled with pride that he would even consider me, knowing that he is a big snob! I wrote that foreword at my beloved Bingo's hospital bedside in a coma as a welcome distraction only to learn that he has a *second* foreword written by someone more famous. Actually, I was the second foreword. That other guy got top billing. I was tempted to try to out-do Todd by having three forewords for this book. But I remembered how awful I felt when Todd did that to me and I took everything Brendon Walsh had warned me about Todd and did the right thing.

If—as is my grand scheme at the end of this book—the foreword is written by Dr Drew Pinsky and I have begged a blurb for the back cover from Ricky Williams and Norm Macdonald, then I have accomplished my goal. That goal being finishing this fucking book and getting back to the road. Starting in a shithole in Champaign, Illinois. I'll thank the people responsible for that show at a later date.

Long after I am dead, the unfinished works of author Adrian Nicole Leblanc will be found in the rubble of a post-armageddon America. I am supposed to be highly profiled in that 13 year-running tome. I don't even know what a tome really means. Nor does she know what a deadline means.

Maybe I should have done more with my life. The harder work will be remembering what I've already done for my next book.

Tracey Wernet will now read this and hit send to the powers that be.

stanhope, dropping mic

INDEX